ROUTLEDGE LIBRARY EDITIONS: BRITISH IN INDIA

Volume 1

BHARATI MUKHERJEE

BHARATI MUKHERJEE
Critical Perspectives

EMMANUEL S. NELSON

LONDON AND NEW YORK

First published in 1993 by Garland Publishing, Inc.

This edition first published in 2017
by Routledge
2 Park Square, Milton Park, Abingdon, Oxon OX14 4RN

and by Routledge
711 Third Avenue, New York, NY 10017

Routledge is an imprint of the Taylor & Francis Group, an informa business

© 1993 Emmanuel S. Nelson

All rights reserved. No part of this book may be reprinted or reproduced or utilised in any form or by any electronic, mechanical, or other means, now known or hereafter invented, including photocopying and recording, or in any information storage or retrieval system, without permission in writing from the publishers.

Trademark notice: Product or corporate names may be trademarks or registered trademarks, and are used only for identification and explanation without intent to infringe.

British Library Cataloguing in Publication Data
A catalogue record for this book is available from the British Library

ISBN: 978-1-138-22929-7 (Set)
ISBN: 978-1-315-20179-5 (Set) (ebk)
ISBN: 978-1-138-24361-3 (Volume 1) (hbk)
ISBN: 978-1-138-28382-4 (Volume 1) (pbk)
ISBN: 978-1-315-26999-3 (Volume 1) (ebk)

Publisher's Note
The publisher has gone to great lengths to ensure the quality of this reprint but points out that some imperfections in the original copies may be apparent.

Disclaimer
The publisher has made every effort to trace copyright holders and would welcome correspondence from those they have been unable to trace.

BHARATI MUKHERJEE
Critical Perspectives

Emmanuel S. Nelson

GARLAND PUBLISHING, INC. • NEW YORK & LONDON
1993

© 1993 Emmanuel S. Nelson
All rights reserved

Library of Congress Cataloging-in-Publication Data

Nelson, Emmanuel S. (Emmanuel Sampath), 1954–
    Bharati Mukherjee : critical perspectives / Emmanuel S. Nelson.
      p. cm. — (Garland reference library of the humanities ; vol. 1663)
    Includes bibliographical references.
    ISBN 0-8153-1173-7 (acid-free paper)
    1. Mukherjee, Bharati—Criticism and interpretation.
I. Mukherjee, Bharati. II. Title. III. Series.
PR9499.3.M77Z79 1993
813'.54—dc20   93-18145
                                                                CIP

For Alpana, Anindyo, and Gurleen

CONTENTS

Introduction
Emmanuel S. Nelson ix

The Inner World of Bharati Mukherjee: From Expatriate to Immigrant
Maya Manju Sharma 3

Bharati Mukherjee as Autobiographer
Pramila Venkateswaran 23

A Question of Identity: Where Gender, Race, and America Meet in Bharati Mukherjee
Brinda Bose 47

Creating, Preserving, Destroying: Violence in Bharati Mukherjee's *Jasmine*
Samir Dayal 65

Sociopolitical Critique as Indices and Narrative Codes in Bharati Mukherjee's *Wife* and *Jasmine*
Janet M. Powers 89

Telling Her Tale: Narrative Voice and Gender Roles in Bharati Mukherjee's *Jasmine*
Pushpa N. Parekh 109

The Aesthetics of an (Un)willing Immigrant: Bharati
Mukherjee's *Days and Nights in Calcutta* and
Jasmine
 Anindyo Roy   127

Toward an Investigation of the Subaltern in Bharati
Mukherjee's *The Middleman and Other Stories* and
Jasmine
 Alpana Sharma Knippling   143

"In the Presence of History": The Representation of
Past and Present Indias in Bharati Mukherjee's
Fiction
 Debjani Banerjee   161

Born Again American: The Immigrant
Consciousness in *Jasmine*
 Gurleen Grewal   181

Love and the Indian Immigrant in Bharati
Mukherjee's Short Fiction
 Mitali R. Pati   197

The Short Fictions of Bernard Malamud and
Bharati Mukherjee
 Carole Stone   213

Selected Bibliography   227

Notes on Contributors   231

Index   235

INTRODUCTION

Emmanuel S. Nelson

At the 1991 Modern Language Association convention held in San Francisco, I organized and chaired a special session titled "Bharati Mukherjee and the Immigrant Tradition." Three presenters on the panel—Alpana Sharma Knippling, Anindyo Roy, and Gurleen Grewal—offered vigorous critiques of what they perceived to be problematic aspects of Mukherjee's art and ideology. As privileged cultural insiders—as scholars who share Mukherjee's upper-middle-class Indian background as well as her immigrant experience in the United States—they challenged politely but confidently some key elements of her work. Mukherjee herself was present at the session, and she responded with an articulate defense of her aesthetics and her politics—a defense that elicited an enthusiastic applause from the audience. The lively intellectual exchange between the author and the critics generated considerable drama; it made the session—in the opinion of many who attended it—a memorable scholarly event. A central objective of this collection of essays is to expand upon and advance the discussion that emerged during that MLA session.

As a Calcutta-born writer who now calls the United States her home after having spent many bitter years in Canada, Bharati Mukherjee is part of a variety of rich literary traditions. Her works can certainly be read in the national context of Indian writing in English and in the international context of the literature of the Indian diaspora. Some of her short stories and works of nonfiction that relentlessly expose and challenge Canadian racism are powerful enough to make her an important figure in the literature of multicultural Canada. Her major narratives of migration, of course, have earned her a significant place in the contemporary literature of the United States. The essays in this volume largely locate her in the American context; collectively, they help define her singular voice in the tradition of immigrant writing.

Mukherjee's complicated politics reflect her multiple (dis)locations; her works reveal the imprint of a complex perspective—a perspective that is simultaneously shaped by her ethnicity, postcoloniality, gender, and migrancy. This complexity, in itself, is not new; after all, there are many immigrant women writers of color who share Mukherjee's predicament. What is fascinating, however, is Mukherjee's determined rejection of the emotional paralysis of exile and her enthusiastic affirmation of the immigrant condition; her remarkable success in forging a coherent vision out of the chaos of her multiple displacements; and her ability to articulate that vision in a voice that is as subtle as it is insistent, as graceful as it is provocative.

The twelve essays that follow the introduction interpret Mukherjee's oeuvre from a variety of critical perspectives. The authors' approaches range from the biographical to the poststructuralist, from cultural analysis to comparative commentary to deconstructive reading. (Contributors to this book quote from different editions of Mukherjee's works.) Such diversity in the contributors' theoretical stances and interpretive strategies enables this collection of essays to serve a key purpose: to offer not only multiple but conflicting perspectives on Mukherjee's art and achievement.

Maya Manju Sharma's "The Inner World of Bharati Mukherjee: From Expatriate to Immigrant" provides an appropriate beginning for a discussion of Mukherjee's life and work. Here Sharma maps the radical transformation of Mukherjee as an artist: from an aloof and alienated expatriate author in emotional and artistic alignment with other exiled writers (such as V.S. Naipaul) to a confident storyteller who has now enthusiastically redefined herself as an artist in the immigrant tradition of American writers (such as Bernard Malamud). The focus of Sharma's essay is largely on Mukherjee's early novels—*The Tiger's Daughter* (1971) and *Wife* (1975). Arguing that both narratives are grounded in selected autobiographical facts, Sharma proceeds to comment on Mukherjee's effective transmutation of those life-facts into powerful fictional statements. Defending Mukherjee against ideologically motivated criticisms—especially from Indian nationalists and Western feminists—Sharma combines her own insights into Bengali Hindu culture with Sudhir Kakar's psychoanalytic theories of Westernized Indian consciousness and offers perceptive interpretations of both novels.

While Sharma outlines in broad terms Mukherjee's transformation from an expatriate to an immigrant, Pramila Venkateswaran, in her essay that follows Sharma's, focuses precisely on that crucial transformative stage. Venkateswaran, in her "Bharati Mukherjee as Autobiographer," identifies *Days and Nights in Calcutta* (1977) as a significant text that marks the nodal point in Mukherjee's personal and artistic development. *Days and Nights* reveals Mukherjee's increasing preparedness to abandon her Naipaulian preoccupation with nomadic alienation and to engage the liberating potential of immigration. *Days and Nights*, co-authored with Clark Blaise, is an unconventional autobiographical narrative that "occupies the indeterminate area between self-portraiture and journalistic reportage, between autobiography and ethnography, between self-writing and cultural anamnesis." On the one hand, the narrative is an effort to expose the predicament of women in a decidedly patriarchal Indian society; on the other hand, it is an attempt by Mukherjee to define her own multiple (dis)locations, examine her increasing discomfort with a variety of Indian cultural practices, and come to terms with her growing realization that the "real" India is vastly different from the imagined "home" of her expatriate nostalgia. Venkateswaran points out that Mukherjee's failure to integrate the tradition of Shakti (female power) into her analysis of women's status in the Indian socioculture renders her portrayal rather synecdochic; nevertheless, Venkateswaran argues, *Days and Nights* offers one of the most compelling examinations of the lives of women in contemporary India. Even more significantly, *Days and Nights* is a pioneering text in the literature of postcolonial expatriation: it systematically destroys, not without considerable personal anguish, the illusion of "home" in a bold attempt to forge a new home and a new identity in another country.

It is this issue of fashioning a new self in a new place that Brinda Bose examines in her "A Question of Identity: Where Gender, Race, and America Meet in Bharati Mukherjee." Specifically, Bose considers the implications of the ways in which Mukherjee inscribes ethnicity, gender, and migrancy in *The Tiger's Daughter*, *Wife*, and *Jasmine* (1989). Focusing on the female protagonists in each of these novels, Bose comments on the complex personal and cultural negotiations that Indian women immigrants face as they struggle to manage the tensions inherent in their conditions. Caught between their memories of India and the promises of America, they confront the need to adapt themselves to traumatic change. Such adaptation—and the immense psychological transformation which it requires—is possible only when the characters unanchor themselves from their nostalgic immobility and begin to engage risk and adventure. But change, Mukherjee cautions, often involves violence—psychic as well as physical—which Bose rightly identifies as a leitmotif in Mukherjee's fiction in general.

This pervasiveness of violence in Mukherjee's fictional universe is the subject of Samir Dayal's "Creating, Preserving, Destroying: Violence in Bharati Mukherjee's *Jasmine*." Jasmine's journey begins in strife-torn Punjab, where terror lurks even in the seemingly idyllic countryside. Her arrival in Florida is marked by violence—

Introduction

the violence of rape and her retaliatory violence of murder. Even the small town in Iowa where she temporarily settles down with a banker proves to be a surprisingly violent place. Dayal argues that this insistent presence of various forms of violence in *Jasmine* is not merely a reflection of the realities of contemporary life everywhere; nor is the novel simply, as Fredric Jameson might suggest, an allegorical enactment of the violence of postcolonial India. Rather, Dayal insists, that the complex and ambivalent functionality of violence in *Jasmine* reveals "the contradictions of postcolonial subject-formation."

While Dayal draws on the theories of postcolonialism to substantiate his arguments, Janet M. Powers takes a poststructuralist approach in her "Sociopolitical Critique as Indices and Narrative Codes in Bharati Mukherjee's *Wife* and *Jasmine*" to offer fascinating deconstructive readings of both novels. Using Roland Barthes's theory of narrative codes that he presents in his *S/Z* and *Image/Music/Text*, Powers explores Mukherjee's provocative sociopolitical critiques of American society as well as the Indian immigrant communities in her works. By identifying significant elements of sociopolitical critiques as function units and by examining them in terms of Barthes's system of structural analysis of narrative, Powers convincingly argues that "the startling turns of plot in *Wife* and *Jasmine*, which might at first be taken as inept writing," in fact, do not "violate narrative logic but . . . join with sociopolitical observations at a higher level to create a new sort of postcolonial narrative logic."

Pushpa N. Parekh's "Telling Her Tale: Narrative Voice and Gender Roles in Bharati Mukherjee's *Jasmine*" offers an equally intriguing interpretation of the novel's theme and structure. While Powers finds the narrative logic of Jasmine uniquely "postcolonial," Parekh argues that the narrative structure as well as the thematic substance of the novel reflect the form and content of classical female-oriented oral tales of India. In these traditional tales the female protagonist's incremental empowerment involves three distinct stages: from a "silent woman" she grows into a "speaking person" before she finally emerges as a vibrant "teller of tales." Parekh identifies in the "complex triad of Jyoti-Jasmine-Jane persona" a comparable pattern of development: Jyoti, "the silent woman" of feudal Hasnapur, becomes the semiliberated, citified Jasmine, "the speaking person" of Jullundhar, who, ultimately, transforms herself into a self-confident and eloquent "teller of tales." Thus Mukherjee revives in her postmodern narrative of immigration the ancient form of female-centered oral folktales of India.

The next four essays in the volume interrogate some of the key aesthetic and ideological assumptions of Mukherjee's work. Anindyo Roy, for example, begins his "The Aesthetics of an (Un)willing Immigrant: Bharati Mukherjee's *Days and Nights in Calcutta* and *Jasmine*" by defining the aesthetics of postcolonial exile that Mukherjee identifies as her artistic credo in her autobiographical *Days and Nights*. Roy then proceeds to examine the specific ways in which Mukherjee deploys these aesthetics in her novel *Jasmine*. He concludes by demonstrating how Mukherjee's "representation and production of the aesthetics of exile as a transnational and cosmopolitan 'epic theme' elide the deep contradictions built within the space of postcoloniality."

Alpana Sharma Knippling, in her brilliant essay titled "Toward an Investigation of the Subaltern in Bharati Mukherjee's *The Middleman and Other Stories* and *Jasmine*," offers an engaging commentary on Mukherjee's representation of the Other. Knippling acknowledges Mukherjee's vigorous and much needed "challenge to mainstream American literary-cultural productions," but she raises two key concerns. First, she questions the ability of Mukherjee—a privileged Bengali intellectual from upper-middle-class Calcutta—to represent in her narratives the economically marginalized and ethnically voiceless subaltern characters. Since Mukherjee on occasion unapologetically asserts her elite background—even speaks of her "Brahminical elegance"—Knippling asks how Mukherjee can so glibly translate the subaltern selves into her own self in many of her short stories that are narrated either in the first person or in the limited third-person point of view. Second, Knippling addresses a related but equally problematic aspect of representation in Mukherjee's fiction: the portrayal of a variety of new immigrants "across the cultural registers of race, ethnicity, gender, and class: Iraqi Jews, Afghanis, Indians from India, Uganda, and Trinidad, etc." In this representation of these "Others," Knippling asserts, there is a questionable homogenization of radical differences as well as a reckless conflation of vastly dissimilar historical and cultural identities. To discount the heterogeneity of ethnic minorities in the United States, Knippling cautions, is to retreat into dangerous notions of essentialism and to become vulnerable to "the imperialist program of assimilation, appropriation, and domestication."

The problem of representation is also the focus of Debjani Banerjee's essay that follows Knippling's. Her "'In the Presence of History': The Representation of Past and Present Indias in Bharati Mukherjee's Fiction" examines Mukherjee's uses of Indian history in *The Tiger's Daughter* and *Jasmine*. In both of these novels, Banerjee asserts, the historical moments which provide the political contexts for the narratives are exploited by the author largely for their sensationalism. For example, in framing Calcutta's Naxalite movement in *The Tiger's Daughter*, Mukherjee stresses the violence but remains largely reticent on the grim socioeconomic circumstances that spawned the revolutionary uprising. Her interpretation of the Naxalite revolt remains mostly "unifocal, drawing on the hegemonic point of view." Similarly, the current political crisis in Punjab dominates the early chapters of *Jasmine*; here again Mukherjee fails to contextualize the separatist movement in Punjab in terms of the troubled history of the subcontinent and her emphasis, predictably, is on the violence. Sikh activism, for example, is presented as mere terrorism. Banerjee argues that these superficial and misleading representations of ideologically charged moments in Indian history in Mukherjee's texts suggest her abdication of her responsibilities as a postcolonial intellectual who finds herself in a problematic yet privileged position as an interpreter of India to the West.

Gurleen Grewal, in her "Born Again American: The Immigrant Consciousness in *Jasmine*," offers a restrained critique of the troublesome politics that she recognizes in Mukherjee's most celebrated novel to date. Grewal concedes that Mukherjee's casting of her Indian immigrant woman protagonist in the familiar image of the American pioneer extolled in frontier novels is indeed "heroic and makes for some dramatic moments." What concerns Grewal, however, is the rather ingenuous and improbable nature of the protagonist's journey: the dramatic transformation of Jyoti to Jane—from a Punjabi peasant woman who is willing to commit *sati* to a reckless middle-class American woman who is willing to abandon her crippled husband in order to elope with a former lover. In narrativizing such a grand metamorphosis, Grewal argues, Mukherjee reinscribes the dominant ideology of the American Dream—a white male myth which insists on the spurious notion that anyone can reinvent himself or herself in America, regardless of race, gender, or class. Mukherjee's seeming complicity with such a conservative ideology also necessitates other compromises—both artistic and political—that Grewal explores in her essay.

The last two essays in the volume focus on Mukherjee's short stories. Mitali R. Pati's "Love and the Indian Immigrant in Bharati Mukherjee's Short Fiction" provides a lively commentary on a number of short stories which comically expose the dilemmas of Indian immigrant men and women who are often neither able to abandon their Old World scripts of romance and sexuality nor thoroughly master the American modes of romantic and sexual self-expression. Mukherjee's expert use of irony, satire, and parody reveals—with gentle humor—how her immigrant characters' "Indian paradigms of love, desire, and romance are deconstructed by their American experiences."

Carole Stone, in her "The Short Fictions of Bernard Malamud and Bharati Mukherjee," offers a useful comparative study of the two immigrant authors. Stone suggests that Mukherjee's adoption of Malamud as a literary model is prompted not only by some of the similarities inherent in their immigrant material but also by her strategic desire to ground herself firmly in the American immigrant literary tradition. Stone's comparative commentary points to the possibilities for a variety of cross-ethnic studies of immigrant traditions in American literature.

This collection of essays, I believe, captures the intensity while broadening the parameters of the discussion that began at the 1991 MLA convention special session on Bharati Mukherjee. But its publication is also an unequivocal acknowledgment of Mukherjee's emergence as a major American writer with an international audience. Her works, collectively, provide us with a poignant chronicle of her own personal search for home, wholeness, and stability. Her greatness, however, derives from her discovery in our immigrant lives of an occasion for art of epic dimensions.

Bharati Mukherjee

THE INNER WORLD OF BHARATI MUKHERJEE: FROM EXPATRIATE TO IMMIGRANT

Maya Manju Sharma

Bharati Mukherjee's early novels, *The Tiger's Daughter* (1971) and *Wife* (1975), explore the conditions of being an Indian expatriate and being an American immigrant. In conceiving the character of Tara in *The Tiger's Daughter*, Mukherjee had already begun to distance herself from the former role; in writing of the aborted Americanization of Dimple in *Wife*, she was already feeling her way into the latter. By the time she wrote *Darkness* (1985), she had identified herself completely with it. The process was a continuous one, so we shall look forward briefly to *Darkness* before returning to Tara the expatriate and Dimple the immigrant.

The years between *The Tiger's Daughter*, *Wife*, and *Darkness* mark a change in the inner world of Bharati Mukherjee and her consciousness. In the Introduction to *Darkness*, she says that until the spring of 1984, "I had thought of myself in spite of a white husband and two assimilated sons as an expatriate" (1). She defines expatriates as conscious knowers of their fate and immigrants—in particular to Canada—as "lost souls put upon and pathetic." The style *par excellence* of the expatriate is irony, as is so clearly shown by Naipaul, says Mukherjee. Exploring what she calls "state-of-the-art expatriation," Mukherjee made use of "a mordant self-protective irony." However, 1984 is a turning point in Mukherjee's sensibility and style. She says, "The book I dream of updating is no longer *A Passage to India*, it's *Call It Sleep*." She thus reveals that she is freed of the debility of expatriate nostalgia by the astringencies of life in the New World. What frees her from the company of persons who surrender "little bits of a reluctant self every year clutching the souvenirs of an ever retreating past" (*Darkness* 3)? By this time—1984—Mukherjee records that in writing the stories collected in *Darkness* she is no longer the aloof expatriate writer using irony that allows her "detachment from and superiority over those well-bred post colonials . . . adrift in the new world, wondering if they would ever belong" (*Darkness* 3).

The stories in *Darkness* are a celebration of change from "aloofness of expatriation" to the "exuberance of immigration" (*Darkness* 3). The dynamic of this growth is present in *The Tiger's Daughter* and *Wife*. In both these novels the author's voice is omniscient and irony her strategy. However, they are not written to imply, as Jasbir Jain says, "total rejection or a ruthless questioning of tradition or a love-hate relationship with the native heritage" (13). Rather, these early novels are travels in what Sudhir Kakar identifies as the "Psycho-Social country" of self shared by many other Indians studying, living, and working for long periods abroad in Europe or the United States: "At some time during this self-chosen exile, a more or less protracted confrontation with the self as battleground becomes almost inevitable" (*Inner World* 12–13). *The Tiger's Daughter* and *Wife* are the record of her confrontation with her self as her battleground. Tara, the protagonist of *The Tiger's Daughter*, comes home to find the niche she left behind seven years ago. Instead she witnesses the fracturing of her Calcutta:

> Not the Calcutta of documentary films—not a hell where beggars fought off dying cattle for still warm garbage—but a gracious green subtropical city where Irish nuns instructed girls from better families on how to hold their

heads high and how to drop their voices to a whisper and still be heard and obeyed above the screams of the city. ("Invisible Woman" 36)

This city that she had left, though comfortable, was not soft even then. And now she is back without her foreign husband and unaware that she is the source of disease in her social universe. That Tara is the alter ego of the author is clear from the autobiographical details in *Days and Nights*; the testings of Tara are also battles in the growth of the author's sensibility from that of the expatriate to that of the immigrant. This change is not arrived at by petulant challenge of tradition, but by deliberately putting the self at risk abroad and at home.

Abroad at first as a young woman of 21, Bharati Mukherjee came to study at Iowa while her younger sister Ranu tried again at Vassar, but was once more overcome by homesickness and went back to Baroda at Christmas. Bharati remained in graduate school, eventually to complete an M.F.A. and a Ph.D. in Comparative Literature. In 1963, during her second year of graduate school at the age of 23, she married Clark Blaise, a fellow student, in the lunchtime hour, forgoing the sacraments and ceremonies of a Bengali wedding.[1] Before and after having children, Mukherjee traveled to India in the summer, to stay connected and to let her husband have quiet in which to write: "India had been a place to send the family on summer vacations so that he could have undisturbed time for writing" (*Days and Nights* Part II 168). Mukherjee's own first novel was written during such a summer break. In his interview with her, Geoff Hancock asks:

Could you tell me about the origins of *The Tiger's Daughter*? Was that your MFA thesis in Iowa?

Mukherjee answers:

No. I wrote a collection of short stories for my MFA thesis. (41)

She goes on to explain that her husband sent off a copy of a well-received short story, "Debate on a Rainy Afternoon," to *Massachusetts Review*. When the story was published, it won honorable mention in "Best American Stories" for that year. Editors from three major publishing houses asked her to write novels; but since "the editor from Houghton Mifflin was the most persistent," Mukherjee wrote the editor that she was very busy finishing her dissertation and teaching full time besides raising two children, "but that as soon as I had a summer break, I'd get to work on a novel. And that's what I did" (Hancock 41). Wife, scholar, mother, teacher, novelist all rolled into one equals Superwoman. Indeed, Houghton Mifflin did publish Mukherjee's first novel, *The Tiger's Daughter*, on November 5, 1971. In *The Tiger's Daughter* and *Wife*, Mukherjee put her experience of Canada—traumatic transformation—behind her and found a voice of her own.

In the summer of 1966 Mukherjee went with her family first to Toronto, then to McGill. Life in Canada—fourteen years of it—tested her spirit to the breaking point. Her essay "Invisible Woman" is a blistering reflection on those years. She writes: "Many including myself left [Canada] unable to keep our twin halves together" (40). By the time she came to write this, she had not only, as we know, married a North American—a child of divorced parents—but also "stayed on for a Ph.D." These two factors, but especially the Ph.D., cut her off forever from "the world of passive privilege" that she had come from. In her Calcutta society, she records: "An MA in English is considered refined, but a doctorate is far too serious a business; indicative more of Brains than beauty and likely to lead to a quarrelsome nature" ("Invisible Woman" 36). She could not really go home no matter how many summers she spent with her family and friends. Her ambition, training, and marriage are wrong for Bengali Brahmin uppercrust life. But in the country of adoption, Canada, there was no welcome either. Mukherjee writes:

From Expatriate to Immigrant

> In Montreal, I was simultaneously a full professor at McGill, an author, a confident lecturer, and (I like to think) a charming and competent hostess and guest—*and* a housebound, fearful, aggressive, obsessive, unforgiving queen of bitterness. Whenever I read articles about . . . women committing suicide . . . I knew I was looking into a mirror. ("Invisible Woman" 39)

Here Mukherjee voices the impossibility of life as a Canadian citizen of color and wife of a North American author—finally the impossibility of being recognized as a Canadian author. Clark Blaise was asked to join the Writers' Union of Canada but Bharati Mukherjee was not—despite the fact that she was a citizen of Canada and he was not. The officials explained that she was automatically included under her husband's name. Later a more truthful confession came: "We did not know how to spell your name, and we were afraid of insulting you." Finally, most truthfully: "Your book was published by an American publisher and we could not get hold of it, so . . ." ("Invisible Woman" 39). That is as close to an apology as Mukherjee was to receive.[2]

Bharati Mukherjee lived in Canada from 1966 to 1980. Ultimately she risked everything—a stable career as a full professor, material and marital stability—to immigrate to the United States, where she found her voice again: "The transformation as a writer and as a resident of the new world, occurred with the act of immigration to the United States" (*Darkness* 12).

The journey starting in 1961 from Calcutta to student-time in Iowa and romance and marriage American campus-style to Canadian citizenship in 1966 and immigration to the United States in 1980 covers 21 years. These are the years of *agon* when in her novels Bharati Mukherjee models so well the "deep and persistent undercurrent of nostalgia almost sensual in character for the sights, smells, tastes, sounds of the country of our childhood" (Kakar, *Inner World* 13). She found the therapy in the act of creating that Kakar described seven years after *The Tiger's Daughter* and three years after *Wife*.

Kakar said that the acts of researching and writing *The Inner World* "have clarified and engaged the deeply Indian Part of myself thereby strengthening a sense of personal and historic continuity" (13). It is indeed this kind of strengthening that occurred through the writing of *The Tiger's Daughter* and *Wife*.

Tara Banerjee, the protagonist of *The Tiger's Daughter*, is modeled in her homesickness on Ranu's experience at Vassar; but her strength to endure that agony, go to "Madison" for summer school, meet and marry the young American David Cartwright, bear two sons, live at 124th Street and Broadway, and go back after seven years, is drawn out of the stuff of Bharati Mukherjee herself. Tara goes home to assess herself—to see whether she can rediscover herself in her birth tradition—to understand how much she belongs and in what manner she is different.

When *The Tiger's Daughter* came out, it was received with extravagant praise. Clark Blaise writes in *Days and Nights in Calcutta* that Satyajit Ray was delighted to receive a copy. He invited both of them to tea, for he very much wanted to meet the author whose first novel had been so highly praised in the *New Statesman*. He promised to share a copy of the review over tea (*Days and Nights* Part I 125–126). Indeed, John Spurling of the *New Statesman* gave her work high praise:

> She has achieved something more in the tradition of *Buddenbrooks* or *The Leopard*. *The Tiger's Daughter* is less grand in scale than either of those books; its tone of voice less ironic than Mann's, less melancholic than Lampedusa's, but a true imaginative explanation of class in decay rather than a sociological description. (26)

However, in *The Tiger's Daughter* Mukherjee wisely does not attempt a family saga but sets about exposing how it feels for a fifteen-year-old girl to leave a sheltered home hedged by class privilege and wealth, come back to it grown to young womanhood—to come home after breaking all the social taboos by marrying a foreigner—and see whether she can find her place at home again. This journey begins in Bombay and concludes in Calcutta, as Mukherjee sets her heroine traveling alone in a train across the Indian subcontinent. In Calcutta she experiences the terrors of a city paralyzed physically and morally in a *gherao* (mobbing). All the questions for which Tara had no information at Vassar will be answered as she continues to witness the crowd's use of its numbers to surround or gherao, paralyzing movement, political demonstration, street and *bustee* (squatter) life, at first from the security of the balcony of the fashionable Catelli-Continental Hotel and finally marooned in a car in the middle of an angry mob. Early on, this woman finds that she is different from her contemporaries in ways that cannot be communicated even if they wished that communication, simply because the society Tara rejoins is without a vision of the West that they could read if they chose to. All America means to that society is gadgets. Her tact and politeness render her unable to articulate her differences. It is this inability on Tara's part that in part upsets Mukherjee's Indian critics.

Something about *The Tiger's Daughter* upsets Indian critics greatly. They seem to share the reaction of Tara's erstwhile schoolmates, who feel she has polluted herself beyond redemption by her foreign education and *mleccha* marriage. "Here in Darjeeling," Jasbir Jain says incorrectly, "she is seduced and this act of seduction is symbolic of her foreignness which is an experience which cannot be undone" (15). The "seduction" is more like rape but, after all, having married a foreigner, she had it coming. The rape itself happens not in Darjeeling, the hill station of the Raj, but in Nayapur and at the hands of Tuntunwalla, both symbolic of the new India.

At the end of the novel, according to Jain, Tara is "rejecting India and her Indianness unable to grasp its meaning, and equally unable to understand the America she is going back to" (15). This is nonsense. Because she has kept faith with the old Bengal represented by her father and Joyonto Ray Chowdhary, Tara has more insight into the Indian predicament than her contemporaries, who distance themselves from the social question entirely. Jain's only evidence that she doesn't understand America is the fact that she wants to go back, and that doesn't really prove the point. After all, her apartment on the edge of Harlem is safer than the Catelli-Continental Hotel in Calcutta.

Mukherjee's Indian critics are continually excoriating her for her "expatriate sensibility," a phrase first used against V.S. Naipaul, and her "incomplete decolonization." In an insufferably condescending piece Sivaramkrishna claims that his subject ("Mrs. Mukherjee") has yet to find her authentic voice as a writer (86). To the average reader, she has a markedly individual voice, but it is one that the nationalistic intellectual refuses to hear as authentic. Jasbir Jain notes that in *The Tiger's Daughter* and *Wife*,

> The main concern is, no matter how we approach these novels, the relationship of the protagonists towards India. The attempt to understand India is clouded by the desire to interpret for foreigners, to judge India by their standards and value systems and this results in a kind of vacuum surrounding the protagonists. They belong nowhere. (18–19)

In contrast, Jain praises the novels of Shantha Rama Rau and Kamala Markandaya, whose protagonists have been exposed to Western education but not succumbed to it: "The questioning has a relevance for the self; it is not undertaken to satisfy the curiosity of some outsider" (19).

To be sure, the absent American husband is a constant point of reference in *The Tiger's Daughter*. Tara clings to the thought of him in an attempt to maintain her identity in a Calcutta changing beyond all recognition. And in fact Mukherjee has an American husband. But in a way the husband serves as the externalization of a foreign point of view. Mukherjee, like her character Tara, had assimilated long before leaving India for good.

Mukherjee actually lived in Europe as a small child and went to school there first. When her family returned to

From Expatriate to Immigrant 11

Calcutta, she attended a convent school created for English girls. There she began to write: "The world of fiction seemed more real to me than the world around me. I started my first novel when I was about nine or ten. It came to seventy or eighty pages. It was about English children and was set in England" (Carb 653). In high school she even wrote a first-person story of Napoleon. Like many Indians of her generation and class, Mukherjee was bicultural from the very beginning.

No one has given greater thought to the identity crisis of the bicultural Indian than psychoanalytic ego psychologist Sudhir Kakar. "The expression of affect without restraint, the being in emotion, the infectious liveliness amidst squalor—in short the intensity of life—is a deeply yet diffusely seductive siren song for Indian Intellectuals" (*Inner World* 13). It is to seek the state of "being in emotion[,] . . . infectious liveliness," to hear the "siren song" of nostalgia, that Tara comes to Calcutta. Mukherjee chooses her characters' names carefully. "Tara Banerjee Cartwright" involves complex layers of wordplay. Tara is the great Goddess of the Tantrics in one of Her forms, the desolate seat of the High Kings of Ireland, the lost paradise of Scarlett O'Hara. Banerjee is Bandhopadyay, the Master of Bondage, as Mukherjee is Mukhtopadyay, the Master of Liberation. Cartwright is the Master of the Vehicle, of that which crosses over (tarati) from bondage to freedom; the Cartwrights were the rancher family who civilized the West on American television during Tara's—and Mukherjee's—early years in the United States.

That Tara's name alludes to *Gone with the Wind* is probably deliberate and certainly important. Social disorder has done to Calcutta what Sherman's army did to Atlanta; more to the point, the Naxilite riots, like the American Civil War, are not some catastrophe coming from outside, but the inevitable consequence of systematic social injustice. Tara in America did not realize this; her nostalgia for the old Bengal was a form of "visionless knowledge." Without Joyonto Ray Chowdhary's opening her eyes to epiphanies of "mystery and death"—and poverty—Tara could have gone on to become a Margaret Mitchell of India, one of many.

The vision Joyonto imparts is important to one named for the *divine* Tara. She must learn, as he is learning, to free herself from the soft vision of a protected past. She must come to understand that the good life of the few is based on immense human suffering, and that all that is born must die and be consumed. She runs from the yogi at the cremation ground because she will not have her palm read. She resists seeing that her own personal destiny is woven into the fabric of birth and death, but she does learn to see that this is true of the society into which she was born.

The gatherings at the Catelli-Continental, at the homes of friends, at the school, and at the Chamber of Commerce's annual charity carnival, the earth tremor and snake at the picnic, the Darjeeling episode of insult and exposure to the unsanctioned eyes of young toughs on holiday, and Tuntunwalla bent on satisfying "heart's matters" in Nayapur all play a role in waking her up to the vision that teases her. The novel ends as it began—at the Catelli-Continental. Except for the forays outside the hotel commanded by Joyonto to give her a breath of fresh air, Tara has never been a part of the crowd. She has always been sheltered, as child, young adult, and woman. Each excursion traumatizes her by bringing her closer to the touch of the masses. She has spent her time viewing the marching world of Calcutta's Park Street from behind its protective balcony, being made quite uncomfortable by Marie Antoinettish impatience. The groups that congregate at the Catelli-Continental—the young women in pastel saris, the old men carrying cherished dogs—watch from the balcony the life of the sidewalk dwellers and the protest marches. This works two ways: those who view are also exposed to the scrutiny of those they sit and comment on all day. They attach no importance to this fact of their being themselves on view. Their sensibilities are shielded by conviction of the righteousness their privileged status confers on them. The eccentric owner of tea estates in Assam, Joyonto Ray Chowdhary, is the only one who realizes how vulnerable the group really is. He watches them meet at the Catelli-Continental to plan parties, do post mortems of functions they attend, discuss each other's lives, and above all sit suspended above the sidewalk of Park Street—jeweled fish in a fancy bowl in which the water level is sinking day by day. It is here Tara witnesses her first and last demonstration when willy nilly she joins the crowd even if it is in an enclosed car—not any more on the balcony. She has summoned her friends to tell them she is returning to the United States, when the marchers riot under the balcony. Joyonto, from the day he vowed to protect the luminous Brahmin child, has tried to prepare her for this moment. One hopes that the vision gives her the creative ability to survive. In her study of the expatriate sensibility Sudha Rai quotes V.S. Naipaul's response to his first journey to India: "It was a journey that ought not to have been made. It had broken my life in two" (15–16). In his effort to understand the workings of Eastern norms—*karma, dharma, moksha*—and balancing the outcome against the Western norms of individuality and freedom, Naipaul misses the safety net, and will have to make his journey to the source again. Mukherjee's Tara, however, is prepared by her early life in Calcutta, Western education at home and abroad, and most importantly by Joyonto Ray Chowdhary not to yield to the abyss that fissures beneath the tightrope she walks.

When Tara/Bharati goes West, she undergoes a new birth in the womb of Vassar and growth in graduate school. The new-birthed consciousness—birthed in dormitories and classrooms by a Western curriculum and consciousness—seeks to hold its history at its center where the knowledge is visionless (*The Tiger's Daughter* 9). Like Henry James' heroine, Isabel Archer, who goes to Europe/Britain, the source of her tradition, for vision in knowledge, so Tara/Bharati must come to the source—the omphalos of all vision—the Catelli-Continental. Thanks to Joyonto Ray Chowdhary, and her years away, Tara begins to exchange vision for insight. At the end of the novel, as she sits shivering in the Fiat, surrounded by a mob, wondering whether she will ever see her husband again, she sees the vision twinkling, pinching, pulling, slapping through the crowd that surrounds the hotel. Bharati Mukherjee, in refusing to state what it is, invites a reader response in decoding the vision. Stanley Fish, an important reader response theorist, says: "The place where sense is made or not made is in the reader's mind rather than the printed page or space between the covers of a book" (Tompkins xvii). What follows is a response.

In *Shamans, Mystics and Doctors* Kakar reminds us that a Tantric has only those desires that the environment is already willing and in a position to satisfy (167). In the penultimate paragraph of *The Tiger's Daughter* Tara has a glimpse of the "vision" that has teased her throughout the novel, but it is a glimpse only, and does not, for her, assume definite form. We are told that it is the vision that has made Joyonto "almost holy"; we may infer that it is intimately connected with the Tantric yogi at the cremation ground and all he represents, and that it is somehow expressed by Joyonto's obsessive, frantic imitations of the early T.S. Eliot. Joyonto has altered himself to fit his environment. The thin old aristocrat has been beaten by the mob while attempting to distract them from Tara's car, and the fat young capitalist has been killed when he leaves the car to save him. At this point Tara sees Joyonto's vision bouncing off the placards and running amok through the crowd boxing ears and pinching bottoms, spreading hysteria through the city. Whether or not she makes it home to America, her knowledge of her Indian origins, which was "visionless" there, is now no longer entirely so.

As we have seen, the Tantric vision transcends nostalgia by revealing the corruptible and corrupting nature of all finite objects of desire. All Tara is left with in the end is her love for her husband, who is, in Tantric belief, only a stand-in for something greater. To the Tantric, human desire is not in the least vain because its objects, though themselves unreal, are symbolic of higher reality. Thus Tara's nostalgia for a vanishing India is itself capable of alchemic transformation from reactionary sentimentality to the stuff of art.

Wife was so different from *The Tiger's Daughter* that many readers didn't know what to make of it (Sivaramkrishna 79). Tara Cartwright returns to India to recover her roots; Dimple Basu does everything she can to obliterate hers. She even induces a miscarriage so that she does not have to bring a child conceived in India into the New World. Rosanne Klass, writing in *Ms.*, the feminist monthly, says that Mukherjee doesn't understand the consequences of such an act for a traditionally raised Indian woman. But Mukherjee understands them all too well: *Wife* is the story of these consequences. For Dimple, as for some Western feminists, abortion is a sacrament of liberation from the traditional roles and constraints of womanhood. She terminates her pregnancy by skipping rope, but that does not mean that the action is undertaken frivolously. Rather, this detail may signify that the action is a frivolous one in a very deep and sinister sense, and that Dimple is aware of this. It is the deliberate repudiation of a moral code for which she has no replacement. Mukherjee's lightness of touch is here no lack of seriousness; Flannery O'Connor is a clear influence.

Dimple's moral and cultural suicide is symbolized and effectuated by an act of abortion, the destruction of an actual or potential human life merely because it has begun, like Dimple herself, in India. This act is pregnant with the destruction of the marriage bond in adultery, and the climactic murder of the husband. As noted above, this comes dangerously close to a critique of feminist ideology by an author who is, by her own admission, fundamentally a moralist:

> My fiction locates very clearly, I think, what's morally right and what's not. But I don't have guys in white hats slugging guys in black hats. There's villainy growing out

of misunderstandings and malice, but there's no Devil. (Hancock 44)

This is from an interview with Geoff Hancock, who asks, "Is infidelity and murder the only solution?" "Dimple thinks so," she replies. "The ending, I guess, is discomfitting" (44). Especially, one might add, for the husband. Mukherjee goes on to explain more fully:

> Dimple's decision to murder her husband is her misguided act of self-assertion. If she had remained a housewife living with her extended family in India, she probably would not have asked herself questions such as, am I unhappy, do I deserve to be unhappy. And if by chance she had asked herself these questions, she might have settled her problems by committing suicide. So turning to violence outward rather than inward is part of her slow and misguided Americanization. *Wife* is a novel that is very dear to me. (Hancock 44)

Dimple's "misguided Americanization" begins when she raises the question of individual happiness, as a Western ideal she has failed to measure up to, or a right she has been denied. From a Hindu religious point of view, *Wife* shows the illusory nature of Dimple's idea of happiness, the hollowness of her American dream. A Judeo-Christian reading of Dimple's progress from abortion would give considerable aid and comfort to the "right to life" crowd, and the specter of this misreading may have provoked the hostile review in *Ms*. Nevertheless, Mukherjee's moral imagination is certainly not a Judeo-Christian one; as she makes clear in another interview:

> I was born into a Hindu Bengali Brahmin family which means I have a different sense of self, of existence, and of mortality, than do writers like Malamud. I believe that our souls can be reborn in another body, so the perspective I have about a single character's life is different from that of an American writer who believes that he has only one life. (Carb 651)

To the Hindu imagination abortion, suicide, and murder are not the ultimate acts they seem to be to the Jewish or Christian conscience. However, the Hindu sees no real point in someone like Dimple's being so anxious about her individual happiness in this one life of many, making herself so much more unhappy. He—or she—might even see a tragic irony in the title *Wife*. Modern Indian society, like the American, gives little honor to wives. According to Lina Fruzzetti the Hindu tradition, especially the Bengali tradition, from which Dimple's progenitors have long departed, is far otherwise:

> In Bengal, the very idea of auspiciousness, or blessedness, is associated with marriage and married women. A new wife (stri) is introduced to her husband's house as a deity, wife, and future mother. Stri, a term carrying a sacred meaning, not only denotes one's own wife but also stands for Laksmi (Goddess of Wealth), Durga (the Mother Goddess), femaleness, motherhood, and womanliness. (123)

In a traditional Bengali household, the man may be king, but the woman is priestess. There is, indeed, a sense in which the husband is God, but the wife is Goddess. Dimple has not rejected this tradition; sadly, she has never known it. Conceived outside any sacral context, the child is misbegotten, fit for destruction in the act of jumping rope, expressive of the fact that Dimple herself is still a child because she has not been initiated into the mysteries of womanhood. Both husband and wife see marriage secularly, as a means toward individual happiness, so there is no reason for faithfulness. In such a marriage the choice of widowhood is something of an act of truth. Fruzzetti tells us what widowhood means to the Hindu:

> A husband gives his new wife the symbols of a married woman: iron bangles and vermilion. Similarly, a woman offers her gifts of a santan [child], her reproductive organs, and her sexuality to her husband. When he dies these gifts are not returned, her reproductive power, her

> sexuality, and her femaleness being permanently removed. This means that the death of a man puts an end to the femaleness of his wife. After the death of the husband, a part of the woman is symbolically dead. The widow is neither a virgin who can be given to others in marriage nor a married woman with a living husband through whom children can be produced. (103)

Dimple's divorce, Hindu style, is thus a kind of symbolic castration, a murder not so much of her inept spouse as of her own stunted womanhood. Her creator's attitude is certainly compassionate, but, as certainly, not approving.

Wife is not a Hindu critique of Western feminism, but it hints at one, and these hints may have unnerved Rosanne Klass, the reviewer at *Ms.*, to the point of resorting to desperate measures indeed. Dimple has an upsetting misunderstanding with the manager of a kosher deli, where the pungent odor and a thumbprint on a sign call up associations of India's ultimate pollution, beef blood. Klass points out that kosher butchering removes all blood, and all but accuses Mukherjee of a contemptuous ignorance of Jews and their customs. In reality, however, it is Klass—not Mukherjee—who is guilty of ignorance.

Firoza Jussawalla praises the modern Indian woman for breaking free of the traditional loyalty to cotton and silk and wearing saris of Japanese synthetics, much better adapted to housework and office work (583). Bharati Mukherjee is another sort entirely. One imagines she would prefer clothing cut in the best Western fashions for the North American climate, out of the best traditional materials. In her fiction Mukherjee handles Western themes and settings as well as characters who are Westernized or bicultural. Yet she is forced to admit that the very structure of her imagination is essentially Hindu, and essentially moral, as we have seen above.

Given Mukherjee's moral and metaphysical commitments, it is all the more remarkable that she should come to see herself as an immigrant American rather than an expatriated Indian. "Language gives me my identity," she tells Hancock, "I am the writer I am because

I write in North American English about immigrants in the New World" (35). Mukherjee's immigration is not so much her move from the Calcutta of the East to the Calcutta of the West (as she affectionately calls New York) by way of Canada, as it is her move from the English of Jane Austen to the American of Walt Whitman. "It's possible—with sharp ears and the right equipment—to hear America singing even in the seams of the dominant culture. In fact it may be the best listening post for the next generation of Whitmans" (*Darkness* 3). Of course Whitman is more than the bard of democratic pluralism. He is also the most persuasive of that long line of American culture heroes who, for whatever mysterious reasons, gravitated toward a Hindu philosophy of life.

For Jussawalla the Whitmanesque dream is a lie covering up the racist reality of America, with which Mukherjee is in fawning collusion:

> Bharati Mukherjee definitely seems to have found her "haven" in the United States, but with this comes an obsequiousness, a pleading to be mainstreamed, to be seen as the next generation of "Whitmans." . . . [I]n Mukherjee's voice there is an admonishment to other immigrants, which when placed in the context of the reality of discrimination rings hollow. (591)

Jussawalla reads the stories in *Darkness* as an attack on the unassimilated immigrant and a justification for his ill-treatment and would no doubt see *Wife* in the same terms. "Do these people deserve America, where life is fluid and accepting? . . . Her [Mukherjee's] answer is no" (590). For Jussawalla, Mukherjee is the leader of a Quisling movement that includes Hanif Kureishi and Vikram Seth:

> Is this criticism of immigrant behavior, then, the counter-hegemonic discourse of the ex-colonized? Or is this the new hegemonic discourse of those who see themselves as assimilated and assimilable? The irony is that in separating themselves and in hoping to be accepted among the mainstream of the majority of the population, these writers only extend and perpetuate a

new colonial mentality, which is perhaps possible in America but *not* possible in the U.K. where there is no arms-opened reception, however colonized and acceptable the post-colonial immigrants might be. (590–591)

To affirm an American identity is not necessarily to pledge allegiance to the forces of racism and imperialism worldwide. To take an affectionate look at the foibles of Indians in Flushing is not to justify the racially motivated beatings in London and Toronto. Nor is Whitman's dream of a pluralistic America an utter canard. Against the immigrants of Whitman's youth, the Irish, Nativists had unleashed an organized campaign of hysteria and violence to make today's skinheads look wimpish indeed, and most of the Irish still refused to mend their ways. By Whitman's maturity they *were* America, or at least New York, which (except to a Whitman) may not be exactly the same thing. If Mukherjee, like Whitman, feels at home in the Calcutta of the West, that does not make her an imperialistic toady.

The easy rhetoric of colonialism and decolonization does not have much to do with immigrant life in America, as Jussawalla half admits, and does not fit the Indian complexities well either. Mukherjee's sense of Indianness is real, but is not limited to the self-concept of modern India. She grew up Bengali in a country where English is an official language and her mother tongue is not, and was in America when half of Bengal won its independence from Pakistan. Dyed-in-the-wool Bengalis feel themselves as expatriated in New Delhi as they do in New York; Mukherjee feels as at home in New York as she would anywhere in India, including the post-Naxilite Calcutta. She is no less Bengali for that. Accepting the role of immigrant, she has not redefined herself as an American. Rather, she has consented to be part of that long procession of peoples who have over the years redefined America.

NOTES

1. See *Days and Nights*, Part I, pp. 158–162, for a portrait of a family wedding, and Fruzzetti's summary of the wedding rituals, p. 140. For a detailed account of the traditions see Fruzzetti, pp. 69–96.

2. While the Canadian Writers' Union does acknowledge its embarrassment at being unable to spell her name, it is extraordinary that M. Sivaramkrishna cannot also get the author's name correct. In his article "Bharati Mukherjee" he insultingly refers to her eleven times as "Mrs. Mukherjee." Her married name is Mrs. Clark Blaise.

WORKS CITED

Carb, Alison B. "An Interview with Bharati Mukherjee." *The Massachusetts Review* 29.4 (1988): 645–654.

Fruzzetti, Lina M. *The Gift of a Virgin: Women, Marriage, and Ritual in Bengali Society.* New Delhi: Oxford University Press, 1990.

Hancock, Geoff. "An Interview with Bharati Mukherjee." *Canadian Fiction Magazine* 59 (1987): 30–44.

Jain, Jasbir. "Foreignness of Spirit: The World of Bharati Mukherjee's Novels." *Journal of Indian Writing in English* 13.2 (July 1985): 12–19.

Jussawalla, Feroza. "Chiffon Saris: The Plight of South Asian Immigrants in the New World." *The Massachusetts Review* 29.4 (1988): 583–595.

Kakar, Sudhir. *The Inner World: The Psycho-Analytic Study of Childhood and Society in India*. New Delhi: Oxford University Press, 1978.

———. *Shamans, Mystics and Doctors: A Psychological Inquiry into India and Its Healing Traditions*. Boston: Beacon, 1983.

Klass, Rosanne. "Indian Wife Lives Soap-Opera Life." *Ms.* (Oct. 1975): 83.

Mukherjee, Bharati. *Darkness*. Markham, Ontario: Penguin, 1985.

———. "An Invisible Woman." *Saturday Night* (March 1981): 36–40.

———. *The Tiger's Daughter*. Boston: Houghton Mifflin, 1971.

———, and Clark Blaise. *Days and Nights in Calcutta*. Garden City, N.Y.: Doubleday, 1977.

Rai, Sudha. *V.S. Naipaul: A Study in Expatriate Sensibility*. New Delhi: Heinemann, 1982.

Sivaramakrishna, M. "Bharati Mukherjee." *Indian English Novelists*. Ed. Madhusudan Prasad. New Delhi: Sterling, 1982. 71–86.

Spurling, John. Rev. of *The Tiger's Daughter*. *New Statesman* (6 July 1973): 26.

Tompkins, Jane P. *Reader-Response Criticism*. Baltimore: Johns Hopkins University, 1980.

BHARATI MUKHERJEE AS AUTOBIOGRAPHER

Pramila Venkateswaran

Days and Nights in Calcutta is created at the intersection of cultures, of postcolonial and "free" worlds, of "tradition" and "modernity," of East and West. Unlike the confessional mode of traditional autobiography, *Days and Nights* occupies the indeterminate area between self-portraiture and journalistic reportage, between autobiography and ethnography, between self-writing and cultural anamnesis. Divided into two parts, the first written by Clark Blaise and the second by Bharati Mukherjee, the dual authorship is itself a comment on the cultural braiding that is an underlying theme in the book. Subverting generic categories, the autobiographies, Mukherjee's particularly, play with the diffusion, tension, and multiplicity of meanings that join to create the picture of the Indian woman's consciousness. Her narrative shows how values separate Western and Indian cultures and merge them, lines dissipate and reappear, and definitions form and collapse. The work reveals the ever-changing relationship between the center and the periphery.

Under the overarching story of her visit to India as an Indian woman married to a Canadian and living as an expatriate in Canada, Mukherjee in *Days and Nights* argues compellingly that Indian women are culturally constructed and sketches the possibilities for the Indian woman to change her destiny. What Mukherjee does recognize is the importance of looking at the "now," the "middle" of women's particular realities, the possibilities for women's liberation which the Hindu imagination does allow despite the overwhelmingly oppressive tradition, and the importance of applying a reinterpreted Hindu philosophy to suit women's particular realities. Curiously, however, while *Days and Nights* derives its power by allowing the collective voices of Calcutta women to take over the narrative, it is its very selectivity noticeably marked with the absence of the tradition of *Shakti* (female power) that denies the reader a complete picture of Indian women's experiences.

The shifting center of Mukherjee's narrative among the myriad characters provides an apt locus for her material, which is the shifting cultural values regarding the woman's subject position in Indian society. As her story moves between herself and the other women, so do her descriptions and evaluations of classes and cultures.[1] Since traditional autobiography,[2] typically an outpouring of the self, would not have been relevant to the material she deals with, Mukherjee combines autobiography with ethnography; her personal story is relevant only insofar as it relates to the outer set of events and the collective identity of Calcutta women. The world outside the self takes on an importance as it would to a novelist or a journalist, such that it provides an area for the narrator to either participate in or observe from the fringes. Her alienation or involvement is contextual; therefore, the center of the narrative constantly shifts according to the context, from the collective to the individual, from the sociohistorical reconstruction of women to individual and personal revelation.

Mukherjee uses concepts such as the "Hindu imagination" and "merging" to shape her ideas and fulfill her goal of documenting the range of Hindu women's experiences in conjunction with her own discovery of identity. Indian women's experiences, as Mukherjee perceives them, seem to adhere to the ambiguous nature of Hinduism. She invents the term "Hindu imagination" to describe the form she uses to shape her work and combines it with her argument for the reconstruction of the woman's self. She uses the term to mean the collectivity of the Hindu woman's consciousness which is ingrained within the mythical tradition that has contributed to constructing her values. The Hindu imagination is a symbolic imagination, whose comprehensive vision encompasses the abstract and the spiritual, the inner and the outer, the tangible and the intangible. Understanding women's experiences within this paradoxical philosophy is particularly difficult, since it demands that we look at female experience within the entirety of the Hindu tradition.

Mukherjee's tacit observation, "In the Hindu imagination, everything is causeless, endless middle" (286) carries her frustration with people's acceptance of their lot and the lack of scientific inquiry into the causes and effects of their reality. While this attitude concurs with the Hindu belief in Brahman and all of creation as beginningless and endless, that all is "middle," it goes counter to the Hindu notion of *karma* by which one's reality is measured according to one's past deeds. The concept of *thirtha* or ford, a crossover point, with its emphasis on the passage itself, is an interesting corollary to the notion of the "middle," the space that is the woman's reality. By beginning her narrative right in the middle of her life, Mukherjee makes it cohere to the Hindu notion of the beginninglessness and endlessness of the Ultimate and of Creation itself. At the same time, her narratives about the Calcutta women and her presentation of herself in the epilogue give the impression that they begin their journey at a definite time and place and some of them, such as the narrator and Meena, are ready to "cross over" to new territories within themselves.

By presenting vignettes of ethnography, she informs us how she and some of the women she encounters shape their lives—the middle or the passage between the before and the after. Her encounters with her friends, many of them former schoolmates, put her in touch with the pulse of women's position in India. Although the women are grounded in reality, each of them trying to cope with the middle of her journey, they explain their experiences in terms of karma. The Hindu belief in karma, the determination of one's fate in accordance with past deeds, has no place for accident. Despite the Hindu belief in karma, accidents seem to play a major role especially in the oppressed person's life, here, the Hindu woman's life, whose drama Mukherjee captures mid-act, as it were. To the Hindu, says Mukherjee, accidents, coincidences, predictions take on the validity of truth. Her autobiography, a chronicle of collective memory and individual self-discovery, is made to seem a product of an accident; losing her house in a fire and getting hurt in a car accident brings her to India and inevitably makes her reflect on her identity and those of the women around her. The birth of a woman is itself an accident as the oppressive social conditions of women seem to suggest. Within the context of the narrative, happiness and sorrow are not explained by present conditions but are judged as karmic. Since women are subjects in society and their individuality is contained, personal happiness for women becomes coincidental to their lives.

Interestingly, the "Hindu imagination," as Mukherjee conceives it, embraces the sublime and the ridiculous, a polarity that aptly characterizes the world she writes about and which she, too, is in—a world in which there exists a gulf between philosophy and culture. While the "middle" is a powerful vision of a person's life, the center of an individual's *thirtha*, or crossing, it is also a vision that is frustrating and oftentimes ridiculous. An apt instance is when Anjali's daughter and her classmates at Loretto House rebel against the decision of the nuns to ban Ezekiel's poem from being reprinted in the college magazine *Palm Leaves* because of its alleged unsuitability. Not being given any explanation regarding the reason for the nuns' pronouncement nor what happened after the rebellion of the students, Mukherjee experiences enormous disappointment and frustration. She remarks that every Indian story—the Indian reality—is marked by "middles"; there are no befores and afters.

India is the narrator's midpoint between her position as an expatriate in Canada and her decision to establish herself as an American immigrant. It is the place where she and her family come to rest, where she rediscovers herself and reevaluates her identity as a woman and as a writer. India becomes a place for "centering" herself, for looking at herself in relation to the Indian community, evaluating her past, and deciding on her future. India is the topoi where the self and the Other, she and women she writes about, the narrator as other and the Bengali community, converge and separate, where cultures collide and collude, and where historical and narrative time meet and diverge. *Days and Nights* is the space that Mukherjee, as woman, as writer, and as immigrant, occupies that is within India and outside it.

On the margins between "abroad" and "home," Mukherjee occupies an ambiguous position. She is the Other both in Canada, a white-dominated country, and in India. As an Indian, her plurality—a Bengali Brahmin with an English education—makes her live on the margins. In Canada, it was easy to become a Canadian citizen, but to be accepted socially as a writer in her own right proved difficult. In India she is "racially invisible"; in Canada her visibility is problematic. She was "the wife of Clark Blaise the writer, who also writes." Ironically, during her visit in India she is the star of Calcutta, the talk of the town, more popular than the Hindi film stars.

She and the characters that people the narrative are sometimes in the center and sometimes on the periphery, depending on the context in which they are situated. As an observer and recorder of the life around her, she is sometimes the "other" and sometimes the participant, and this confusion creates a problematic position for her as a writer. As Salman Rushdie aptly puts it, his in-between-ness as a Pakistani writer in England makes him at one and the same time an insider and an outsider in his society (Rushdie 19); he is British, Indian, or Pakistani, central or marginal, depending on the situation. Living on the cultural divide, Mukherjee feels absorbed by the elasticity of Hindu culture and at the same time alienated by its rigidity and hierarchy. Note that just as she is an insider and an outsider, Indians themselves live inside and outside the definitions and communities they create. For example, Anjali's parties are open only to the "Number One" executives and their wives, and the party for Anjali becomes a strategy of self-definition. Also note that Mukherjee uses other images to emphasize the division between inside and outside, which contradict Hindu philosophy's insistence on the transparency between Brahman and Atman. For example, the riots on the streets as opposed to the calmness within middle-class households, the poor outside, as opposed to the rich within, and the surging crowd outside the theater and the glitter of wealth within, all emphasize division.

The question of the writer's identity within an ever-shifting center, therefore, becomes a vexed issue in this work. Mukherjee, perceived as a "foreign returned" woman married to a white man, feels she is leading two lives, one with her family and another outside it. She is accepted by her family, but outside it she is seen as an Indian woman with a white escort. Caught in tension between the family and the world outside, she lets the collective voice take over the work. Mukherjee sees herself through the eyes of others. She is seen as a local woman who has done well. She represents the career woman, who is independent economically and has equality in her marriage. It is through what others say of her that we learn how she is viewed by Indian society. For example, Mukherjee observes that when she meets *dimma* (grandmother), who is bedridden, she slips a hundred rupee note into her hand, which a visitor spots and is enraged by. The woman's anger stems, Mukherjee observes, from her own lack of economic independence. At another time when she is interviewed in *Desh*, Clark's act of pouring the tea becomes symbolic of the power relation between the

Blaises. Set against the backdrop of Indian households where the husband, generally speaking, expects his wife to wait on him, the teapot incident becomes news. By showing how others perceive her, Mukherjee exposes the position of women in Indian culture: the wife's apparent lack of economic independence and her seeming subservience to the husband.

In describing women in Calcutta, recreated through interviews with them, recounting of slices of stories from the epics, retelling newspaper stories involving women, and describing her parents' relationships with her relatives, friends, and herself, Mukherjee observes that the women hold one common value: serving the husband as the primary duty of the good Indian wife. Social position to a large extent dictates women's experiences. Depending on their positions in society, women feel either accepted or alienated. Accepted if they concur with tradition and rejected if they dissent, women are controlled by their tradition. While the collectivity of tradition is supportive for women, as seen in the joint family households and Jaya's marriage, since values in that collectivity are male-generated, women's subjective experiences are often in tension with the collective voice.

Questions pertaining to the identity of the Indian woman and the narrator's identity, at once collective and individual, are the subjects of the autobiography. Mukherjee reads herself and the lives of Calcutta women within the configurations of the Naxalite uprising, the remnants of anachronistic British culture among the upper class, and the collective hold of age-old Hindu tradition. She locates women's experiences in the Hindu tradition replete with Sita and Savitri role models who exemplify acceptance, selflessness, and *pativrata* (husband worship) as the ideals for the wife and mother. Self-abnegation, the definition of the ideal wife in the *Ramamyana* and in the story of Satyavan and Savitri, which form part of the powerful oral tradition internalized by most Indian males and females, stands in conflict with the values of self-assertion and self-actualization women hold in public life, especially if they are in positions of power. Despite their Western education, the upper-class women Mukherjee speaks with identify with their tradition and equate husband with god. Veena and Anjali, upper-class Bengali wives, live in mansions cut off from the surging and volatile life outside, with its class and caste riots and the Naxalite revolt. Their lives are spent focused on domestic life and supporting their husbands' businesses by entertaining, attending parties, going to the horse races, a reality that seems unconnected with that of middle-class women like Mukherjee's relatives, who are more in touch with socioeconomic realities. What does connect the classes, however, is their unavowed faith in the *pativrata* ideal.

The wives of the "Number One Executives" whom Mukherjee interviews are proud of displaying their identity which they receive from their husbands. Married to men of status in society, these women are proud of their position. A woman is seen not for what she is but what she represents about the family. Her background, social and familial, is primary. Even her beauty is culturally constructed: fairness and fullness are the measures of feminine beauty. Wealth, social class, and caste play important roles in a woman's life; they dictate her destiny. All her energies are directed toward finding a good husband, since her tradition values marriage as her salvation. Arranged marriage, with its rules of "courtship," dowry, and ritual, ultimately is humiliating to the woman but she still prefers to be married rather than be stigmatized as a spinster. And for the woman to live independently is still for many Indians an alien concept. Marriage and motherhood are still seen as a woman's ideals.

Clark Blaise, the witness to Mukherjee's narrative, perceives that despite Indian society's overwhelming demand that women be submissive, accepting, and self-sacrificing, some women have the rebel in them. Jaya, despite the humiliation of being rejected by several suitors on account of her dark skin and thin figure, comes across to Blaise as vivacious and spirited. She is totally in control of her life once she "chooses" to marry Arun, and her family accepts him despite his lower caste status. Blaise sees in Indian women a power that exists despite the overwhelming rigidity of the male dominated tradition. Jaya's marriage, with its attendant complexities, such as dowry, wedding arrangements, and elaborate rituals, seems to Blaise a metaphor of Indian life: "the ritual with all its irregularities just happens to work" (161). What he notices about the inventiveness within the rigidity can be said of women and the way they deal with their oppressive realities. Within society's rigid definitions of marriage Jaya manages to find happiness, although personal happiness is seen as relational to the community, or is subsumed by that of the husband and children within the family.

Beneath the collective traditional voices stir the undercurrents of rebellion: Anjali's daughter and her classmates at Loretto House battle with the nuns to include a poem that the nuns have labeled "unsuitable." Meena goes to college to get her degree despite family opposition. Someone's sister becomes a Naxalite leader. Someone marries out of caste and is shunned by her family. Some women manage careers and family. While the collective for women means support and solidarity, it is at the same time confining for the independent woman, since her society does not value women's personal freedom and happiness.

With the help of ethnographic data and stories from the local newspaper and the grapevine, Mukherjee describes the kinds of experiences women are subjected to. Despite being educated and having a career, women have to wait on their husbands. A young woman had to flee India because she couldn't bear being physically abused by her mother-in-law and her husband. While these are stories among the middle class, among the lower classes the stories are just as poignant. Bitto, a widow in a North Indian village, is hunted by her family and the local police and is killed along with her lover. For a woman to want a family after she is widowed is a transgression according to the conventional Hindu code of ethics.

The pockets of anger rumbling beneath the surface calm are revealed to us in the stories of Meena and other intelligent women who make great sacrifices to accomplish their personal goals. As Mukherjee points out, despite the odds these women resist the cultural norms prescribed for them. Her reports on the Marwari woman, Meena, especially, is a moving account. She captures the little details about Meena and her environment, the antiseptic Marwari household, its subtle sense of wealth, and the utter quietness of the women in that joint family who make themselves neither seen nor heard. Meena's story, quoted and reported in the third person by Mukherjee, is gripping on account of its apparent simplicity. For Meena, reading a book was the ultimate act of rebellion in a family that did not value a woman's education because they believed that it would interfere with her ideals of wifehood and motherhood. Her final words to Mukherjee, "Now I am determined to be a teacher, to modify my community. . . . If they don't let me teach I shall be at the end of my tether" (236), is more potent than any feminist slogan. Ideas of women's liberation in such a tightly knit social structure are reduced to, as Mukherjee states, cooking from time-saving recipes. When liberation for women is so trivialized, even reading a book or getting a job is a major rebellion. Moreover, the woman's individuality is quashed with the religious brainwashing. Sita-Savitri role models retain everyone's veneration. Despite the collective stereotyping of women as docile, unassertive, and obedient, the "weird" woman continues to emerge, fighting against an oppressive society by spreading the word that a woman has individual rights to "own property, work, study, vote, divorce, and remarry" (236).

In Mukherjee's narrative, Meena's account becomes symbolic of the resistance and rebellion threatening to challenge a crippling tradition. What comes across in the documentary is that the possibilities for women to establish their identity and find personal happiness do exist but either through alienating the family or by negotiating with the family. Either way entails suffering on the part of the woman. Collectivity, therefore, stands in tension with individuality. While the individual may experience support in belonging to the collective, she might be resented for establishing her individuality. In the Indian context the collective makes women powerful, but the internalized tradition makes them passive and accepting. The collective voices in Mukherjee's work are loud and without irony state that the woman belongs in the home, that she should be a *pativrata*, and that she obtains identity from her husband. When the wives "made conventional small talk about the dishonesty of servants, the general deterioration of the moral fiber, and the woman's place being in the home, they intended no irony" (213). But on the fringes of this tight circle, Mukherjee meets women who have defied the cultural demands and made their own choices in marriage and vocation. While it is true, as Friedman points out, that women see themselves as part of a collective, the potential for women to see themselves as "different from cultural prescription is part of their collective identity, since their "collective identity can also be a source of strength and transformation" (Friedman 39). The Indian woman's experience is ambiguous; while the message of Hindu philosophy as expressed by society is that she should transcend self in order to achieve union with the Ultimate, in reality she wishes to assert her individuality even if it means rebelling against the collective. Since the Hindu tradition is paradoxical, where negation of self intersects with action (an assertion of self), women who rebel attempt to maintain the balance between their individuality and the collective.

The shifting cultural values between East and West and between tradition and modernity are played out within the dialectic between merging and separateness and between self-reinvention and self-suppression. Mukherjee uses the term "merging"—philosophically the union of Brahman and Atman—as a healing process for all kinds of separateness—between castes and classes, men and women, the center and the margin. Although merging is a Hindu concept, the reality in India tells us otherwise: walls are built to separate rich from poor, upper castes from lower, men from women. In *Days and Nights* Mukherjee anticipates the value in merging that her characters in the short stories and *Jasmine*—immigrants in the United States—discover. Merging becomes the ideal balance between ghettoization and melting. But merging, she discovers, will always be in tension with self-preservation, imaged in the building of compound walls around houses, creation of "colonies" within teeming cities, erecting barriers between classes, and creating values to keep women separate from men. Self-preservation is always the weapon of the dominant group, be it the British imperialists, the Brahmins, or the middle and upper classes. In her narrative, Mukherjee shows that caste, class, gender divisions, and their attendant values, such as the primacy of the family, contribute to maintaining one's separateness. For example, as a young girl Mukherjee kept herself to her room, away from her family, so she could develop her own sense of what she was. Mukherjee finds that women crave isolation just as much as they crave companionship. For instance, the women keep to the serenity of their households, away from the Naxalites, and do not bother to inquire into the reason for their revolt, thus drawing a boundary between themselves and the *tamasha* (confusion) of the world.

So the possibility for reinvention of the self, the recreation of the woman's self, within the rigid matrices of Indian society reveals the plasticity of Hindu philosophy. For example, the Hindu concept of rebirth can be interpreted symbolically to suit women's lives. As we see in all of Mukherjee's works, rebirth is seldom an abstract phenomenon; it is experienced in the here and now. Her characters, for instance in *Middleman and Other Stories*, take on new identities, each identity fluid and separate from the previous ones. In a way *Days and Nights* anticipates what she explores in other works—the possibilities for women to remake themselves, as seen in the Marwari woman, Meena. Confined within the collective, upper-class and middle-class Calcutta, women submerge their identities in those of their husbands and families. Hinduism, with its emphasis on self-sacrifice, makes self-invention irrelevant, except for spiritual knowing with its union of matter and spirit, which is the only liberation not restricted by gender. Mukherjee interprets rebirth as fluidity and change, physical and spiritual renewal. It also suggests the plasticity and elasticity of the self. And this characteristic of rebirth makes it part of the Hindu imagination that is all-encompassing and amorphous, and allows logic and coincidence, reason and irrationality to coexist.

Freedom and power are built into Hindu philosophy, but in the institutionalized forms of the religion these concepts are subsumed by patriarchal oppression. Savitri and Sita—ideals of Indian womanhood—hold sway in the minds of Indian men and women and reinforce their collective thinking, but powerful individual female figures, such as Draupadi and Radha, occupy the fringes of the Indian social drama. Draupadi as intellect and Radha as pure erotic being are suppressed by the Hindu imagination, but they are nevertheless present. In the recreation of the woman's self, these aspects of her self can come to the fore. But in India, as Mukherjee observes, the erotic is taboo, and women's intellect is developed only during their years at schools such as Loretto House, where the women prepare themselves for the competitive marriage market.

Although Mukherjee is seen as the "free" woman, she was not recognized as such in the West; but she is treated with respect and even fanfare in India where a woman, although culturally bound, can experience spiritual freedom. For example, women artists through the ages in India wrote mainly devotional literature as an expression of their liberation: Meera expresses this in her erotic surrender to Krishna; Kamala Das in her autobiography most compellingly tells us that after searching for happiness by exploring her sexuality, she finally discovers in Devi and Krishna her true spirit. From these examples we learn that part of the Hindu woman's consciousness is to regard oppression as physical rather than mental, and that Shakti ultimately belongs to the spirit. It is not a passive force, but is active and shares the creative-destructive paradox of Kali.

Mukherjee, while rendering the collective "middles" (experiences) of Calcutta women, leaves a void in her work. The absence that looms large is that of Kali, patron goddess of Bengal, also worshipped as Devi or Amman in the South. Women, whatever socioeconomic parameters they live in, realize their power to shape their lives, and this power is not new, but stems from the same tradition that provides them with the *pativrata* model. Although Mukherjee places women within their culture, she reads them partially. Since Indian culture is a multilayered cake, so to speak, to say that the Sita-Savitri paradigm explains women's experiences is a synecdochic representation of Indian culture. Women's resistance to male power has a long tradition in India. In order to understand the difficult "middle" of Indian women's experiences, one has to understand the cultural content that shaped it.

One of the tasks that modern historians and sociologists of Indian culture have undertaken is to reconstruct the beginnings of women's position in India in order to understand their experiences within the current sociohistoric conditions and formulate ways in which women can alleviate their oppression. Women's position in India is deeply connected with the basis of Hinduism, fundamental to which is the concept of Shakti. Shakti is the female generative force basic to all action in the universe. Central to the meaning of Shakti is the proposition, "Action and power are female," as opposed to the proposition built into the Western belief system that the "female is powerless and passive" (Egnor 1). According to the Markandeya Purana, the goddess Shakti was created by Brahma, Vishnu, and Shiva to battle with Mahishasura. Imbued with all the masculine attributes, which the three gods willingly gave her, she kills Mahisha and grants a boon to the bull that he rode. His wish is that his body not be destroyed. Yet another legend from the Markandeya Purana is about Kaushiki who is released from Parvati to defeat Raktabija, a demon. When Raktabija multiplies himself, Kaushiki projects another self, Kali. With mouth wide open and tongue lolling out, she laps every drop of blood from Raktabija and thus wipes out all the demons. In the Mahishasura episode, the Goddess is created by the gods for their specific need. In the Raktabija episode, she is created in a terrible form by Parvati, and she does her battle on her own, without any weapons handed her by the gods. In these two myths are "exemplified the treacherous nature of the female. On the one hand she is devoted, self-disciplined (chaste), and ready to sacrifice (for men); on the other, she is sexual, anarchic, destructive, and bloody" (Mitter 79). Kali, or Shakti, therefore suggests enormous female prowess that men feel need to be contained. Hence in the epics, Sita and Draupadi, versions of Shakti, suppress or channel their superior strength "along strictly generative, ritually sanctioned lines" (Mitter 80). This notion of power and containment is the cultural diet of Indians.

Egnor explores in her article the resolution of the contradiction between Shakti and oppression. She discovers that suffering (*turpam*) with intense patience (*porumai*) ultimately makes women powerful. In Tamil culture the importance of endurance (*tankum sakti*) is stressed in order to achieve power over the oppressor. Usually the power is spiritual, since intense suffering brings one closer to spiritual experience. One can see this concept emphasized again in the *bhakti* (divine love) poets, like Meera Bhai and Aandal, who asserted their power through complete surrender to God, and experienced the merging between the physical and the spiritual, the Brahman and the Atman.

The idea of the powerful woman is very much part of the culture that has devised ways to channel this superior energy. "Nothing in Hindu culture prevents a forceful woman—intelligent, ambitious, ideally well-connected, and with a 'manifest destiny'—from mounting to the top, where she is surrounded by praise and entreaty" (Mitter 80). Therefore it is up to the woman to find a means of manifesting her Shakti, either as Kali, or Draupadi, or Sita, or any other empowered figure.

When we understand how woman's power traditionally appears alongside her containment, Mukherjee's narratives about Calcutta women, from the suppressed to the rebellious, need to be seen within this context. Mukherjee's interpretation of Sita and Savitri as models of women who surrendered totally to their husbands is one-sided. While *pativrata* may be an internalized ideal, Indian women also admire Sita's fidelity, single-mindedness, and her final act of vanishing into the flaming lap of mother earth as a neat repartee to Rama's demand that she undergo the test of fire for the second time to prove her chastity. Similarly, Draupadi may be seen as the ideal of wifely devotion, but she is also seen as the symbol of the intellect. She is the only person in the *Mahabaratha* who questions Yuddhishtira's dharma. Nancy Falk argues that Draupadi's formidable speeches are accepted in the epic mainly on account of her role as woman and as wife. Although her role as woman makes her subject to Duryodhana's ridicule and renders her powerless, her role as wife—because it enjoins on her the responsibility of participating as an equal in the religious rituals—allows her to speak out as her husband's equal. "For religious purposes—which means both for ritual purposes and also in the observance of the dharma, the woman formed a unit with her husband" (Falk 103).

As Joanna Liddle and Rama Joshi explore in their book *Daughters of Independence*, the main difference between Western women and Indian women is that in the West women were considered inferior by society, whereas in India, women were deemed powerful and therefore had to be controlled (49). Hence, despite the repeated subjugation of women, especially after Manu's Laws came into effect, and with the influence of the Islamic and British cultures, fighters for women's liberation, both men and women, continued to emerge in India.[3]

Education for liberation is a slogan Indians associate with the Independence movement. But, in fact, education for women had always been stressed as part of the culture. Of course, education was another means by which women were commodified; a woman had to be well educated so she could be worthy of her husband. She was educated not for herself but to fulfill her husband's needs. Notions of women's education as a means to their liberation existed side by side with the more widespread notion of education as another means of controlling them morally. Mukherjee's description of the Loretto House girls falls into this latter category; they were educated so they could marry into status and high society. However, their mothers are conscious of the freedom of the mind that education effects, especially for women. As Mukherjee mentions in her book, her mother's threat to her relatives to equip her children with a "formidable education" (228) shows that she knew that the intellect is a superior weapon that liberates women—an idea that has been with Hindu culture since the Vedic times, but had become yet another means to control women.

The absence of Shakti, traditionally a source of power, renders Mukherjee's narrative a partial anamnesis of the Indian woman's position. The importance given to knowledge, both as spiritual and cognitive power, as an integral part of Shakti, symbolized in the goddess Saraswati, as well as in Draupadi, is central to Mukherjee's identity. We learn that her "gift of the pen" renders her different from the Loretto House girls, but in her selective rendering of the Hindu culture we don't see this marriage between intellect and power in Indian women.

Mukherjee's experience is apart from the traditional collective internalization of Shakti, the power in women to create and destroy, a power, as Susan Wadley observes, that is acquired through suffering (*tapas*), a power that stands in paradoxical relation to oppression. Although Mukherjee herself does not realize it, the narratives of women, such as Meena, Jaya, Kamala, and the woman who maintains a long-distance marriage, tell us that women negotiate within their families in order to achieve a compromise. This power to negotiate is a demonstration of women's power and the dual message in our tradition—of power and control—makes such negotiations possible. In these stories we know the outcomes of these women's negotiations, unlike the frustrating "middles" of stories of rebellion in which we do not know the reasons or the outcome.

Salman Rushdie in *Imaginary Homelands* asks a question that is crucial to writers living on the cultural divide. He asks, "How are we to live in this world?" This question could also include others: How is the woman writer to live in this world? And how is the woman to live in this world? Mukherjee's answer to the last two are subjects of her short stories and her novel, *Jasmine*. In *Days and Nights*, she deals with these questions in the epilogue to the narrative. As an Indian woman, she has to reinvent herself, even if it means relinquishing her past completely. There is no sense, she believes, in holding on to a past that does not qualify one's reality with meaning.

Anticipating the characters in her short stories, Mukherjee decides that she is an immigrant, not an exile. India is a place she can never live in. While growing up in India, she discovers that to be a woman "was to be a powerless victim whose only escape was through self-inflicted wounds" (228). Her terrible revelation paves the way for her to establish her identity as a writer. Her trysts with the great English, Russian, and Bengali writers and her own ability to write make her different and destine her to follow a path distinct from the pattern of life of the Ballygunge girls.

Although she feels emotionally attached to her friends and family in India, she feels both as a woman and as a writer she needs to move in another direction and call that home. Having felt different from her fellow Indians all along, she resorts to another collective, that of the cultural enclave of North America, particularly the United States, where, she explains in her introduction to *Darkness*, a merging of oneself with the mainstream culture is possible, unlike in Canada, a mosaic, where the immigrant is always seen as different.

Her inability to return to India and the sense of her difference from other Indian women find resolution in her art—the marriage of the American and the Hindu imagination. It is the blending of two disparate imaginations that vitalize Mukherjee's unique craft. But what is at issue here is how the woman writer lives and writes on the cultural divide. Unlike the writer in exile who writes about a lost home, Mukherjee feels that as an immigrant writer she needs to focus on her present surroundings and invent "Indias of the mind" (Rushdie 10) with the help of a constantly evolving imagination. Like her fictional characters, she looks forward, since to deal with her present reality, she feels that reinvention of self, not nostalgia, is her strength.

Although Mukherjee uses the symbolic imagination in Hindu tradition to look at the ambiguity of women's realities, she hardly finds any redeeming feature in the tradition as far as women are concerned. The message that comes across crystal clear to immigrant writers like herself is to wed their unique craft to the reality they are in—the immigrant reality; instead of living in and writing about the past, she chooses to wed the Hindu imagination to the American imagination that she has imbibed. While this message carries the banner of hope and optimism for women, urging them to mold their destiny rather than accept it, her narrative ignores the fact that her message is rooted in the tradition she deplores. As the authors of *Daughters of Independence* argue, because of the tradition of female power, women have the possibility to effect changes by using the very instruments used to suppress them. Since self-sacrifice is deemed ideal for women, sacrifice itself can be used as a form of resistance, "by depriving the other as well as the self, of something that they both value, or by raising a reciprocal sacrifice from the other" (Liddle and Joshi 225). Blaise astutely remarks, "Family, family, family. In India all is finally family" (*Days and Nights* 92). So it is within the family where mechanisms of change can begin through "negotiation of compromises" (Liddle and Joshi 225). The self-consciousness Mukherjee sees as sustaining women and which she promotes in her fiction is more in line with the American notion of individuality rather than the Hindu notion of self-surrender, which is spiritual surrender that is exemplified in contemporary writers such as Kamala Das, and the *bhakti* poets, such as Meera and Aandal.

Unlike Maxine Hong Kingston, who rediscovers something sustaining in her Chinese tradition[4] and Rushdie, who creates imaginary homelands from the "shards of memory,"[5] Mukherjee does not. Her year in India makes her realize that although Hinduism saves people from losing faith totally, the cynicism and irascibility of the outside ultimately invades households; she finds familial love stifling. Just as she finds kinship to be oppressive, she finds that writing as a Third World writer about her homeland is restrictive. In the penultimate section of the book, she sees a ghost of an uncle who had died years ago—a scene that carries metaphoric value. India will exist in the immigrant writer's work as a ghost, a friendly one that visits her occasionally. Although India will be part of the life of her imagination, it will not be central to her writing. It can only remain a friendly specter in the background; as she declares later, there are new epics she must explore in the country of immigrants she will be living in. Her realization that she was one of them (Calcutta women) would become years later her defiant announcement in her article in the *New York Times* "I am one of you now" (1) to her American readers. In that one sentence she asserts herself as an American in the immigrant tradition.

NOTES

1. Sidonie Smith describes the shift of the autobiographer from the "I" to "multiple locales" as one which brings about a shift in the center of the narrative, such that "the formerly peripheral becomes central, [and] the central moves away toward the periphery as other locales assume precedence" (157).

2. See William C. Spengemann, *The Forms of Autobiography* (New Haven and London: Yale University Press, 1980), especially the introduction, for an account of autobiography as self-biography and problems of self-definition.

3. Susan Wadley argues that South Indian women are more liberated than North Indian women and gives several cultural and historical reasons for this difference. Despite the foreign invasions, the South was not as affected as the North because of its geographic location. Also a look at South Indian literary traditions will give us clues about the position of ordinary women during the reign of the Cholas and the Pandyas. For more details on the subject, refer to Sara Mitter (*Dharma's Daughters*).

4. Kingston's persona Ink in *The Woman Warrior* is caught between two worlds, Chinese and American. In her mother she sees two Chinese traditions: the belief that the wife is a slave and the notion of the woman as a warrior. Her mother identifies with the mythical woman warrior, Fu Ma Lan; Ink also identifies with the latter and finds that her identity with her mother as warrior lends her the strength to break out of silence.

5. Salman Rushdie remarks in *Imaginary Homelands* that it is the present that he finds foreign, whereas the past is home. Only in the images of the past recreated in art can the immigrant writer feel finally at home.

WORKS CITED

Egnor, Margaret. "On the Meaning of Sakti to Women in Tamil Nadu." *The Powers of Tamil Women.* Ed. Susan S. Wadley. Syracuse University: Foreign and Comparative Studies Program/South Asian Studies, 1980. 1–34.

Falk, Nancy. "Draupadi and the Dharma." *Beyond Androcentrism: New Essays in Religion.* Ed. Rita M. Gross. Billings, Montana: Scholars Press, 1977. 89–114.

Friedman, Susan S., "Women's Autobiographical Selves." *The Private Self: Theory and Practice of Women's Autobiographical Writings.* Ed. Shari Benstock. Chapel Hill: University of North Carolina Press, 1988.

Kingston, Maxine Hong. *The Woman Warrior.* New York: Knopf, 1976.

Liddle, Joanna, and Rama Joshi. *Daughters of Independence: Gender, Caste and Class in India.* New Brunswick, N.J.: Rutgers University Press, 1991.

Mitter, Sara S. *Dharma's Daughters: Contemporary Indian Women and Hindu Culture.* New Brunswick, N.J.: Rutgers University Press, 1990.

Mukherjee, Bharati. "Immigrant Writing: Give Us Your Maximalists!" *New York Times Book Review* (28 August 1988): 1, 28–29.

_____, and Clark Blaise. *Days and Nights in Calcutta.* Garden City, N.Y.: Doubleday, 1977.

Rushdie, Salman. *Imaginary Homelands: Essays and Criticism 1981–1991.* London: Granta Books, 1991.

Smith, Sidonie. "Construing Truths in Lying Mouths: Truthtelling in Women's Autobiography." *Studies in the Literary Imagination* 23 (Fall 1990): 145–163.

Spengemann, William C. *The Forms of Autobiography: Episodes in a Literary Genre*. New Haven and London: Yale University Press, 1980.

Wadley, Susan. "The Paradoxical Powers of Tamil Women." *The Powers of Tamil Women*. Ed. Susan S. Wadley. Syracuse University: Foreign and Comparative Studies Program/South Asian Studies, 1980. 153–170.

A QUESTION OF IDENTITY: WHERE GENDER, RACE, AND AMERICA MEET IN BHARATI MUKHERJEE

Brinda Bose

Ethnic women in America are clearly twice-marginalized: by virtues of their ethnicity and their gender. The central figures in Mukherjee's novels *The Tiger's Daughter*, *Wife*, and *Jasmine*—Tara, Dimple, Jasmine—fight two simultaneous battles against marginalization during their early expatriate experiences in America; coming as they are from (an)Other world, their very identities are in question in America, calling out for a re-visioning and a re-defining at the start. The moments of change/transformation/re-incarnation are crucial because, though the exercise is assertive/powerful/celebratory in its mainstream movement, the echoes at the margins valorize the anxieties of expatriation.

The identities that Mukherjee's women eventually emerge with exemplify the characteristics of a whole new breed in this country, the "ethnic" who is also "American." The process of finding their identities must be a matter of intense struggle: with the self, with tradition, with the wonders and horrors of a new culture, with growing aspirations, hopes, and desires. Where gender, race, and the American experience meet in Bharati Mukherjee, the intersection is fraught with the tension of combat, even when the combat itself needs to be identified in subtextual moments.

Mukherjee's women do eventually find their distinctive voices, but not before they have battled violently with the images of their own selves as representations of "Otherness"—exotic yet silent, capable yet repressed. More often than not, these women have grown up in Indian families which, in the wake of the British Raj, amalgamated Western ideas with traditional beliefs; this often finds the young women emancipated but confused. Cultural roots retain their hold in insidious ways; though in times of fear and indecision Mukherjee's Westernized Indian women return to seek the comfort of traditional faiths, they increasingly discover it to be cold—and so the quest for a new identity continues. If "acquisition of Americanness" is an ethnic concern, spanning language, dress, and behavioral codes, then these women have another acquisition to battle for first: the acquisition, and retention, of an individual female identity that no longer needs to conform to traditional (in this case, Indian) patterns.

Apparently, Mukherjee's growing concern is that these newborn identities should not suffer from the terror of marginalization, a concern that is probably legitimate to immigrants everywhere. When she sets out her critical agenda in the introduction to *Darkness*, she describes her stories as ones of "broken identities" and "discarded languages," but nevertheless these identities are fired by a passion and a "will to bond [themselves] to a new community" (2). Tracing a development through Mukherjee's work, from her early novel *The Tiger's Daughter* to *Jasmine*, one finds that this community is, ever-increasingly, a celebration of what the author obviously considers the spirit of America, a spirit that defies homesickness and nostalgia in order that one may savor the "exuberance of immigration" (*Darkness* 2). As a subject position, this exuberance has its advantages as well as its problems. An advantage, of course, is that the immigrant gets to enjoy his/her transformation from a

A Question of Identity

nervous resident (or illegal) alien into a full-blown American and is able to justify his/her choice of homeland by fitting into the New World with aplomb. The problem remains: it is not easy to overcome the "aloofness of expatriation" (*Darkness* 3), nor is it painless to sever oneself from the roots and traditions of the culture that one comes from. The question that then arises is, how authentic is the voice that seeks to forget such trauma? According to Sneja Gunew,

> the whole notion of authenticity, of the authentic migrant experience, is one that comes to us constructed by hegemonic voices; and so, what one has to tease out is what is not there. One way of doing this (if one has knowledge from a particular culture), is to say: but look this is what is left out, this is what is covered over . . . and then to ask, what readings are not privileged, what is not there, what questions can't be asked?[1]

Certainly, more and more is left out as Mukherjee's women evolve from the homesick Tara who returns home to find herself peculiarly alienated, through Dimple whose confusion turns violent, to the liberated Jyoti-Jasmine-Jase-Jane who makes a lifetime-for-every-name look like a possibility for any exuberant immigrant. What gets covered over in the flurry of change and action is the conflict and the confusion of "the whole cross-cultural business"[2] as Gayatri Spivak puts it, the trauma of getting used to the idea that one is not going to be completely at home in either place—or burying that idea in a heap of excitement about becoming, and being, "American," as Jasmine does so well. The greatest interest of these stories still lies, however, at those critical junctures when decisions need to be made, when old habits and beliefs have to be discarded for more daring fancies. While *The Tiger's Daughter* is primarily a prolonged tale of this conflict, and *Wife* shares many more of these moments with the reader than does the third novel, *Jasmine*, it is Jasmine's story that is best told—though what we get out of it depends largely on how sensitive we are to the questions that are never asked.

To do this, we probably need to apply Spivak's reworked theory of marginalization to what is glossed over in Mukherjee's texts; that is, we need to pay attention to the shadows of anxiety that hang over even the most joyous (centered) moments: "I would like to re-invent [marginality] as simply a critical moment rather than a decentered moment[,] . . . the place for argument, the place for the critical moment, the place of interests for assertions rather than a shifting of the center. . . ."[3] I am assuming that there are two levels of marginality that we are dealing with here: the marginal protagonist, in terms of where she comes from, and the marginality of what she does not say, in terms of her covering up anxieties in order to fit more easily into the new life. Both need to be read "as not simply opposed to the center but as an accomplice of the center" (Harasym 156), because it is at the margins that the most crucial moments of the texts are played out.

Duality and conflict are not merely a feature of immigrant life in America; Mukherjee's women are brought up in a culture that presents them with such ambiguities from childhood. The breaking of identities and the discarding of languages actually begin early, their lives being shaped by the confluence of rich cultural and religious traditions, on the one hand, and the "new learning" imposed by British colonialism in India, on the other. These different influences involve them in tortured processes of self-recognition and self-assimilation right from the start; the confusion is doubled upon coming to America.

Tara of *The Tiger's Daughter* belongs to a Western-educated Indian family which no longer believes that girls should only be taught to keep house, cook, and pray. She is sent to a convent school for a proper education in the "English medium," and then to college in America at the age of fifteen. However, cultural roots still reveal themselves in unexpected ways: the prim nuns of St. Blaise's in Calcutta may teach Tara all about lady-like poise and self-control in the face of adversity, yet Tara, sitting in her lonely room at Vassar a few years later, remembers the comforting array of little gods and goddesses her mother used to worship at home and prays to Kali, the Hindu goddess of power, to tide her over many awkward moments with the polite and inscrutable Americans (*The Tiger's Daughter* 11). And yet she marries an American, and when she visits India many years after she had first left it, she discovers that though the world she had been born into is gracious and welcoming still, she cannot any longer find the self that had once belonged to it. Even as those symbols and icons that had struggled to sustain her from afar become real all over again, she realizes that the return is no idyll, and there are reasons for the prodigal to feel trapped and abandoned both at the same time.

One has to wonder, then, what would have happened if Tara, instead of feeling alienated in that educated Bengali society, had allowed herself to fit comfortably back into those patterns—how would she have coped with the return to her adoptive country and American husband? (As it stands, one may presume that she will be somewhat relieved at the end of her holiday in India.) The immigrant experience, Mukherjee firmly believes, may be analogized as a series of reincarnations, deaths of earlier existences followed by rebirths full of promise; this is borne out consistently by the tales of Tara, Dimple, and Jasmine, even while Mukherjee hails immigrant Indianness "as a set of fluid identities to be celebrated" (*Darkness* 3).

The celebration does not come easy, as Mukherjee's young women find out, and much of the difficulty arises from an inability to divorce oneself completely from one's past—though in terms of progression, Jasmine does it far better than Tara and Dimple. Memory evolves into a political and ideological signifier in the fiction of Bharati Mukherjee, as her protagonists alternate between the desire for remembering and the need for forgetting, with its accompanying pain. If the dominant ideology in this fiction is that of the West as colonizer and male as master, with the subaltern constituted of the new immigrants from the Third World (especially women, here), then for these characters assimilation and acceptance in the new culture appear impossible if the past is not forgotten. This forgetting, however, can hardly be accomplished without guilt and pain—and this is the rite of passage for Tara that *The Tiger's Daughter* documents.

Tara's memory has played tricks on her during her prolonged expatriate experience in America—as memory is wont to do. She had been homesick and lonely in her early years abroad, then grown wistful and romantic with faint longings that nudged her consistently through her changing lifestyle to the extent that she hung Indian scarves around her apartment and curried hamburger "desperately" despite her American husband's protesting stomach (*The Tiger's Daughter* 34). Even at these points she is yet to learn, as Mukherjee comments elsewhere, that as long as she clutches at "souvenirs of an ever-retreating past" she will "never belong, anywhere" (*Darkness* 2). And belonging is all-important, even if it means the discarding of nostalgia in order to wholly embrace the New World.

Salman Rushdie, in *Imaginary Homelands*, talks of being reminded by an old photograph that "it's my present that is foreign, and that the past is home, albeit a lost home in a lost city in the mists of lost time."[4] Obviously, this is the nostalgia that Mukherjee is working against: Tara will feel herself to be an expatriate and an alien for as long as she conceives of India as the only country she can really belong to, and the only way the movement toward becoming an exuberant immigrant can be launched is by burying the ghosts of the past. Though *The Tiger's Daughter* is not autobiographical, as Mukherjee has stated, some of Tara's experiences on her return to India are reflections of the author's reactions upon returning home: "There were just so many aspects of India that I disliked by then. So a lot of my stories since are really about transformation—psychological transformation—especially among women."[5]

The concept of transformation itself changes to reincarnation as one moves from Tara to Dimple and Jasmine: it seems as if Mukherjee concludes that a gradual and gentle transformation is not spirited enough for the sweeping adaptations that are required of the immigrant who wishes to belong to the world she has chosen to be in. Sneja Gunew raises this issue in a discussion on multiculturalism with Gayatri Chakravorty Spivak:

> What is very much a question for me at this moment is that if you are constructed in one particular kind of language, what violence does it do to your subjectivity if one then has to move into another language and suppress whatever selves or subjectivities were constructed by the first. (Broe and Ingram 419)

It would appear that for any of Mukherjee's women who might legitimately feel, like Spivak, that "I am bicultural, but my biculturality is that I'm not at home in either of the places" (Harasym 83), the first selves and subjectivities must be violently transfigured to meet the need of being at home in the adopted homeland.

Violence is a key word, a leitmotif in Mukherjee's fiction, and the "psychic violence" that she thinks is necessary for the transformation of character is often emphasized by an accompanying physical conflict of some sort. The level of violence escalates as one moves from Tara's horror as she is, in two climactic scenes, seduced by a middle-aged politician and stranded in the midst of a bloody political riot, to Dimple's frenzied killing of her husband, and finally to Jasmine's reincarnation as an avenging Kali in her desperate bid to find a foothold in the American way of life. Tara is convinced by these experiences that she needs to discard her past and embrace her home away from home, and to her this is a physical wrench; both Dimple and Jasmine are eased into the notion that if circumstances require that they do more than merely escape, they must do so to save themselves. For them, murder evolves into an acceptable signifier for discarding nostalgia and starting over; it is neither the end nor even merely the means to an end: it is a beginning.

Once the home-country has been relegated to the recesses of rejected memory, and the new life is looked forward to with hope, the process of defining a new identity can begin. And these processes have to begin, necessarily, with a growing awareness of the freedom of expression (ushered in with a dose of violence in many of these cases). As genteel women from backgrounds that did not privilege the power of change for the female gender—though Tara, who belonged to the liberal elite of Calcutta, was better off than Dimple of the pretentious middle-class home and Jasmine, the village belle with dreams of learning English—to speak, to touch, to feel for oneself are goals worth pursuing. Spivak says, "It is not a solution, the idea of the disenfranchised speaking for themselves, or the radical critics speaking for them; this question of representation, self-representation, representing others, is a problem" (Broe and Ingram 416), but in order to be able to locate oneself in the new multicultural world, clarifying these issues becomes a necessity. For Mukherjee's women who grew up in a traditionally repressed society it means, importantly, a discovery of their own sexuality; finding voice is also, for the first time, speaking of the body. In *Wife*, the newly married Dimple accompanies her husband to America generally supportive of his intention to break away from the pettiness of their middle-class existence in India, but obviously she is not the docile "wife" her rather traditional spouse expects her to be even in the new country. She shows, in fact, the makings of a rebel quite early on, when she aborts her child in the privacy of her bathroom before they leave for America. (Perhaps this engenders in her the notion that it is possible to rid herself of what she doesn't want.) And so she arrives in America, naive and untrained, certainly, but psychologically prepared to broaden her perspectives. It is not so much that she has to discard all that her traditional upbringing has taught her about the married state, rather that she has to transform it to suit her changing self as she discovers it to be in a strange situation. Mukherjee has said:

> ... the kinds of women who attract me, who intrigue me, are those who are adaptable. We've all been trained to please, trained to be adaptable as wives, and that adaptability is working to the women's advantage when we come over as immigrants. . . . For an Indian woman to learn to drive, put on pants, cash checks, is a big leap. They are . . . exhilarated by that change. They are no longer having to do what mothers-in-law tyrannically forced them to do. (*Iowa Review* 19)

With the exhilaration come fears, trepidations, doubts, mistakes—and violence, both psychological and physical. More and more through Mukherjee's novels, as the trepidations and doubts get overtaken in the flurries of action and activity, what is glossed over in terms of psychological torment is compressed into desperate violent acts. This enhances the tension of the combative moments when decisions and choices are made, and Mukherjee considers it a necessary experience for the remaking of the self in terms of the new immigrant aesthetic. When asked, "Do you see immigration as an experience of reincarnation?" Mukherjee has answered, "Absolutely! I have been murdered and reborn at least three times" (Connell, et al. 18). Dimple is murdered and reborn many more times, until she needs to murder in order to be reborn.

Each time, the new births that are engendered by some violent fracturing of norms are accompanied by great pain, but Dimple is helplessly caught in the gripping quest for a new female American identity. The two acquisitions culminate in a momentary ecstasy when she indulges in an afternoon's extramarital digression with a "genuine American," but a happy guiltless amalgamation seems impossible: despite her pleasure at the escapade, prudence still warns her that she must not "do it again" (*Wife* 202) because she cannot allow herself to complicate her life. The complications, however, are far too compounded already, and it is not caution but abandonment that is required of her. In moments of despair, Dimple has been contemplating suicide.

The fact that she finds another way out of her miserably married state is a comment on her new life as an immigrant woman in America, which molds her personality into the shape of her future. Mukherjee has explicated on this idea: ". . . [I]n a bizarre way, my stuff is meant to be optimistic. Dimple, if she had remained in Calcutta, would have gone into depression, and she would have found a very convenient way out for unhappy Bengali wives—suicide. . ." (Connell, et al. 20). It may be interesting in this context to consider Spivak's suggestion that the regulative psychobiography for Indian women was "sanctioned suicide."[6] Is the fact that Dimple discards this option to privilege her selfhood then indicative of her buying into the culture of hegemonic Western liberal feminism? Mukherjee sees it as progress:

> In the United States, she suddenly learns to ask herself "self"-oriented questions. Am I happy? Am I unhappy? And that, to me, is progress. So, instead of committing suicide, turning society-mandated violence inward, she, in a misguided act, kills the enemy. . . . [I]t's meant to be a positive act. Self-assertive. (*Iowa Review* 20)

The enemy she kills is the traditional Indian husband whom she has outgrown; but in the evolutionary process that leads her to this final act of self-assertion, Dimple is forced to enact many metaphorical murders upon her own senses. The murders are in step with each successive realization of how far she has traveled from her nascent being in India, and in the margins of these tiny crucifixions lies the story of the struggle to evolve into a whole new entity. To her husband, who is completely unaware of this distancing movement (from expatriation toward immigration, perhaps), she confesses that she is troubled by the fact that she does not dream about Calcutta any more; not grasping at all the danger of this discarded past, he is relieved that she is no longer fretting and teasingly warns her about becoming "too American" (*Wife* 112).

If "too American" signifies a politics and an ideology that affirms selfhood in particular, then it is quite certainly what Dimple is in the process of becoming. She may still "feel more comfortable in a sari" (*Wife* 155), but as Mukherjee is surely trying to imply, the violent transformations of her psyche are more dangerous because of these shrill protestations. There is a simultaneous fracturing and evolving of identity going on here, in terms of both ethnicity and gender, which is true of the experience of multiculturalism. As Trinh T. Minh-ha points out, the moment at which one discovers that the personal ("the ethnic me, the female me") is also the political is crucial, because one cannot annul the other:

> . . . the choice that many women of color feel obliged to make between ethnicity and womanhood: how can they? You never have/are one without the other. The idea of two illusorily separated identities, one ethnic, the other woman (or more precisely female), again, partakes in the Euro-American system of dualistic reasoning and its age-old divide-and-conquer tactics.[7]

Since it appears that Mukherjee's women do at some points feel obliged to make that choice, it is imperative to know what the options represent. To Tara and Dimple and Jasmine, continuing to be Indian would necessitate a return to being the kind of daughter, sister, wife, and widow that tradition demanded of them—decorous, submissive, and loyal—but it seemed highly incongruous in the contexts of their present lives; becoming an American presented the possibility of power to change their fates. Such a possibility is always heady, and one can perhaps see how the exhilaration of the moment could successfully hide the underlying anxieties, especially when it is really those anxieties that are driving the women to seek the power of change. Ultimately, it is not the traditional role models that the women reject, but the fact that they can no longer reconcile the models to their circumstances. What drives them to react with violence, then, is their frustration at other people's inability to understand their changing needs and desires, now that they are no longer confined to the social and cultural patterns of their past.

In fact, confinement becomes a major issue in Mukherjee's work, as the women demonstrate their quest for freedom in all aspects of their lives. Dimple has become a prisoner of the ghetto in Flushing, Queens, and being an educated and thinking woman, she is unable to accept the contradictions of this existence; hence her descent into depression, madness, and murder. The murder itself may be "ambiguous" (Mukherjee's term) in many ways, but it is essentially symbolic of Dimple's assertion of power at a critical juncture. Jasmine finds herself in a similar Indian ghetto in New York, and she too cannot bear the incongruity of being a housebound young widow in a city and a culture where possibilities are supposed to be endless.

The very essence of *Jasmine* resides in the concept of endless possibility: lifetimes of experience are crammed into a few years in the life of its young female protagonist as Jasmine is put through the most gruelling confrontations with death (of her husband Prakash), murder (of Half-Face who raped her), assault and crippling (of Bud), and suicide (of her neighbor Darrel). She is for a while the mother of seventeen-year-old Du (an immigrant like herself); she is expecting the child of a crippled man whom she leaves for the man she thinks she actually loves (Taylor). The picaresque, surrealistic, no-holds-barred ethos obviously has a message beneath the action: that change and adaptability are the key to survival, and that the successful immigrant has the instinct.

There are many questions lurking in the margins of this tale, not least regarding the improbability of a young unschooled village girl from Hasnapur, Punjab, blossoming so quickly into the "adventurous Jase" in jeans and T-shirts and sneakers. Jasmine, moreover, appears to be happy to wipe out most of her history, except for occasional memories of her slain husband Prakash. She has no sentimental longing to return to her homeland: she has the spirit of the true immigrant, despite being the most improbable one. Though she is no writer, she seems to embody what Mukherjee has said of herself: "I left India by choice to settle in the U.S. I have adopted this country as my home. I view myself as an American author in the tradition of other American authors whose ancestors arrived at Ellis Island" (Carb 650).

Though Jasmine comes to America with the crazy notion of erecting a funeral pyre for her dead husband's clothes on his (intended) university campus and burning herself on it, once again the notion of sanctioned suicide (sati in this case) is rejected when America offers other possibilities. By grasping at the dream of a new life, Jasmine (like the others) feels compelled to sacrifice most of her original self, because both the ethnicity and the womanhood that she identified with have to be massively reworked. Minh-ha has talked of the impossibility of separating "ethnic" and "female"; in terms of the complete reconstruction of the self that Jasmine subjects herself to, it appears that to discard the notions of womanhood that she had till then nurtured (of a widow's aspirations culminating in suicide), she needs to discard her ethnicity too—the only way that she can cope with the freedom of choices thrust upon her, intellectual and sexual, is to see herself within the construct of a new "American" woman.

Mukherjee explains her perception of violently changing identities by calling upon the Hindu religious belief in reincarnation, which is an interesting—if marginalized—way of linking ethnicity with the new womanhood she celebrates in her work:

> I believe that our souls can be reborn in another body, so the perspective I have about a single character's life is different from that of an American writer who believes that he only has one life. . . . As a Hindu . . . I believe in the existence of alternate realities, and this belief makes itself evident in my fiction. (Carb 651)

This notion of alternate realities most obviously manifests itself in the women's changed sexual behavior. Dimple's brief but momentous affair with an American man is merely the foreshadowing of the choices that are to terrify as well as liberate Jasmine. In Mukherjee's fiction, a woman's sexual freedom often functions as a measure of her increasing detachment from traditional sexual mores and, correspondingly, of her assimilation in the New World through her rapid Westernization/Americanization.

In a bizarre sort of way, Jasmine is released from her traditional identity as a de-sexed widow soon after she arrives in America, for in being raped by Half-Face, murdering him, and walking out of the scene of the crime in full possession of herself, she has already transgressed all the norms she would have been expected to live by. Afterward, as she grows more confident in her powers to shape a new identity for herself, she is able to express her sexual desires more candidly; this culminates in her decision to reject her earlier intention of staying with the crippled Bud (whose baby she is having by artificial insemination), and to leave with Taylor, grasping at yet another chance at happiness. As she asserts, she is not merely choosing between men; she is symbolically asserting her right to try and reposition the stars instead of passively accepting her fate. In America she has learned that nothing lasts forever, so she need not condemn herself to a life she does not particularly want. While freeing herself from duty, however, she does also reject the man who had renamed her Jane and had refused to acknowledge her roots; she chooses Taylor who loved her Indianness, so perhaps this is an indication that having worked out the complications of a new identity, Jasmine is now ready to come to terms with her past, making the marginal the accomplice of the center in the final analysis.

Negotiating power from the margins is a tricky proposition at best, and it is possible that in the intricate battle to forge a new self in a strange land, the trauma of a lost identity is drowned with every surge of hope. Mukherjee's ethnic American women are, as she says,

A Question of Identity

"between roles. . . . There isn't a role model for the 'Jasmines' or the 'Dimples'. They have to invent their roles, survive and revise as best as they can" (Connell, et al. 23). While they survive and revise, they remain for a while suspended between two worlds, until they have to choose between them in order to find a space to inhabit. The New World, in which they must now "intervene" and "negotiate" (Spivak's terms, Harasym, 72), holds promise of a new selfhood as well as new battles against marginalizations. Self-assertion, however, is a power that these women are only beginning to enjoy.

NOTES

1. Sneja Gunew, in conversation with Gayatri Chakravorty Spivak on "Questions of Multiculturalism," in *Women's Writing in Exile*, ed. Broe and Ingram, 414.

2. Gayatri Chakravorty Spivak discusses issues of biculturality (Indian/American) and the problems of representation, self-representation, and representing others with Angela Ingram in "Postmarked Calcutta, India," in *The Post-Colonial Critic*, ed. Harasym, 82.

3. Spivak in an interview with Harold Veeser on "The New Historicism: Political Commitment and the Postmodern Critic" in Harasym, 156.

4. Salman Rushdie ruminates on being an Indian writer in England, and on writing about India from the outside, creating fictions, "imaginary homelands, Indias of the mind" in "Imaginary Homelands," in collected essays and criticism with the same title (1991), 9.

5. Mukherjee in an interview in *The Iowa Review* in 1990, 15.

6. Spivak, "Can the Subaltern Speak? Speculations on Widow Sacrifice" in *Wedge* 7/8 (Winter/Spring, 1985).

7. Trinh T. Minh-ha discusses the perceived duality of ethnicity and womanhood, within the construct of "Difference: A Special Third World Issue" in *Woman, Native, Other* (1989), 104.

WORKS CITED

Broe, Mary Lynn, and Angela Ingram, eds. *Women's Writing in Exile.* Chapel Hill and London: University of North Carolina Press, 1989.

Carb, Alison B. "An Interview with Bharati Mukherjee." *The Massachusetts Review* 29.4 (1988): 645–654.

Connell, Michael, Jessie Grearson, and Tom Grimes. "An Interview with Bharati Mukherjee." *Iowa Review* 20.3 (1990): 7–32.

Harasym, Sarah, ed. *The Post-Colonial Critic.* New York: Routledge, 1990.

Minh-ha, Trinh T. *Woman, Native, Other: Writing, Postcoloniality and Feminism.* Bloomington and Indianapolis: Indiana University Press, 1989.

Mukherjee, Bharati. *Darkness.* Markham, Ontario: Penguin, 1985.

———. *The Tiger's Daughter.* New Delhi: Penguin, 1990.

———. *Wife.* New Delhi: Penguin, 1990.

Rushdie, Salman. *Imaginary Homelands: Essays and Criticism 1981–1991.* London: Granta/Penguin, 1991.

Spivak, Gayatri. "Can the Subaltern Speak? Speculations on Widow Sacrifice." *Wedge* 7/8 (Winter/Spring 1985): 1–9.

CREATING, PRESERVING, DESTROYING: VIOLENCE IN BHARATI MUKHERJEE'S *JASMINE*

Samir Dayal

> There are no harmless, compassionate ways to remake oneself.
> *Jasmine* (29)

How should one understand the violence in which Bharati Mukherjee's fictional universe is steeped? It is a gross truism and simplification to suggest, as some readers have done, that it is a "reflection" of what is after all a violent world. The functionality of violence in Mukherjee's recent novel *Jasmine* is complex and ambivalent, as it is in her earlier *The Tiger's Daughter*, *Wife*, *The Middleman and Other Stories*, and even in the nonfictional *Days and Nights in Calcutta*. That complexity and that ambivalence, it may be argued, coincide with the contradictions of postcolonial subject-formation, as I show in this reading of *Jasmine*.

The protagonist of the novel is both a victim and an agent of violence and she is not the only such figure. Violence is the other face of power; gaining an understanding of it involves grasping the play—and the staging—of power structures, particularly in the postcolonial diasporic context. Moreover, violence manifests itself not only in social and political but also in psychosexual and psychosocial realms. The novel is an account of Jasmine's coming into her own as a woman, killing in order to live.

Jasmine's journey of self-discovery, taking her from a feudal condition to her migrancy and exile in the West, is marked by violence. The syntax of her self-articulation is a parable for the social transformation of the Indian postcolonial. As if by parabolic symmetry, the ongoing transformation of postcolonial India is punctuated by eruptions of sectarian violence. The obverse of the euphoria of Independence was the horror of Partition. The horror has continued in the unceasing violence between Muslims and Hindus, the bloody fighting in Bangladesh, the unresolved Kashmir problem. Before Indira Gandhi's "Emergency" quelled it, the Maoist Naxalite violence in Bengal was another formidable chapter in postcolonial Indian history. The violence associated with the militant Sikh factions agitating for a new Khalistan in Punjab refuses to disappear and in fact is the matrix of Jasmine's emancipatory struggle. As India moves toward modernity, it threatens to crack, if not "Balkanize" itself. At the level of ethnic nationalism, where the debate between tradition and modernity is most luridly apparent in modern India, India's progress toward the twenty-first century is nothing if not violent.[1] But for the characters in Mukherjee's novel, the West to which Jasmine goes is equally violent, in different ways. Not only as an epiphenomenon of modern life, and not only as what Fredric Jameson might call a national allegory, violence is a central theme of the novel.

The important characters in *Jasmine* are hyperconscious of a species of entropy and seek not so much the fantasy of escape from entropy but, ironically, some form of acceptance, or embrace, of it. That embrace is often the occasion for radical self-transformation, even destruction of "self," but the transformation is exothermic, generating a tremendous energy—an expression of *élan vital*.

It is not a contradiction, then, to suggest that in accepting violence as somehow ineluctable, Mukherjee's characters are also in search of a heightened sense of self mapped at the moment that the geometry of their entropic universe is negotiated. A wholly apt epigraph from James Gleick's *Chaos* inducts the reader into the world of *Jasmine*: "The new geometry mirrors a universe that is rough, not rounded, scabrous, not smooth. It is a geometry of the pitted, pocked, and broken up, the twisted, tangled, and intertwined."[2]

The self, in such a universe, undergoes an abyssal of identity. In an early short story called "The World According to Hsu" the female protagonist, traveling rootlessly abroad, among a "collection of Indians and Europeans babbling in English and remembered dialects," reflects paradoxically that "[n]o matter where she lived, she would never feel so at home again."[3] Jasmine, having constantly to acknowledge that she is never "at home" and is instead perpetually a nomad, finds her differential sense of who she "is" complicated by a compulsion to return obsessively to some putative "original" or vestigial Indianness.

Her husband, Prakash Vijh, is her prime mover, encouraging her to recognize herself as a victim of a "feudal" power structure, so as to emancipate herself from it. Jasmine's more or less conscious struggle out of this feudal structure is homologous with the struggle of postcolonial subject-formation. The simple village girl Jyoti may have harbored the illusion of fixed identity. But as a woman—as Jasmine—she learns to resist a final or simple reversion to the ossified stereotype of the feudal Indian wife and to subvert the West's desire to territorialize her, to render familiar her strangeness.

That Jasmine is marked for violent transformation is evident in the first words of the novel, which describe a scene of foretelling: an astrologer predicts her early widowhood and subsequent exile. Jasmine's description of herself at seven as "scabrous-armed" (3) echoes the words of the book's epigraph. By contrast, her sisters, whose arms are "butter-smooth" (4), are unprepared to undergo the processes of radical change. When she mockingly rejects the astrologer's prediction, the astrologer chucks her hard on the head, and she falls. Her forehead is marked with a star-shaped scar, which her sisters see only as a liability. Jasmine, however, shouts defiantly that it is her "third eye" (5) that enables her, like sages, to see the invisible. The bleeding stigmata portends her endless self-transformation: it "glows, a spotlight trained on lives to come" (21).

The astrologer's prediction (which turns out to be accurate) introduces the theme of the debate the Third World incessantly conducts with itself—the debate of tradition versus modernity. Prakash, Jyoti's husband, considers himself modern and citified and rejects many traditional values, but traditionalists, such as her friend Vimla, are alarmed at such subversion. Prakash, confident that he can defeat entropy and control the chaos, is determined to be an engineer and wants to go to America, in order to defy fate and to escape mediocrity. Prakash, Jyoti/Jasmine's Professor Higgins, tries to redeem her from her fatalist complacency. He cautions her against the feudal mentality which he feels is the reason for India's malaise; he argues that it is the women of India who will ultimately redeem the nation from its "backwardness."

Jyoti/Jasmine notes acidly that Prakash's nonviolence was a principle he observed at home as well as preached publicly: she acknowledges that he never hit her. The point takes its edge from the staggering rates of domestic violence in India, where, as Elisabeth Bumiller observes, many men take it as a "prerogative" that they may, in certain circumstances, beat their wives.[4] Prakash and his friends are emancipated—political (Nehruvian and Gandhian) idealists, disrupters, and rebuilders (77)—but they are thin voices against the lost, violent souls that threaten to introduce anarchy. The Nehruvian or Gandhian tenets of nonviolence have not prevailed over internecine violence in India.

Sukkhi, his imagination inflamed by the separatist rhetoric of *khalsa*, or "purity," preached by the Sikh leader Sant Bhindranwale, rejects the rational peacemaking counsel of Prakash. He and his fellow separatists, the Khalsa Lions, terrorize and dominate the area. The most lucrative local activity in Hasnapur is smuggling liquor and guns (49). The village men's talk that Jyoti/Jasmine overhears revolves around the violent politics of her surroundings; the Sikh militants, she realizes, are terrorizing the area. Even Masterji, her progressive teacher, meets a violent reward for his mild, enlightenment advocacy of peaceful change toward modernity. Sukkhi and his fellow revolutionaries scoff at his rationality: they chop off his beard and pump bullets into him.

Jasmine's father, Pitaji, imagined he could see death coming from far off—that he would die calmly and with dignity. Instead, he dies "horribly," gored by a bull he never saw coming. A Lahori friend tries valiantly to elaborate what Jasmine later admits is a "soft" if traditional eschatology to explain this death: that life is merely an elaborate illusion. Young Jyoti buys into this fatalist eschatology, often vilified in Orientalist descriptions of the Eastern mind, to give meaning to apparent absurdity: she figures that perhaps her father's accidental death was merely a part of god's plan to facilitate her falling in love with Prakash and expedite her departure to the United States. But here Jyoti is also refusing to capitulate to despair, to the almost unbearable excess of reality (43). She seeks hope in the ordinary and control, however trivial, over chaos. For example, she goes to her friend Vimla's house to play with the electric switch. By turning the light on and off at will, she feels "totally in control" (44).

Her desire for "control" is remarkable in her stiflingly patriarchal situation. In the Hasnapur gender hegemony, women were not to participate in the filthy world of commerce; but men, the purveyors of that economy, are sustained as well as soiled by it (50). Encouraged to seek an education by Masterji, she even declares her scandalously unladylike ambition to become a doctor. This is regarded, naturally, as a symptom of madness by her father and by her father's mother, Dida, who blames Jasmine's insanity on her relatively freethinking mother and on the imminent end of the world—for was this not what scripture described as Kali Yuga, the Age of Chaos, of Violent Destruction? (51–52). Because Jasmine's mother, Mataji, was supportive of her daughter, she of course was beaten by her husband but in the morning she assures Jasmine that she should continue to dream of becoming a doctor. But Mataji remains always faithful to her husband, prepared to go to the traditional extreme of trying to commit sati.

In rural Hasnapur, violence is almost a necessary element of a woman's life. Girls, even at birth, are regarded as "curses," signs of divine displeasure. Jasmine was one of several daughters; when the midwife brought her out, she "had a ruby-red choker of bruise around [her] throat and sapphire fingerprints on [her] collarbone" (40). In New York, when she relates this incident to Taylor and Wylie, the liberated, sophisticated Western woman "misses the point," and "shriek[s] at my 'foremothers'" (40). "My mother," she explains, "was a sniper. She wanted to spare me the pain of a dowryless bride. My mother wanted a happy life for me" (40). The woman's lot, when not mitigated by a man's benevolent intervention and "protection," is bleak: "bad luck dogged dowryless wives, barren wives. They fell into wells, they got run over by trains, they burned to death heating milk on kerosene stoves" (41).

The transformation of the "feudal" wife Jyoti into the modern, English-speaking Jasmine, inevitably, involves a violent baptism in Prakash's blood. A Khalsa Lion bomb kills Prakash on the eve of the young couple's scheduled departure for the West, for that other paradise. Transformed into a bloodthirsty woman, Jasmine demands the assassin Sukkhi's death from the police.

The novel's association of violence with transformation is its leitmotif: "[t]here are no harmless,

Violence in Jasmine 71

compassionate ways to remake oneself. We murder who we were so we can rebirth ourselves in the images of dreams" (29). Violence demystifies stability and identity for Jyoti, eventually disabusing her of her craving for security. It steels her for a heroic self-destruction as a feudal wife and for her remaking abroad: in violent destruction may lie the seeds of creation.

The imperative to control her life justifies, in Jasmine's mind, her pragmatic readiness to use violence; in fact, she views recourse to violence as an affirmation of the will to live. Discovering a thick staff while out gathering wood in Hasnapur, she recognizes it as a weapon in what is tantamount to an act of self-redefinition; she closes her fist over the top of the staff and she feels "a buzz of power" (54). Faced with a rabid dog when out with the women of the village, she kills it with a single stroke. But this is an act of self-defense: she has projected onto the dog her fear of the always imminent rapist.

And perhaps the apocalyptic moment of Jasmine's self-assertion occurs on the occasion of her actual violent rape by Half-Face, on the threshold of the New World. In killing Half-Face, she experiences an epistemic violence that is also a life-affirming transformation: "For the first time in my life, I understood what evil was about. It was about not being human. . . . It was a very simple, very clear perception, a moment of truth, the kind of understanding that I have heard comes at the moment of death" (116). In that act of violent self-transcendence, she becomes Kali, the goddess who drinks (evil) men's blood: "I extended my tongue, and sliced it. Hot blood dripped immediately in the sink" (118). Demonized into Kali, she becomes "Death incarnate" (119); but the culmination of her emancipatory journey toward self-assertion will involve other demonizations, requiring an accession to a ghostliness and a disillusionment with reified selfhood.

Murdering to create, Jasmine learns she must also be something always already different—a necessity Gloria Anzaldua describes:

> For centuries now, . . . it has always been a world of the intellect, reasoning, the machine. Here women were stuck with having tremendous powers of intuition experiencing other levels of reality and other realities yet they had to sit on it because men would say, well, you're crazy. All of a sudden there's a reemergence of the intuitive energies—and they are very powerful. And if you apply them in your life on the personal and political plane then that gives you a tremendous amount of energy—it's almost like a volcano erupting.[5]

Jasmine instinctively understands the link between violence and the dissolution of identity. Although she is deeply ambivalent, she recapitulates the Eastern figuration of self as nothing; but that negativity is coupled powerfully and ambivalently with the "positive" image of Kali. During her tenure as Duff's—and Bud's—"caregiver" she is a conscientious protectress; in her pregnancy by Bud, she is creative. Jasmine is a destroyer but, like Kali, she is also ultimately a preserver, and an agent of the life-force. For Kali is an aspect of the Indian trinity—Brahma, Vishnu, Shiva.

The three modes or aspects of that Absolute, in Hindu theology, are not crudely differentiated. And in *Jasmine*, it is often hard to separate perpetrators from victims, destruction from creation, and violence from its opposites. That sex—a manifestation of the life-force—should obliterate ersatz distinctions between destruction and its antipodes is utterly appropriate. The Little Death of orgasm promises renewal and wholeness. Or, to turn it around, the moment of ecstasy is the moment of self-annihilation. The obliquities of sex speak through Bud, the ruined king, who can seek wholeness—a cognate with health and healing—only in the "ek-stasis" of sex. Sex, as experienced by the wife of a man in a wheelchair, is complicated, an expression of affection and love, but also lust, duty, and violence, and it requires shape-shifting, as we read in richly ambivalent language: "[Bud] likes me to change roles, from caregiver to temptress, and I try to do it convincingly, walking differently, smiling. . . . His upper body is enormously strong, the bench press of love. . . . What kills me . . . is the look of torture, excitement, desperation on Bud's face as he watches me" (36). Nor is violence easily avoided. Jasmine may have escaped from the violent, feudal world of an Indian village. But violence continually threatens the idyll of the alien in her new world. In New York, "Jase's" burgeoning family intimacy with Taylor and his daughter Duff is shattered by a chance encounter with Sukkhi, who shows up blandly pushing a hot-dog cart (188). Jasmine/Jase escapes to Iowa, where she believes miracles can still happen; but there, too, she learns that violence is a constant wolf at the door. She keeps the house locked when Bud is not at home, for she knows that even small Midwestern farm communities are not without violence.

The farmers of Iowa, like the peasants of Hasnapur, are "hemmed in by etiquette. When they break out of it, like Harlan Kroener did, you know how terrible things have gotten" (11). In Iowa, it is all repression, repression—until the repressed returns as violent eruption. The usually placid Harlan, angered at having had a loan request turned down by Bud, shoots him in the back before turning the gun upon himself, fatally (190–192). Bud's own immobility has made him more excitable, more stressed, because more repressed. His explosions occur in the bedroom: orgasm is his release, his cry of pain. Darrel commits suicide when he can no longer contain his many financial and romantic frustrations; but just before he ends his life, he seems to Jasmine quite in control of his life. And a tenant farmer goes out to feed his pigs and shoots himself; hours later his wife finds his body in the manure pit. Then again there is the nameless Osage man who "beat his wife with a spade, then hanged himself in his machine shed" (156).

This catastrophic violence that lies just beneath the skin of the quotidian is meticulously but offhandedly catalogued by Jasmine, as though to banalize it, as though the victims, the perpetrators, and the observers of the violence were benumbing or anaesthetizing themselves against an excess of reality. Bud survives the attempt on his life but asks the doctor to throw out the deformed slugs that had bounced off his bones. For Taylor's friends in New York, experience should lead to greater self-knowledge; for Jasmine, "experience must be forgotten, or else it will kill" (33).

Like Jasmine, her adopted Vietnamese son Du tries to innoculate himself against the omnipresent violence by inhabiting it, erasing the neat distinctions between violence and its presumed antidotes. Du watches a lot of violence on television, like the average American child. But he is an extraordinary audience, because he, like his adoptive mother, has undergone the experience of Third World violence, although he seems to Jasmine strangely untouched by it. Their acute awareness of violence is perhaps their strongest bond. When Jasmine prompts him with the affectionate confession that she has killed a man, he surprises her with his response that he too has killed and, in fact, more than once. He represses and banalizes his knowledge of the threatening entropy of the universe in an attempt to detach himself from that disturbing knowledge—to gain control over life, which threatens at any moment to be nudged into chaos. When Jasmine tries to throw the careful cover off that repressed knowledge of violence, he refuses to cooperate. He listens to her lurid stories of India but does not reciprocate. Decompression, simple confrontation of violence, is too threatening for Du, even though he is otherwise toughened. He is able to stand in -35 degree cold in a Hawaiian T-shirt while the native Iowans are in coats and he had never before seen snow or known such cold (14). His toughness, like that of Jasmine, is an externalization of his will to live; his denial, like Jasmine's, is an expression of his survival instinct.

That instinct may often translate into ease of assimiliation. Du seems to adjust to life in Iowa rather quickly. But Jasmine recognizes that assimilation has its own ambiguities.[6] When Jasmine and Du watch, on television, an INS (Immigration and Naturalization Services) raid in which two illegal Mexican immigrant workers are apprehended, Jasmine sympathizes with their uncertain circumstances. But Du's reaction is more ambiguous. When one of the INS officers wouldn't uncuff one of the Mexicans long enough to wipe his face after he had thrown up, Jasmine thinks she hears Du mumble an expletive, but she is not sure whether his anger is directed at the officers or at the Mexican.

Du embraces and inhabits a violent, if private, schematization of the world in which he lives, without becoming part of it. This nearly yogic discipline is modeled after the Eastern notion of detachment; he is like Wayne Patel in another story by Mukherjee, who aspires to a "saintly" detachment—"Love and pain: in the saint's mind there is no separation."[7] Du is an "engineer," like Prakash, of all the machinery in the world, seen and unseen. He transfigures and projects his violent background into a savage, unruly hybridity both like and unlike Jasmine's: "My transformation has been genetic; Du's was hyphenated" (222). Du's tinkering is a projection of his violent past onto his repressed and outwardly calm present and is linked to his future. Even before becoming an immigrant in America, Du has had two other lives—one in Vietnam, another in a refugee camp. Now he is on his way to study engineering at Iowa State University (157).

One finds no simple distinctions between Jasmine as destroyer and Jasmine as caregiver. Karin calls her a "tornado" (215). And Karin should know. As seen through Karin's eyes, Jasmine's affectless, selfish destruction of Karin's marriage to Bud makes her his femme fatale. Jasmine, as Jane Ripplemeyer, certainly destroys Karin's home, not out of malice or groping acquisitiveness but rather out of a desperately selfish nomadism, a continual urge to "homelessness" and exile that is at the same time an inturned modality, the preservation of a precarious and interminably mutable sense of self. She destroys, or is reconciled to the destruction of, one "home" after another, even her own. In New York she meets Kate, in whose gloriously untidy (that is, deliberately unconventional) apartment she also meets the pet iguana Sam. With Sam,

Jasmine feels an immediate fellowship. Exiles from a home that can never be reclaimed, they are both inhabitants of what the book's epigraph has identified as "a universe that is rough, not rounded, scabrous, not smooth. . . ." Jasmine's impulse to destroy her habitat is linked to a suspicion of habit, to a disillusionment with the Yeatsian fantasy of rootedness in any one dear place. It is also linked to a displacement of a notion of reified or stable identity. When she leaves Bud at the end of the novel with Taylor and his adopted daughter, she is reentering the circle of self-directedness and self-emancipation, which, however, never produces a fixed self.

Migrancy, a perpetual subtext of Mukherjee's fiction, is figurally repeated as displacement and deferral of unitary selfhood. Jyoti escapes from a childhood and adolescence circumscribed by a feudal economy in Hasnapur to become Jasmine, although she herself does not fully understand the homology between her feudal situation and the colonization of mind and body. She discovers that her strength lies not in cleaving to an elusive, or illusive, unity of identity, but in perpetual and vigilant internal exile, a legacy Prakash unwittingly left her in weaning her from her "feudally" simple impulse to unambitious wifehood and motherhood.

Jasmine's temporary refuge with the Vadheras is an encounter with the insubstantiality of identity. But the Vadheras' incomparably pale ghostliness is a kind of vacuity. Mr. Vadhera is frozen in a sclerotic lie intended to cover up his humiliating and ghoulish job as a sorter of human hair; Mrs. Vadhera is caught between the simulacra of two lives, one in America and the other endlessly rehearsed on videotapes of Hindi films she watches—she dreams of both, having neither. Since coming to America, Jasmine herself has felt caught between two different worlds, divided between near-feudalism and modernity.

Jasmine discovers identity as *différence*, as a multiply split subjectivity: Jyoti/Jasmine/Kali/Jase/Jane. These subjectivities are, furthermore, determined by their

Violence in Jasmine

belatedness: she does not remain simply Jyoti or anything else, but recognizes her multiplicity and ghostliness only *after* the violence involved in the destruction of each of the momentary condensations of self into particular named identities, each ghostly. She perpetually haunts, and is haunted by, her ghostly identities. Her mother had cautioned her that husbands are like onions because they reveal themselves layer by layer (82). And, although her mother did not point this out, onions are also empty at the heart. Jasmine understands her own ghostliness in a more radical sense and forsakes a root identity: she recognizes within her Jasmine the caregiver but also Jase the tireless adventurer. She is thrilled by the conflicting forces within herself. That is, she thrills to the contradictions and ambivalences of her new postcolonial self. She becomes a perpetual nomad and hybrid in the most radical sense; she shuttles between differing identities.

James Snead has suggested that hybridity is a challenge to notions of "universality."[8] Similarly, Homi Bhabha, in a discussion of the hybridity of colonial Indians as a form of resistance to colonial discourse, observes that "[w]hen they make . . . intercultural, hybrid demands, the natives are both challenging the boundaries of discourse and subtly changing its terms and setting up another specifically colonial space of power/knowledge."[9] Gillea Deleuze and Felix Guattari have observed that a minority literature is characterized in part by a deterritorialization of the space of power/knowledge. Anzaldua, similarly, hints at the subversive power of non-singularity, hybridity, "foreignness," and ambivalence:

> You say my name is ambivalence? Think of me as Shiva, a many armed and legged body with one foot on brown soil, one on white, one in a straight society, one in the gay world, the [man's] world, the women's, one limb in the literary world, another in the working class, the socialist, and the occult worlds. A sort of spider woman hanging by one thin strand of web.
> Who, me confused? Not so. Only your labels split me.[10]

The stability of identity is as horrific to Jasmine as it is to Anzaldua's woman, because the promise of security is unmasked as a delusion, and the displaced and decentered self is recognized as empowering. Jasmine simultaneously registers exhilaration and a *frisson* of terror at the prospect of exploding the delusion of unitary identity: while "Plain Jane" is all she wants to be for Bud, she realizes that it is merely a role, like many others, that she plays. Although she prays that her idyllic job as Duff's "day mummy" would be a permanent one, she sees that all stays against violence, entropy, destruction are at best temporary, at worst ephemeral and illusory. She feels safe with Du but acknowledges that he too will one day leave to step into his own future.

As a teenage peasant, Jasmine had ingenuously disavowed the political, discounting the colonial Indian past and the violence of the postcolonial present as too remote to pertain to her: she states that she was born eighteen years after the division of the subcontinent into India and Pakistan and that her village, Hasnapur, was not a "violent" (*Jasmine* 44) place at all. Her disavowal reinscribes a certain Indian postcolonial anxiety to deny what Frantz Fanon insists upon, namely, that in postcolonial societies recently liberated from colonialism, "the atmosphere of violence, having colored all the colonial phase, continues to dominate national life," and violence is always and everywhere "just beneath the skin."[11] Here, the constant sense of living in what Fanon calls, in a different context, "an atmosphere of violence" is internalized as a mental climate. In *Jasmine*, Mukherjee may not be explicitly concerned with violence in *historical processes*, but the political is always in the background, and violence is never far from the threshold of the postcolonial's consciousness.[12] The task of decolonization, therefore, continues to be imperative. As Ashis Nandy observes:

> It is now time to turn to the second form of colonization, the one which at least six generations of the Third World have learnt to view as a prerequisite for their liberation. This colonialism colonizes minds in addition to bodies

and it releases forces within the colonized societies to alter their cultural priorities once for all. In the process, it helps generalize the concept of the modern West from a geographical and temporal identity to a psychological category. The West is now everywhere, within the West and outside; in structures and in minds.... We are concerned with a colonialism which survives the demise of empires.[13]

Nandy here extends Fanon's discussion of violence as a necessary mode of resistance to the rhizomatic persistence of "The West" as a colonialism of the mind. The psychologistic struggle upon which Nandy insists may provide a crucial background against which to understand the effectivity or functionality of the violence that surfaces in *Jasmine*. Mukherjee's obsession with this theme is certainly evident in Jasmine's journey of self-discovery as deliberately or necessarily homeless, immigrant, diasporic. Jasmine, "shuttling between lives" (*Jasmine* 76, 77), obsessively rehearses her journey Westward, in a critical reversal of the colonizer's journey to the colony. The postcolonial diasporic travels to the former colonizer's territory, if not to "tropicalize" it (in Salman Rushdie's phrase), then to deterritorialize herself or himself. Following Fanon, Andrew Gurr observes that an artist born in a "colony" is "made conscious of the culturally subservient status of his home and is forced to go into exile in the metropolis as a means of compensating for that sense of subservience."[14] But the artistic freedom and scope thus gained comes at a price: to deconstruct the rhetoric of Otherness, to reproblematize the meeting of East and West, is to raise once more disturbing questions about selfhood and nationhood.

Mukherjee's expatriate protagonist recapitulates Fanon's notion that "[t]he native is always on the alert, for since he can only make out with difficulty the many symbols of the colonial world, he is never sure whether or not he has crossed the frontier.... The native's muscles are always tensed. You can't say he is terrorized, or even apprehensive. He is in fact ready at a moment's notice to exchange the role of quarry for that of hunter" (Fanon 53). We return, then, to the point made at the outset of this essay, that violence manifests itself not only in the social and political but also in the psychosexual and psychosocial realms.[15]

Fanon's "own coming to self-consciousness," depended on "his dislocation from the 'actual Third World,'" as Gates reminds us, drawing upon Albert Memmi's account (Gates 468). Fanon, "whose mother was of Alsatian descent, grew up in Martinique thinking of himself as white and French . . . [;] his painful reconstitution as a black West Indian occurred only when he arrived at the French capital" (Gates 468). It is only when Fanon recognizes himself as "an interloper" in Paris that he is able to recognize the need for the self-assertion of the New Man of no color, in the double session of postcolonial and psychoanalytic discourses.

As Gates observes, "Fanon's current fascination for us has something to do with the convergence of the problematic of colonialism with that of subject-formation."[16] Gates also quotes Edward Said's observation that Fanon and Aimé Césaire "jab directly at the question of identity and identitarian thought, that secret sharer of present anthropological reflection on 'otherness' and 'difference.'"[17] The interesting question in *Jasmine*, I have tried to suggest, is what kind of identity effect, if any, is actually achieved. As Said argues, what Fanon and Césaire "required of their own partisans, even during the heat of the struggle, was to abandon fixed ideas of settled identity and culturally authorized definition."[18] Jasmine instinctively grasps that self-assertion does not necessarily imply a confidence in a stable, reified self. Her struggle to maintain her precarious sense of self registers the effectivity of violence in the continual articulation of her precarious subjectivity in the world.[19]

Needless to say, to try to *understand* the effectivity of violence is not to endorse violence per se. As postcolonial migrant and as female body, Jasmine is at once the victim and the agent of violence. While the banalization of violence may be in some instances an attempt to repress a terrible knowledge of impending chaos, what is often disturbing about Mukherjee's fiction is its tendency to transmogrify violence into a kind of cynical game. In a short story called "The Imaginary Assassin," a young boy rejects his father's conventional dreams of immigrant success and harbors "a secret fascination with a different kind of immigrant, Sirhan B. Sirhan," only to learn that his senile grandfather had preceded him in dreaming a twisted dream in which he, not Nathuram Godse, had assassinated Mahatma Gandhi.[20] In *Wife*, the protagonist repeatedly imagines murdering her husband and hiding his body in the freezer—a scheme whose extravagance she says "delights" her, making her feel "very American somehow, almost like a character in a TV series"—and didn't "women on TV [get] away with murder"? Eventually Dimple realizes her liberating nightmare in a disturbingly celebratory act of violence.[21] In *The Tiger's Daughter*, violence is always just beyond the carefully maintained order of middle-class life. In *The Middleman and Other Stories*, likewise, almost every story is steeped in some form of violence.

If Jasmine seems too blithe and unfeeling in the way she leaves Bud, even though she regards it as necessary, she seems heartless too in the way she seems to shrug at Karin's suffering. And is it because she cannot afford to acknowledge pain, or is it simple callousness that makes her indifferent to Darrel's declaration of love for her and to his subsequent suicide? Jasmine's sensibility, like that of several other protagonists in Mukherjee's fiction, is not so much forlorn as deracinated, even to the point of cynicism. Perhaps this cynical postcolonialist sensibility proceeds from a recognition that, as Susan Suleiman puts it, "[e]ven the 'Third World' and 'women of color' . . . can be shown . . . to be caught up in the logic of the simulacrum and in the economics of multinational capitalism. In today's world, one can argue, there are no more places *outside*; the 'Third World' too is part of the society of the spectacle."[22]

There *is* something spectacular and sensationalist about the violence associated with Mukherjee's characters. The cynical or cauterized amorality of their embrace of violence stems from an instinctual recognition that if every place, including the so-called Third World is assimilated to the status of simulacrum, of spectacle, then it is also true that for the diasporic every place is no place, that all places are homeless, uncanny (*Unheimlich*). Divorced from a set of "home rules," Mukherjee's characters (sometimes bitterly) mock morality, defy normalcy, demolish home.

Aggression is, in one cliché, a masculine trait; Mukherjee's women, in acknowledging or even embracing violence, mock that cliché, as if to say, it is not only men who can wield violent power. At the same time, there is a danger that Mukherjee's women are "masculinized"—that they occupy and speak the same conflictual language of violence, even if for different reasons. There is something fearful, in addition to something admirable, in Jyoti's transformation into the Kali figure through the murder of Half-Face. Granted that Half-Face is her rapist, this response to violence with violence is troubling, even if justified as self-defense.

Mukherjee can sometimes solicit an affective response of fear or loathing, as for instance in a story called "A Father." Mr. Bhowmick, driven mad by his modern daughter's betrayal of his most cherished traditions, batters her artificially inseminated but nevertheless pregnant belly with that archetypal symbol, a rolling pin.[23] But perhaps the language of Mukherjee's fiction is most disturbing when it becomes the language of conflictual engagement or an egotistical jockeying for hegemonic power, or when it is simply "delighting" in real or imagined violence. My reading of Mukherjee's fiction is generally sympathetic. But it is also possible that male readers, such as myself, will respond differently from female readers, and that feminist readers differently from others. I cannot here go into the hermeneutics of those horizons—I raise the point to stress the complex and ambivalent effectivity of violence in Mukherjee's identitarian fables.

NOTES

1. Rey Chow, writing about violence in China, notes that historians "tirelessly" tell us that "modern East Asian history is the history of 'Westernization.' . . ." But the formula of "Westernization," with its trappings of rational progress, should not result in the forgetting of other, indigenous dynamics at work in the East's lurch toward modernity. See Rey Chow, "Violence in the Other Country: China as Crisis, Spectacle, and Woman," in *Third World Women and the Politics of Feminism*, 89.

2. James Gleick's *Chaos*, quoted as an epigraph in Bharati Mukherjee, *Jasmine* 44. All subsequent references will be within the text.

3. Mukherjee, "The World According to Hsu," in *Darkness*, 56.

4. See Elisabeth Bumiller, *May You Be the Mother of a Hundred Sons: A Journey among the Women of India*, 11.

5. Gloria Anzaldua, "La Prieta," in *This Bridge Called My Back: Writings by Radical Woman of Color*, ed. Cherrie Moraga and Gloria Anzaldua, 205.

6. See Gayatri C. Spivak, *The Post-colonial Critic*, 38, 42. Spivak, like Edward Said, insists on disengaging identity from location—and both caution that assimilation into the foreign (Western) culture is far from an unmitigated good.

7. Mukherjee, "Saints," in *Darkness*, 155.

8. James Snead, "European Pedigrees/African Contagions: Nationality, Narrative, and Communality in Tutuola,

Achebe, and Reed," in *Nation and Narration*, ed. Homi K. Bhabha, 234. See my "Talking Dirty: Salman Rushdie's *Midnight's Children*," *College English* 54.4 (April 1992): 431–445.

9. Homi K. Bhabha, "Signs Taken for Wonders," in *"Race," Writing, and Difference*, 179. First published in *Critical Inquiry*'s special issue of Race, Writing, and Difference (September 1985).

10. Gloria Anzaldua, "O.K. Momma, Who the Hell Am I?: An Interview with Luisah Teish," in *This Bridge Called My Back*, 223.

11. See Frantz Fanon, *The Wretched of the Earth*, 71, 76. Fanon insists on the complex functionality of violence. He writes that "decolonization is always a violent phenomenon," and this is the case "[a]t whatever level we study it," including the "relationships between individuals" (Fanon 35–36). Decolonization "is the veritable creation of new men" (36). The native "is declared insensitive to ethics; he represents not only the absence of values, but also the negation of values. . . . He is the corrosive element, destroying all that comes near him" (41). This "Manicheism," as Fanon terms it, at times "goes to its logical conclusion and dehumanizes the native . . . turns him into an animal" (42). But he knows he is not an animal, "and it is precisely at the moment he realizes his humanity that he begins to sharpen the weapons with which he will secure its victory" (43). His "eagerness, the fact that he openly brandishes the threat of violence proves that he is conscious of the unusual character of the contemporary situation and that he means to profit by it" (74). Speaking particularly of "the governments of recently liberated countries," Fanon maintains that "[t]he atmosphere of violence, having colored all the colonial phase, continues to dominate national life, for, as we have already said, the Third World is not cut off from the rest" (76). Thus David Caute can say that in Fanon, "[c]olonialism is violence, political, military, cultural, and psychic; only a counter-violence operating in the same spheres can eradicate it." Although Fanon rejected the Gandhian tactics of nonviolence "as an inauthentic form of decolonization," as Caute characterizes it, Fanon's early "existential view of violence as a form of radical, humanistic self-assertion by the individual" is really "nonviolent violence, in fact"; it was transformed into a "systematic theory of the

necessity of collective, revolutionary violence in the Third World" (Caute, 88).

12. Gilles Deleuze and Felix Guattari, trans. Robert Brinkley, "What Is a Minor Literature?" 13–33.

13. Ashis Nandy, *The Intimate Enemy: Loss and Recovery of Self under Colonialism*, xi. First published in 1983. Nandy wants to "take[s] the idea of psychological resistance to colonialism seriously." (xii) This resistance, as a form of self-assertion, is fraught with danger:

> Today, when "Westernization" has become a pejorative word, there have reappeared on the stage subtler and more sophisticated means of acculturation. . . . It is possible today to be anti-colonial in a way which is specified and promoted by the modern world view as "proper," "sane" and "rational." Even when in opposition, that dissent remains predictable and controlled. It is also possible today to opt for a non-West which itself is a construction of the West. . . . The most violent denunciation of the West produced by Frantz Fanon is written in the elegant style of a Jean-Paul Sartre. The West has not merely produced modern colonialism, it informs most interpretations of colonialism. It colours even this interpretation of interpretation. (xii)

14. Andrew Gurr, *Writers in Exile: The Identity of Home in Modern Literature*, 8.

15. Violence is often regarded as a symptom of a social pathology. As Arnold Feldman suggests, "Violence is conceived as being *incidental* to the basic character of social structures and processes. Indeed the very conception of social structure ordinarily excludes the source of structural destruction." (See Feldman, 111.) Citing Feldman's remark, Lewis A. Coser suggests that it is an unrealistic and "domesticated vision of the social order" that acknowledges violence only as a symptom of a pathology, minimizing the structural features which give rise to violence, and obscuring the complex *function* of violence. Coser argues that violence plays an important threefold role in society—as a "road to achievement," as a danger signal, and as a catalyst for social change. As he goes on to argue,

> Participation in such violence offers opportunity to the oppressed and downtrodden for affirming identity and for claiming full manhood [or, in Jasmine's case, full womanhood] hitherto denied them by the powers that be. Participation in revolutionary violence offers the chance for the first act of participation in the polity, for entry into the world of active citizenship. (Coser 343)

Coser turns to Frantz Fanon's argument that "violence incarnates absolute *praxis*. . . . Violence once assumed permits those who have left the group to return to their place and to be reintegrated. Colonial man liberates himself in and through violence." The colonized, in other words, is reborn through violence, *on his or her own terms*. Similar considerations, Coser argues, "may also account for the otherwise puzzling fact that women, normally much less given to violence than men, have played leading roles in classical revolutionary movements and in . . . modern liberation movements . . ." (344).

16. Henry Louis Gates, Jr., "Critical Fanonism," 458.

17. Edward Said, "Representing the Colonized: Anthropology's Interlocutors," qtd. in Gates, 458.

18. Ibid.

19. See David Caute, *Frantz Fanon*, 93. Caute observes that "Hannah Arendt, having drawn attention to [Georges] Sorel's debt to Henri Bergson's concept of *élan vital*, remarks that Fanon 'was greatly influenced by Sorel's equation of violence, life and creativity. . . .'"

20. Mukherjee, "The Imaginary Assassin," *Darkness*, 181–189.

21. Mukherjee, *Wife*, 195, 213. First published by Houghton Mifflin, 1975.

22. Susan Rubin Suleiman, *Subversive Intent: Gender, Politics, and the Avant-Garde*, 196.

23. Mukherjee, "A Father," *Darkness*, 73.

WORKS CITED

Anzaldua, Gloria, and Cherrie Moraga, eds. *This Bridge Called My Back: Writings by Radical Women of Color.* Watertown, Mass.: Persephone Press, 1981.

Bhabha, Homi K. "Signs Taken for Wonders: Questions of Ambivalence and Authority under a Tree Outside Delhi, May 1817." *"Race," Writing, and Difference.* Ed. Henry Louis Gates, Jr. Chicago: University of Chicago Press, 1986.

———, ed. *Nation and Narration.* New York: Routledge, 1990.

Bumiller, Elisabeth. *May You Be the Mother of a Hundred Sons: A Journey among the Women of India.* New York: Random House, 1990.

Caute, David. *Frantz Fanon.* New York: The Viking Press, 1970.

Chow, Rey. "Violence in the Other Country: China as Crisis, Spectacle, and Woman" in *Third World Women and the Politics of Feminism.* Ed. Chandra Talpade Mohanty, Ann Russo, and Lourdes Torres. Bloomington: Indiana University Press, 1991.

Coser, Lewis A. "Some Social Functions of Violence." *Black Politics: The Inevitability of Conflict. Readings.* Ed. Edward S. Greenberg, Neal Miller, and David J. Olson. New York: Holt, Rinehart and Winston, 1971. 340–351. First Published in *The Annals,* 364 (March 1966): 8–18.

Dayal, Samir. "Talking Dirty: Salman Rushdie's *Midnight's Children.*" *College English* 54.4 (April 1992): 431–445.

Deleuze, Gilles, and Felix Guattari. Trans. Robert Brinkley. "What Is a Minor Literature?" *Mississippi Review* 11 (Spring 1983): 13–33.

Fanon, Frantz. *The Wretched of the Earth.* Trans. Constance Farrington, with a Preface by Jean-Paul Sartre. New York:

Grove Press, 1968. First published as *Les Damnes de la terre*. Paris: François Maspero, 1961.

Feldman, Arnold S. "Violence and Volatility: The Likelihood of Revolution." *Internal War*. Ed. Harry Eckstein. New York: Free Press, 1964.

Gates, Henry Louis, Jr. "Critical Fanonism." *Critical Inquiry* 17 (Spring 1991): 457–470.

Gurr, Andrew. *Writers in Exile: The Identity of Home in Modern Literature*. Sussex: The Harvester Press, 1981.

Mukherjee, Bharati. *Darkness*. New York: Penguin, 1985.

———. *Jasmine*. New York: Grove Weidenfeld, 1989.

———. *The Tiger's Daughter*. Boston: Houghton Mifflin, 1971.

———. *Wife*. New York: Penguin, 1987. First published by Houghton Mifflin, 1975.

Nandy, Ashis. *The Intimate Enemy: Loss and Recovery of Self under Colonialism*. Delhi: Oxford University Press, 1989. First published 1983.

Said, Edward. "Representing the Colonized: Anthropology's Interlocutors." *Critical Inquiry* 15 (Winter 1989): 223.

Snead, James. "European Pedigrees/African Contagions: Nationality, Narrative, and Communality in Tutuola, Achebe, and Reed." *Nation and Narration*. Ed. Homi K. Bhabha. New York: Routledge, 1990.

Spivak, Gayatri C. *The Post-colonial Critic*. Ed. Sarah Harasym. New York: Routledge, 1990.

Suleiman, Susan Rubin. *Subversive Intent: Gender, Politics, and the Avant-Garde*. Cambridge, Mass.: Harvard University Press, 1990.

SOCIOPOLITICAL CRITIQUE AS INDICES AND NARRATIVE CODES IN BHARATI MUKHERJEE'S *WIFE* AND *JASMINE*

Janet M. Powers

In an interview with Bill Moyers, Bharati Mukherjee offers her view of immigrant attitudes and thus insight into the literature of immigration. Stressing the similarity between the experiences of all immigrants from the Third World, Mukherjee asserts that America offers "romanticism and hope" to those coming out of cultures of "cynicism, irony, and despair." The United States, she insists, offers the opportunity to "dream big" and to "pull it off," actions that are not possible in a traditional society. Yet, immigrants lead dangerous lives: they can't take shelter in traditional values, but neither do they know the rules of the dominant culture. Thus, newcomers to North America lead "raw, raucous, messy lives," which contrast strongly with the "small crises" of settled, suburban lives.[1]

The literature of the dominant culture generally deals subtly with such small crises in terms of a single cultural code. Literature of immigration, however, is a variant of postcolonial literature, which complicates the reader's task by introducing multiple cultural codes. A distinguishing trait of postcolonial fiction is the introduction of new linguistic elements and sociopolitical critique into the literature of a dominant culture. Moreover, it is the collision of values, expressed via multiple cultural codes, which, in terms of action, often generates satire, misunderstanding, or violence. Therefore, postcolonial literature is frequently unsettling to a society that prides itself on homogeneity or predictable behavior. The multiple codes of Mukherjee's novels expose both the paradoxical energy and emptiness of American society as well as the antithetical combination of flexibility and adherence to tradition displayed by Indian immigrants to the United States. Through dagger-like observations, Mukherjee's characters comment on the insanity of the lives they lead as Third World peoples adjusting to a fast-paced, mercenary society.

In searching for a critical theory which will take into account the functions of multiple cultural codes, the work of Roland Barthes, who early insisted on the plurality of the text, seems particularly useful. A truly integrated text, suggests Barthes, is founded on a "syntax of embedding and enveloping" (*Image* 118), best understood as a process of "ceaselessly substituting meaning for the straightforward copy of the events recounted" (*Image* 119). Barthes' way of explaining meaning, as "an incessant play of potentials whose varying falls give the narrative its dynamism or energy" (*Image* 122), is highly appropriate for analyzing the novels of Bharati Mukherjee. Perceived in this way, as counterpoint to sequential elements of narrative, Mukherjee's sociopolitical critique becomes essential to the startling turns of plot in *Wife* and *Jasmine*, which might at first be taken as inept writing. Sudden decisions to murder, changing one's name, or settling down in small-town America, are seen not to violate narrative logic but rather to join with sociopolitical observations at a higher level to create a new sort of postcolonial narrative logic.

In "Introduction to the Structural Analysis of Narratives," Barthes asserts that a narrative is made up entirely of functions, each of which signifies in different degrees (*Image* 89). He refers to integrational functions as *indices*, which may refer to character, feeling, atmosphere, a philosophy, or even a narrative agent, and which generally require some deciphering. Through the process of integration, claims Barthes, the global signifieds of a number of scattered indices are joined at a higher level (*Image* 122). Thus, the function of narrative, as Barthes explains it, is not mimesis or representation but creation of an "enigmatic" spectacle. Reality lies "in the logic there exposed, risked, satisfied" (*Image* 124).

Because these two novels deal with the immigrant experience, both immigrant Indian and resident American lifestyles come in for their share of sociopolitical critique. Indeed, it is this use of multicultural indices which is the hallmark of postcolonial literature. In *S/Z* (1974), Barthes introduced another way of interpreting texts: through the isolation of *lexia*, or fragments of the text, each of which may have three or four different meanings. He proposed five major codes under which all textual signifiers can be grouped. Because three of these, the seme (semantic unit), the symbolic grouping, and the cultural code, establish "permutable, reversible conditions outside the constraints of time" (*S/Z* 30), they are more useful in referring specifically to Mukherjee's sociopolitical critique. The other two codes, the hermeneutic and the proaretic, deal with plot and action, respectively.

This essay will demonstrate how both of these critical theories illumine the sociopolitical commentary generated in Bharati Mukherjee's novels of the Indian immigrant experience in the United States. The earlier theory, collected in *Image-Music-Text*, will serve for an analysis of *Wife*, using the notion of indices as they integrate with higher levels of action and narration to generate a system of narrative. The five cultural codes described in *S/Z*, in turn, will enable us to examine in *Jasmine* the sociopolitical commentary which punctuates the text. Taking as our assumption that sociopolitical observations largely constitute cultural and symbolic codes, we will discover that the multiple cultural code is particularly the province of the immigrant writer. However, in both novels, the cultural handsprings demanded of postcolonial peoples resident in the West are presented in terms of the hermeneutic and the proaretic as well as through semic, symbolic, and cultural codes. The critical concept introduced earlier in *Image-Music-Text* will be particularly helpful in allowing us to perceive links between cultural observations made by the third-person selective narrator of *Wife*, who describes the plight of immigrants in a hostile city, and the actions which those characters perform. In deconstructing such a narrative, however, one arrives first at the highest level, that of narration, which embodies the code by which the narrator and reader are signified throughout the narrative (Barthes, *S/Z* 110). That level, in turn, gives intelligibility to characters, which are units of the second or actional level. The major part of the narrative, however, is derived from the first level, that of functions.

Because sociopolitical critique tends to refer both to doing and being, Barthes' two major classes of functions, distributional and integrational, would logically come under consideration. For our purposes, however, we will work merely with indices, which belong to the latter group and tend to involve a functionality of being (rather than doing) and metaphoric (rather than metonymic) relata (*S/Z* 93). Discovering what an indicial notation "is for," in turn leads to higher levels, those of characters' actions or of narration. Part of a "parametrical relation" extended over an episode, character, or entire work, a typical index will involve deciphering, thus enabling the reader to learn to know a culture, a character, or an atmosphere (*S/Z* 96).

I

In *Wife*, we index the apartment of an Indian engineer and his wife living in urban America, by noting the furnishings in the living space occupied by Meena and Jyoti Sen: wall-to-wall carpet, TV, a combination tea

Sociopolitical Critique

trolley and warming tray, stereo set, bookcase with eight engineering books, transistor radio, tape recorder, and plastic flowers (52). Because there are no chairs, we realize that the Sens never entertain Westerners in their home, a point confirmed in conversation noting their disgust with beef eaters and American insincerity, insecurity with the English language, and projected losses on inexpensive furniture for those returning home. This particular index, however, has further ramifications for understanding the world in which Dimple Basu is expected to live: one of isolation from American culture except through the medium of television, which so thoroughly terrifies her with endless accounts of violence that she will not venture forth alone. Yet television also empowers her to a final rebellious act against the role of the traditional Hindu wife, a role unsuited either to modern India or to the United States.

The presence of plastic flowers, implying a love of flowers in a temperate climate where they are expensive rather than abundant, also suggests a certain parsimoniousness and acceptance of what is tasteless and artificial. A satiric reinforcement of those qualities occurs later, when we learn that Meena does Ikebana arrangements with plastic flowers yet sees no irony in the act. At the level of actions, Dimple, who hates both the furniture and the flowers, finds an acceptable outlet for her desire "to break and smash each piece" by breaking off three plastic petals. Yet she cannot throw out the torn petals, for she feels guilty, "as if she had intended to throw out parts of her own body," so she puts them into safekeeping with her passport, health certificate, and gold jewelry (*Wife* 104–105). Her body, that of "the good Hindu wife," has by now become for her a piece of plastic, easily molded, like the parts of a doll. Toward the end of the novel, we are told that she is falling apart in the manner of "a very old toy" that has been played with too roughly (*Wife* 212).

In the same apartment living room is a wall hanging which has further implications for both the level of actions and the level of narration. Although an image of Rama might be typical of any Indian dwelling and therefore functional merely on the level of discourse, the framed batik hanging of Rama and his court, with Sita hip-deep in flames, forms an index of atmosphere with reference not only to exile but to a horrendous act as yet unknown to the reader (*Wife* 53). Like Sita, the good Hindu wife, Dimple has left Calcutta and gone with her husband to the "forest," enduring not only physical discomfort but also psychological distress. Yet because of the prison inadvertently created by Dimple's fear of New York City, her insensitive husband, and the expected immigrant wife's role, she becomes vulnerable to "kidnapping" by Milt Glasser, who is Ravana in American guise. Unlike Sita, Dimple does not insist on chastity; nor does she reward the husband who tries, belatedly, to rescue her from despondency. The flames in which she is tested are those of reality; because she cannot truly be Sita, she does not survive, but implodes like a star.

Description of a character in someone else's conversation can also serve to index that individual in ways that later become meaningful at the level of action. Ina Mullick, for instance, is first presented as someone who might give Dimple "bad ideas"; she chainsmokes, goes to night school, and is seemingly Americanized. When we actually encounter her, she appears in dark glasses, white pants, and a knotted shirt which leaves her navel exposed; the effect is "chillingly sexy" (*Wife* 74). Her dress alone indexes her as an Indian woman who has abandoned her modesty and adopted American attitudes toward sexuality. We learn that she belongs to a women's group, is apparently having an affair with Milt Glasser, and is bitterly unhappy.

Ina, who has a graduate degree in physics from Calcutta University, has similarly been forced into the role of "the good Hindu wife" but has refused to be trapped by it. Yet her wild exploration of American lifestyles is not only an object of ridicule in the Indian community but represents the sort of forbidden freedom available only to a

Bengali wife whose husband has not looked after her properly. For Dimple, Ina functions as an opposing parameter to the constraints imposed by that sector of the Indian immigrant community which never ventures forth into the larger culture. With great difficulty, Dimple must somehow steer a course between these role models, neither of which is suitable for her. As a college-educated woman whose natural curiosity about the world has been blunted both by traditional role expectations and illusions about love gleaned from films and magazines, Dimple struggles to please her husband.

Amit, meanwhile, struggles to retain proper authority in the marriage, insisting that television, other Indians, and a baby are enough to keep any wife occupied. Truly a stroke of genius on Mukherjee's part are the imaginary advertisements through which Dimple tries to characterize her ever-so-rational engineer husband. She envisions him in a Macy's suit sitting next to Johnny Carson or in an *Esquire* ad smiling up at her from a typewriter and asking her to get him a Grant's. Trying to manage her culture shock by imitating his cool unflappability, she constructs a Dewar's Profile of a man whose traditional attitudes make no sense in the light of his decision to emigrate to the United States. Although we index Amit through the medium of advertising, as refracted through Dimple's mind, we begin to understand that he is, in fact, utterly irrational. Although he doesn't want Dimple to wear pants, he persuades her to drink beer. He memorizes jokes (five a day) methodically in an effort to become more like the Americans he works with. He urges Dimple to go out and meet other Indians but won't permit her to accept a job offered by one.

Perhaps the most devastating critique of immigrant Indian culture is contained in the letter to Miss Problem-Walla, which Dimple writes after her relationship with Milt becomes more complex. "Is love to be measured by physiological symptoms?" (*Wife* 202–203), she wants to know, trying to cope with a question that growing up in India has not prepared her for. But sadly, though modeled after the American institution of Ann Landers, Miss Problem-Walla deals only with beauty problems, not with human relationships. For as letters to the editor imply (*Wife* 27), in Indian society, societal roles are spelled out and the ideal celebrated. No other sorts of problems should exist for a married woman; or if they do, they should be resolved as Sita solved hers: with chastity and absolute faithfulness. Yet for Dimple, who has not yet ventured into American society, writing to Ann Landers is out of the question. Her virtual imprisonment within societal roles is evident in the fact that she has no one with whom to discuss her problem. Choosing Miss Problem-Walla is the ironic act of a young woman still trapped within the expectations of polite Bengali society, yet wrestling with options offered by American society.

To Dimple, however, the dominant society seems to be one of violent extremes. Everything she sees on television deals with love, but everything she reads in the newspaper is about death. Murder, as it randomly occurs in the city, is particularly frightening. Meena advises her not to do the laundry alone, at risk of being mugged in the basement of the building. Screaming police sirens in the night remind her of the dangerous world beyond her apartment. Her "gallery of monsters" includes alcoholics, dope fiends, black men in leather jackets, small dark Hispanics, and Puerto Rican girls in tight clothes (*Wife* 120). Dimple's first overt act of violence against Amit is to lunge at him with a paring knife because she imagines him to be a burglar sneaking up on her. Later, a man whom she has seen on the elevator slips into her apartment uninvited, horrifying her.

Even Americans seem aware that theirs is a violent society. Milt Glasser invites Dimple to an absurdly Roman show, a piece of performance art called "The Bull's Eye," in which a man runs around in circles in Madison Square Garden while spectators throw darts, javelins, and arrows at him. Although Milt may be putting Dimple on, he speaks glibly of how the intention of the piece is to redeem a violence-ridden society by estranging the audience from

Sociopolitical Critique

violence, though clearly it could feed the violence as well (*Wife* 202). This exaggerated index of the American preoccupation with death seems to bear out Dimple's earlier observation that in America, talking about murders was like talking about the weather (*Wife* 99). Dimple's exaggerated expectation of the violence awaiting her in New York is disappointed when she sits a long time on a public bench, hoping to be attacked, yet experiences nothing but Amit's wrath.

Dimple, of course, imagines that all of the violence is outside and fails to see the violence within her own being. An avid television viewer, she understands all too well that murder and death result from "love gone awry" (*Wife* 73). In her case, however, it might be said that murder results from "the good Hindu wife" ideal imposed on a naive but intelligent young woman. Having to dwell in an Indian ghetto in an alien culture, however, is only part of the problem. Amit is not Dimple's first victim; her baby, conceived in India, was aborted with the help of a skipping rope because "it cluttered up the preparation for going abroad" (*Wife* 42). The skipping rope is a particularly felicitous index of Dimple's character. She responds to her pregnancy as a woman bent on self-fulfillment, unwilling to restrict herself to the role of wife and mother. She looks on emigration to America as a chance to refashion herself, perhaps by taking evening classes and becoming a librarian.

Thus, we can say that Dimple literally skips out of her pregnancy, just as she would like to skip out on her husband after she has come to know Milt Glasser. She talks herself out of the idea that she is committing murder by stressing that it was unplanned. This first act of violence, however, sets the pattern for others to come. Her wounding of Amit with the paring knife and his later decapitation are similar acts of impulse, though born of a deep hostility to her role as the good Bengali wife in an arranged marriage. Dimple's way of killing, "deliberately, excitedly" (*Wife* 188), is contrasted with that of Ina and Leni, for whom things don't die accidentally. Thus a cactus which dies of overwatering becomes another ironic index of Dimple's inability to thrive in her overprotected domestic environment. The spontaneity and unpredictability of death as it affects Dimple seem to her very different from the randomness, intolerance, and detachment with which Americans kill.

The cultural ironies implicit in these observations are significant, of course. Americans, whose culture is celebrated for passion and love marriages, have assumed the detachment which, in the *Bhagavad Gita,* Hindus are traditionally exhorted to strive for. Meanwhile, Dimple, a young woman for whom religious ideals have never been particularly meaningful, instead turns to soap operas for her values. Frustrated by her inability to find love in an arranged marriage, she experiments with an affair but is hopelessly unable to manage a moment of intimacy with Milt. Their attempt at lovemaking ends with a comparative study of underwear and Dimple's much too formal conversation. Blue bikini briefs, which serve as an index of Milt's rather casual attitude toward sexual involvement, are something Amit would never wear; even Dimple prefers to look at them through Marsha's sunglasses in order not to be embarrassed (*Wife* 196).

The purple-tinted sunglasses are perhaps the most typical index of American culture. For Dimple, they are a disguise, borrowed from the West, just like Marsha's clothes and the apartment in which she is living. She also wears Amit's pants and socks and momentarily enjoys the excitement of dressing in other people's clothing. But after her botched afternoon with Milt, she feels worse than ever, cut off now from him and more than ever from Amit and the other Indians. Her borrowed disguises no longer have the power to distract. Purple sunglasses no longer transform reality but instead force her to see her situation for all of its intolerable emptiness. That Dimple has reached the end of her rope is quite obvious. We are prepared for an act of violence.

Yet because the author has been leading us astray at the level of narrative, by hinting at Dimple's suicide through lists of ways to die, the first-time reader is still rather surprised by the ending of the novel. However, indices of the skipping rope and the dead cactus, along with her observations about them, have earlier revealed that Dimple is capable of killing excitedly and intentionally. Thus, the murder must be seen as wholly logical. Moreover, through earlier indices functioning as sociopolitical critique, Mukherjee has prepared us quite well for the murder of Amit. By juxtaposing the image of Sita hip-deep in flames against descriptions of an apartment without chairs, as well as broken plastic flowers, Amit's Dewar's Profile, Milt's blue bikini briefs, and violence in American society, the writer presents a set of indices which collaborate to make sense of Dimple's murder at the level of actions.

Being forced to look at the smallest indices of the narrative is a discipline which Barthes' approach to narrative structure imposes on the reader. One cannot consider these in isolation, however, for the narrative is always integrated among its various levels. Integration, thus, is a vertical process in which each level gives unity to the units of the level below in such a way that "each unit is perceived at once in its surfacing and in its depth" (*Wife* 122). The process of integration in *Wife* is the act of finding unity in the discrete indices of violence both within and exterior to Dimple, so that the final act of violence is seen to be isotopic.

II

In dealing with the second novel, *Jasmine*, in which immigrants are "wily participants in the dominant culture,"[2] we will employ Barthes' theory of narrative codes as set forth in *S/Z*. However, rather than identifying particular lexia which contribute to the general sociopolitical critique of each novel, we will deal with each of the codes separately. In the process, we will discover how the five codes, the seme, the symbolic grouping, the cultural code, the hermeneutic, and the proaretic, operate to create the particular sort of novel which we can refer to as postcolonial. Three of these codes operate much like indices in the previously examined theory of narrative structure. Yet, in *S/Z*, Barthes has refined his analysis in order to distinguish more carefully among types of indices. Similarly, the hermeneutic and proaretic codes, which deal respectively with plot and actions, tend to correspond with what Barthes referred to previously as "the level of actions." The theory of narrative codes tends not to be hierarchical but rather involves a vision of narrative as a grid.

The first code, or seme, is "a connotator of persons, places, or objects, of which the signified is a *character*" (S/Z 190). Although Barthes claims that semes of objects or atmospheres are rather rare, it is evident that in postcolonial literature such is not the case. However, Barthes claims that semes are usually linked to an ideology of the person: "the semic raw material . . . completes what is proper to being" and "fills the name with adjectives" (S/Z 191). As Barthes explains the role of the seme in a classic text, the person is essentially a cluster of semes, usually represented by a proper name, or a pronoun, which enables a character to exist outside the semes of which it is constituted.

Understanding the seme is crucial to appreciating *Jasmine*, a novel in which changing the name of the character amounts to changing the semes which constitute it. The potential of fluidity, which Mukherjee attributes to American culture, is epitomized in the hermeneutic and proaretic codes by the main character's metamorphosis from Jyoti, a Punjabi village girl; to Jasmine, a loving and devoted Hindu wife; to Kali, incarnation of a destroying goddess; to Jazzy, a "remade" nonimmigrant; to Jase, a nanny in the home of a New York college professor; to Jane, live-in partner of a bank official in Iowa. Each of these character transformations is marked by changes in behavior and personality, such that

Sociopolitical Critique

her successive "rebirths" seem analogous to Hindu transmigrations of the soul. Barthes' semic code, identified by adjectival lexia, distinguishes shifts in semes which accompany name changes.

If we examine the semes associated with each of the six permutations, we discover that while some semes disappear, certain qualities do in fact "transmigrate" from one young woman to the next. Jyoti, born in the Punjab, the fifth daughter and seventh of nine children, is a survivor. This quality, perhaps more than any of the other semes associated with her, remains constant. Having survived her mother's attempt at female infanticide, as well as her sniping, Jyoti excels at her studies but is also capable of killing in self-defense, in this case a rabid dog. Both intelligent and beautiful, she demonstrates her strong will by fending off a matchmaker and her parents' attempts to marry her off to a Ludhiana widower. Free to marry whom she pleases, she is attracted intellectually to Prakash before she ever meets him and elopes with this gentle, kind, intelligent young man committed to modern ways. He and his friends share similar semes: "disrupters and rebuilders, idealists" (*Jasmine* 77). It is Prakash who effects her transformation from Jyoti to Jasmine.

Because he is a city man, Prakash wants to remove Jyoti from the village of Hasnapur and make her into a modern, urban woman. To break off the past, he also gives her a new name, Jasmine. Prakash insists that she is too young at the age of fifteen to become pregnant and so turns her away from the traditional role of the good Hindu wife content with babies and housekeeping. Jasmine demonstrates initiative by running a Ladies Group raffle in their building and selling detergent for a commission but doesn't tell her husband about her business ventures. When his dream of studying electronics in the United States is cut short by Sikh extremists, Jasmine resolves to journey to the United States to commit sati.

A number of the semes generated thus far, Jasmine's strong will, her ability to survive the worst, and her initiative, prepare her for her encounter with Half-Face, a war veteran who rapes her after her arrival in Florida as an illegal immigrant. Outraged by the violation of her person, she assumes attributes of Kali, becoming "death incarnate," by slicing her tongue and murdering her rapist. Half-Face, who treats Jasmine merely as a sex object, has only generic names for her: "honey," "baby," "prime little piece." It is Lillian Gordon who rescues Jasmine, teaches her to walk and dress like an American, and also gives her an American nickname, "Jazzy." Donning a T-shirt, tight cords, and running shoes, the nonimmigrant abandons her village sidle, as well as her modesty.

These clothes, however, along with her new name, must be set aside when Jasmine moves in with the Vadheras, who expect her—a widow—to dress and behave modestly. Mukherjee uses no name at all, and virtually no semes, to describe Jasmine during her stay in the immigrant Indian community. Instead, Mukherjee offers semes which critically assess the Flushing ghetto in which Jasmine finds herself: "fortress of Punjabiness," "apartment of artificially maintained Indianness" (*Jasmine* 146). A single seme sums up Jasmine's unhappiness in this environment: "a prisoner doing unreal time" (*Jasmine* 148).

Obtaining a forged green card, Jasmine finds a job as a nanny to Duff, adopted daughter of Taylor and Wylie Hayes, and during the course of her two years with them undergoes another transformation. Taylor renames her, of course; she becomes Jase, a woman well on her way to become an American, blowing most of her salary in stores along Broadway. Unlike Jyoti, who would have saved, and Jasmine, who lived only for Vijh, Jase lives with considerable recklessness. Witness to an American divorce, Jase falls in love with Taylor, who shares many of the same semes as Prakash: he is unfailingly kind, never condescending, and proud of her achievements (*Jasmine* 187).

Yet it is actually Taylor's world that Jase falls in love with, the seemingly magical world of middle-class Americans. She aspires to become the person they thought they saw in her. Yet, stresses the first-person narrator, Taylor didn't try to change her. She changed of her own volition, blooming into an adventuress. Her odyssey with Taylor and Duff cut short by a chance encounter with her husband's murderer, Jase resolves to go to Iowa, which although flat, is a place where one could still expect miracles (*Jasmine* 197). Iowa, where Duff was born, holds in store yet another transformation: from Jase to Jane, unmarried partner of a fifty-year-old banker.

Bud Ripplemeyer's attraction to her is presented as a form of Orientalism: to him she is exotic, mysterious, and intensely sexual (*Jasmine* 200). By other men, she is mistaken for an Asian bar girl and labeled as a whore. Mary Webb expects her as an Indian to be into channeling, gurus, and out-of-body experiences. As Jane, she finds herself a preserver, caring for a crippled man and bearing his child. In first breaking up a marriage and later deciding against a life of Old World dutifulness, she takes on the identity which Bud's wife assigns her in a dream: a tornado, leaving behind a path of destruction. Yet she also has the virtue of having stayed with Bud through his ordeal, of having been faithful in trying times. Thus, she vacillates between aspects of Siva and Vishnu, remaining more Indian than she realizes.

Two important semes help to close the narrative. In describing the particular farming practices on Bud's farm, Jane, like Karin, identifies the family values as "puritan," yet for the first time uses the first-person plural: "We're puritans" (*Jasmine* 237). Thus, she identifies herself as an American and no longer as an immigrant. Moreover, in the final lines of the novel, Jane shows that she is not ready to accept Karin's label of a destructive tornado (*Jasmine* 241). Instead, she describes herself as "greedy with wants and reckless with hopes," values which are typically American, born of fluidity and speed of transformation, qualities of both the American character and its landscape.

In moving to an examination of the symbolic code, we will analyze just three groupings which have the properties of multivalance and reversibility. Barthes notes that in dealing with the symbolic code, "the main task is always to demonstrate that this field can be entered from any number of points" (S/Z 19). A particularly apt symbol for the immigrant experience is Sam, the marine iguana kept as a pet by Duff. Out of his habitat and painfully ugly, he, like Jase, is a long way from home. Not unlike the transformation of Saladin Chamcha, presented by Rushdie in *The Satanic Verses*, the iguana suggests ways in which one's identity can be misread and changed in the process of immigration. Jase holds the reptile on her lap, something she would never have done in India, and responds by noting her own transformation with astonishment.

Another sort of transformation is represented by the developer's purchase of the Flamingo Court Motel, scene of Jasmine's rape, and Lillian Gordon's property, way station for Kanjobal Indians and illegal immigrants. Advertising a Key West-style cottage as part of a mixed-use vacation and residence community called Paradise Bay, the developer literally turns hell into paradise (*Jasmine* 138). Such fluidity, viewed by Jasmine as very American, causes her to react with a passing wave of nausea and the observation that she feels like a stone hurtling downward, unable to stop or slow her descent. In addition to the cultural transformation required of all immigrants to anywhere, the individual transplanted to the United States must also cope with a shifting world in which nothing, not even the landscape, stays the same.

Fluidity is also apparent in the ease with which Americans slough off spouses and adopt children. When Wylie and Taylor are divorced, Jase comments that in America, nothing is so terrible or wonderful that it won't disintegrate (*Jasmine* 181). It was the hardest lesson for her to learn: monuments, agreements, even families, must constantly undergo transformation, even in Iowa. Although presented as the last puritan stronghold, Iowa is where Duff was born to a university student and given up for adoption. And Iowa is where Jase's arrival causes a small-

Sociopolitical Critique

town banker to leave his wife of many years. Finally, Iowa is where Bud and his Indian partner adopt a fourteen-year-old Vietnamese boy, whose own response to living in America is characterized by his genius for scavenging, adaptation, and appropriate technology. Du's practice of recombinant electronics, symbolic of the general gene pool alteration effected by immigrants, points to the ultimate transformation of American society.

The cultural code, according to Barthes, consists like the others of "fragments of something that has always been *already* read, seen, done, experienced" (S/Z 20). Specifically, cultural codes reference a science or a body of knowledge without going so far as to construct the culture they express (S/Z 20). When Jase describes how boys in her village torment geckos and contrasts that violence with American willingness to puree lettuce for a large pet iguana, dual cultural codes are at work. Nirmala Vadhera's insatiable appetite for Hindi films references the network of video outlets available in the United States to Indians who prefer to isolate themselves from the English-speaking people of the dominant culture. Another set of dual codes reveals that the immigrant culture itself is split between the educated younger generation working in the United States and their older parents, who complain of no grandchildren, too-thin daughters-in-law, and nontraditional authority patterns (S/Z 147).

When writing of Indian culture, Mukherjee inevitably feels compelled to explain to her American audience what lies behind certain cultural codes. Thus, she indicates that in India, where the groom's mother is a virtual "tyrant" in the house, each woman in turn looks forward to her opportunity to tyrannize her daughters-in-law. But in the United States, where the younger woman may have a job, the mother-in-law is incapable of wielding authority. Although Barthes implies that the writer need not construct (or reconstruct) the culture that lies behind the codes, we note that some reconstruction is indeed necessary if readers from the dominant culture are fully to appreciate the text. The Indo-English writer faces a similar problem, even when writing of events in India. Various writers have solved this problem by using footnotes or elaborate endnotes, while others, perhaps less successfully than Mukherjee, have woven cultural reconstructions into their narratives.

Such cultural reconstruction, however, is not necessary when writing of the dominant culture. Thus Mukherjee can use the word "puritan" as a cultural code and know that, for her readers, a full constellation of attitudes is called up by that word. What Mukherjee does, however, is to construct for her East and West Coast readers, as well as those from India, the puritan attitude toward farming by calling attention to the Iowa practice of clearing all dead stalks from the fields because it appears "businesslike" (*Jasmine* 237). Even Taylor's prescription for dealing with objects bought by TV marketing—to draw an imaginary shade on the screen—to make it go away, is a variation on the puritan habit of keeping meanness out and goodness in (*Jasmine* 210).

Although it is the beauty of this response to things intolerable that compels Jane to leave Bud for Taylor and Duff, such an escape is seen as inadequate in the face of true evil. Both Du and Jane, as well as the Hmong refugees quilting in Iowa church basements, have faced death head on and killed in self-defense. Thus, immigrants are presented as persons who have, in the past, not been able to pull down the shade, but who have also risked much to come to a culture where such a solution is possible. Yet Darrel's suicide and the evil machinations of the Aryan Nation Brotherhood remind us, via the proaretic and hermeneutic codes, that all is not well in the land of happy endings. And indeed, when Jane announces clearly her philosophy of life, it is essentially a Hindu vision: she dreams of neutralizing harm in a universe where goodness and evil square off at every moment (*Jasmine* 203). This vision, coupled with her Hindu appreciation for transmigrations, enables Mukherjee's character to accept the "enormous psychological and social dislocation" which becoming an American requires.[3]

Barthes' two theories of narrative have in fact proven quite helpful in deconstructing Mukherjee's novels. However, in the process of utilizing his methodologies, we have isolated several characteristics of the literature of immigration and, therefore, of postcolonial fiction, which prove counter to Barthes' observations. First, semes of objects or atmosphere are not particularly rare in Mukherjee's novels of immigration. Second, multiple cultural codes are frequently required to present a contrast between former and present values or expectations. Finally, more cultural reconstruction is required in the novel of immigration than in a narrative dealing with a single cultural code. In general, however, notions of "embedding" and "indices," integrated with levels of action and narration, help us to see how expertly a novel such as *Wife* is constructed. Similarly, three of the narrative codes offer superb avenues by which to explore sociopolitical critique in Mukherjee's novels. Using either of these approaches should prove fruitful when dealing with any literature of immigration.

NOTES

1. *Conquering America with Bharati Mukherjee*, Videocassette. Prod. Bill Moyers.

2. Neela Seshachari, "Indian Immigrant Writing in America: Reconciling the Two Worlds."

3. *Conquering America with Bharati Mukherjee*, Videocassette. Prod. Bill Moyers.

WORKS CITED

Barthes, Roland. *Image-Music-Text*. Trans. Stephen Heath. New York: Hill and Wang, 1977.

———. *S/Z*. Trans. Richard Miller. New York: Hill and Wang, 1974.

Conquering America with Bharati Mukherjee. Videocassette. Prod. Bill Moyers. Public Affairs Television, 1990. 58 min.

Mukherjee, Bharati. *Jasmine*. New York: Grove Weidenfeld, 1989.

———. *Wife*. Markham, Ontario: Penguin, 1987.

Seshachari, Neela. "Indian Immigrant Writing in America: Reconciling the Two Worlds." MLA Convention, Washington, D.C., 29 December 1989.

TELLING HER TALE: NARRATIVE VOICE AND GENDER ROLES IN BHARATI MUKHERJEE'S *JASMINE*

Pushpa N. Parekh

Among traditional oral stories, myths, and folktales in India, the theme of marriage and gender roles are central. As A.K. Ramanujan in "Telling Tales" points out, the "woman-centered tale" in particular, begins, rather than ends, with marriage (246). Unlike the male-centered tales in which the hero figure wins the bride as a reward, "in the woman-centered tales, as in the classical analogues of *Sakuntala* and *Savitri*, it doesn't seem enough for a woman to be married. She has to earn her husband, her married state, through a rite of passage, a period of unmerited suffering" (Ramanujan 247). It is only in the end, through the "telling of her own story to a 'significant other' (often through a device, like a talking doll or a lamp)" that the "silent woman" becomes a "speaking person" (248). In the traditional tales, however, the "silent woman" and the "speaking person" are still constructs of the "teller of tales"; the voicing or unvoicing of their story is embedded in the cultural context and value system of the "teller." Significantly, in the traditional stories, neither the "silent woman" nor the "speaking person" challenges the assigned gender roles in marriage. By internalizing the prevailing definition of a woman's role in marriage as one of suffering and endurance, the tales present the outcome of the story, that is, happiness in marriage, as a reward for these self-sacrifices. A heroine figure from Hindu mythology, Savitri, challenges Yama, the God of Death, to return life to her husband, Satyavan, as narrated in the Puranas. She uses wit and intellect and displays courage in achieving this end. Pleasing Yama with her intellectual agility and wisdom, Savitri obtains a boon from him; he agrees to grant her any wish she desires, except the life of her husband. With clever forethought and presence of mind, Savitri asks that she be blessed with progeny, and Yama grants her this wish. Her observation that she, as a "chaste woman," cannot have children if her husband is dead wins over Yama. He finally surrenders Savitri her husband (Jagannathan 21). It is not surprising that traditional patriarchal renderings of Savitri's tale tend to emphasize a woman's "chastity" and "goodness," rather than her intellect and wisdom, as her reasons for her victory over death and as qualities befitting the final reward—return of her husband and marital bliss.

Bharati Mukherjee, the writer of immigrant tales in America, underscores the reinvention of the woman-centered oral tale in the narrative structure and thematic content of *Jasmine*. She unravels the triple voice-strands in the complex triad of the Jyoti-Jasmine-Jane persona. Jyoti, "the silent woman," is *foretold* and *told* a certain kind of existence and identity. In the traditionally feudalistic Punjab, in an environment of fatalism, caste-ism, and classism, the power of speech is usurped by the dominant male figures. In the family-centered society, these figures are the father, the brothers, and eventually the husband. Jyoti, as her name implies, is a "light" that brightens a household—a very traditional name rich with associations of the woman as the Lakshmi goddess figure. She is visible but apparently unheard. So do all the forces in her environment train her to become, despite her inner outrage and conflict. Jyoti begins her life as a "silent woman" *foretold* by the village astrologer of her "widowhood and exile" (*Jasmine* 1); *told* by her mother (as much a product of the feudalistic society as its silent

Narrative Voice and Gender Roles in Jasmine   111

critic) that the bruise around her throat was to spare her the agony of a dowryless marriage (*Jasmine* 35); *told* by her grandmother Dida that Jyoti's personal courage, exhibited in her courageous killing of the mad dog, was inconsequential (*Jasmine* 50). With Prakash, her husband, she begins a new life. She is *told* to adopt the more modern values of a city woman. Renamed as Jasmine, the protagonist wryly reflects on the paradoxes and ironies inherent in the converging of the two worlds—feudal and modern. At first, caught between the interspaces of these two worlds, Jasmine's voice reflects her desires and feelings as an echo of her training and conditioning in a feudalistic environment. She wants children at the age of fifteen because women in the village were beginning to talk. Prakash begins the process of retraining Jasmine: the overthrow of feudal mentality involves a redefinition of gender roles within marriage. Jasmine's preconditioned voice is trained by Prakash to argue and fight if she does not agree with him—to *want* for herself, a lesson that Jasmine learns as she later empowers her voice with speech. Within the parameters of socially accepted gender roles and their defiance by her husband, she moves from the position of being *told* to that of *telling*.

With Prakash's brutal death and Jasmine's odyssey into self-exile and illegal entry into the Florida backwater, begins the telling of the "speaking person's" tale—one of struggle, violence, wonder, despair, survival, and transformation. This telling is perhaps the most haunting part of the narrative—alternating between the fluidity of voicing through self-reflection, interior monologue, and figurative language, mythologizing her new experience through the oral medium of creating "new proverbs" to the strain of unvoicing through narrative pauses, mental blocks, and silence by volition.

During this phase, Jasmine recasts her role as the observant traveler, the restless sojourner, as well as the intrepid adventurer. Hurtling from the confines of an Indian widow's bleak imprisonment, she runs into the harsh brutality of illegal entry, rape, and murder in

America. The ensuing silence of horror that cloaks Jasmine's world is literalized in her cutting of her tongue; Goddess Kali-like, she pours blood from her mouth on Half-Face, the modern avatar of evil. In Jasmine's inarticulation is exemplified her silent power to transform her self-image as Lakshmi, goddess of domestic bliss, to Kali, the war goddess. Unlike Dimple Dasgupta, the protagonist in Mukherjee's novel *Wife*, who "loses sight of reality as she sinks into the world of television . . . she kills her husband as he complacently eats a bowl of cereal" (Rustomji-Kerns 658), Jasmine has a goal in sight. Any thought of self-destruction in the spotless bathroom of the motel where Half-Face had raped her comes to a fierce end. She prepares herself for her mission of self-immolation after burning her husband's suit under the palm trees of the college campus in Tampa. It is a bizarre goal, but one born out of despair, anger, and frustration at the violence of traditional customs as well as progressive, modern societies.

The voiceless Jyoti as Lakshmi and the tongueless Kali are both "silent women"—postcolonial products as well as critics of those aspects of both traditional and, ironically, even modern cultures, "specifically located in the arena of female sexuality," that are "most oppressive for women" (Katrak 168). Neither passive submission nor active violence is the norm by which Jasmine seeks to define her identity. It is in Lillian Gordon's home, a place of refuge for outcasts and illegal aliens, that Jasmine recovers, in stages, her self and through that her voice. Her passage, as she journeys, both literally and symbolically, across the landscape of America, is no longer any woman's passage. It is the passage of an immigrant woman, specifically an illegal, postcolonial, immigrant woman. Initially, she must by choice become voiceless, invisible, and indistinguishable, adapting an American way of talking and walking, while she keeps the remnants of her past self hidden within her. Straddling two cultures, Jasmine undertakes a journey that involves a physical, an emotional, and a strongly intellectual awakening. From the illegal alien entry to the "day mummy" stage of her life, the voice that tells her story is fraught with questions, doubts, laconic rejection, and bemusing acceptance of the intriguing and often puzzling aspects of the American culture. Faced with the option of total silence within the regimental and studied maintenance of superficial rituals and cultural adherence in the Vadhera's household (where watching Indian movie videos daily is a family's pathetic clinging to the commercialized form of "Indian" culture), Jasmine chooses independence and self-reliance. In the American family, the Hayes household, Jasmine's rueful acceptance of the role of "day mummy" to Duff, reflects on the anxieties that underlie an American working mother's life, on her own role and sense of worth. Wylie and Taylor accept her for who she is. This period in Jasmine's life is the most restful and comforting, emotionally and psychologically. Intellectually, however, it is a phase of minute observations of, complex inner deliberations on, and keen involvement in, her new environment. Then, suddenly, Wylie decides to leave Taylor to take her chance at "happiness" with Stuart. To Jasmine, growing accustomed to a world where cause and effect sequences are essential links to a logical explanation of events, Wylie's apparent "reasonless" abandoning of Taylor and Duff is a jolt back to the inexplicable and unexplainable nature of human action. Instead of fate or destiny or an unknown power being responsible for a family's break-up, Jasmine witnesses an American woman, Wylie, deliberately choosing to leave. Jasmine's inner monologues and silent reflections capture her deliberations on cultural differences and an immigrant woman's emotional adherence to her traditional beliefs while intellectually exploring the new avenues opened to her by the modern value systems. There is a sympathetic nuance to her voice as she appraises the two cultures, Indian and American, and rejects the possibility of adopting either one, in isolation from the other, as the only area for an immigrant woman's growth.

Mukherjee, herself an immigrant woman, had battled with outright racism in Canada and its "devastating personal effects" (Carb 652). In the Introduction to *Darkness*, Mukherjee refers to her experience of "a movement away from the aloofness of expatriation, to the exuberance of immigration" (3). Jasmine, like Mukherjee and so many immigrants, contemplates on the ironies of exclusive "preservation" or "assimilation." She concludes from observing the Vadhera family's total immersion in preserving the old ways of an Indian lifestyle: they are afraid to lose their grip on anything because of fear that they may lose everything. In contrast, the Hayes family confirms for Jasmine that in America nothing really lasts forever. The subsequent experience of an almost idyllic state of family life with Taylor and Duff affirms to Jasmine the indefatigable nature of the human will to acquire and sustain a space of its own. As "Jase," she is accepted by Taylor as an equal. Considerate, kind, and genial in many ways, Taylor doesn't attempt to change her. Yet she changes, even as Mukherjee and other immigrants have done. The ironies of life, however, pursue Jasmine in the reappearance of the Sikh assassin, Sukhwinder, who had murdered her husband in India. Jasmine, reminded of her illegal status, cannot call the police or seek justice, even as she could not in an earlier instance when Half-Face had raped her. She again becomes "voiceless" and seeks sanctuary away from New York in Iowa.

Jasmine's flight to Iowa and her name change to Jane is indicative of a slow but steady immersion into the mainstream American culture. Drawing tentative parallels between Iowa and Punjab and disrupted lives of the farmers in both places seems a psychological mode of survival for Jane. From the special and unique nature of her evolving "Jasmine" self, Jane becomes, as her name implies, a nonentity, even a conscienceless "gold digger" in Karin's words (*Jasmine* 174). From the "Sati-goddess" Jyoti (*Jasmine* 156) to the Kali-Jasmine to "adventurous Jase" (*Jasmine* 165) to "Plain Jane" (*Jasmine* 22) has been an eventful, uneven odyssey; the protagonist's name changes as well as her shifts in places of residence become metaphors for an immigrant woman's "process of uprooting and rerooting" (Carb 648). Dubiously recognized for her mysterious Eastern qualities or her unique culinary skills, Jane is expected to eventually become Bud Ripplemeyer's wife and the mother of their expected child. Jane, however, is a complex blend of the "silent woman," "the speaking person," and the "teller of tales." As the "silent woman" she accepts the almost preplanned, prearranged, tailor-made itinerary of a certain predictable way of life with Bud. But her increasing sense of isolation and loss of self in this suffocating world is heightened by her inability to share with Bud her memories or reflections on the past, which are a part of her identity as much as the present is: Bud prefers not to discuss her Indian past with her. Handicapped as a result of a shooting by Harlan (a disgruntled farmer whom Bud had denied a loan to), Bud slowly sinks into a self-centered existence in which the most natural feelings of sexual passion have to be artificially created. Ready to sacrifice her own happiness and dreams, Jane almost acquiesces to become Bud's wife. It is through Du, their adopted Vietnamese son, that Jane wishes to sustain her identity as an "immigrant." All the forces in Iowa would eventually freeze her to conformity or continual alienation. Bud is uncomfortable with her tales of Hasnapur. He wishes her silent, and Du, driven to quickly become thoroughly American, only cursorily listens to Jasmine's stories of India. Although Jane senses in Du a fellow-survivor, she realizes she cannot remake herself through Du. He escapes Iowa and its imprisoning milieu, to seek his own sister and revive his own identity. Pondering upon her own past, Jane as the "teller of tales" frames her "silence" and her "speaking" with a historical reality and substantiates them with personal significance. In evaluating her past and present and anticipating her future, Jane confronts the complexity and multiplicity of her identity as an immigrant woman.

 Appearing self-possessed and patient, Jane, as we discover her through her interior monologues, is seething.

Likening herself to a "tornado" (*Jasmine* 190), she wonders about the changes that are yet to reshape her destiny. Baden, Iowa, offers her Bud's desperation or Darrel's self-pity—a place where Jane realizes she will be lonely regardless of Bud's presence or absence. The very land, America, that had taught her to become the "speaking person" could close her up and make her feel "millennia old" (*Jasmine* 30). In "telling her tale," the Jane and Jasmine selves of the protagonist seek to blend their "wants" and "dreams" into possibilities and realities. The range and texture of the narrative voice reiterate the immigrant woman's personal journey as a new questing pioneer's movement from self-denial to self-realization. Tonal shifts and choice of metaphors invest the telling of the three stages of Jasmine's evolution with a language that operates at various levels of meaning and creates its own resonance.

The narrative voice of the protagonist, speaking in the first-person point of view, reflects her choice of rhetorical tools in telling her tale. An interesting point made by Liew-Geok Leong in the essay, "Bharati Mukherjee," in *International Literature in English: Essays on the Major Writers*, needs consideration: "The voice of Jasmine, surprisingly articulate and assured, is not always believable, given her background and circumstances; it is her creator's voice that takes over and speaks for her, the result perhaps of too close an identification with the subject" (494). It is a legitimate point which needs illustration. In many ways the unevenness of voice in Jasmine reflects the precarious nature of her identity and existence. Living on the edge, on the "margins" as it were, Jasmine lunges into the safe and unsafe expanses with almost a heady assurance. She can be aggressively outraged by the racist condescension of mainstream America that marvels at Third World Du's driving skills and scholastic achievements. At the same time, it is strained and unbelievable as Jane's voice, as is revealed when she compares herself to Charlotte Brontë's Jane Eyre. The literary allusion is a direct product of

Mukherjee's, rather than Jasmine's, "Anglicized life," attending "an elite school for girls run by Irish nuns who followed a heavily British and European curriculum" (Leong 487). Instances of this kind of improbability of voice and character are, however, reflective of the relatively early stage of Mukherjee's own writing. *Jasmine* transcends these limitations through the richness of tonal variations that compounds the building tempo of the novel.

The memory of Jasmine's personal history and environment shapes and directs the reception of her present experiences and context and is often countered by the accruing of new memories of newer experiences. This double perspective of the shifts in time and space and their impact on the psyche of the immigrant woman can be explored through the tonal shifts with which the Jasmine-Jane protagonist concretizes her emotional and intellectual reality. Fear, anger, pain, bitterness, confusion, silence, irony, humor, as well as pathos underline her observations as she discovers for herself the undefined median between the preservation of the Old World and the assimilation into the new one. Painful recollections of the past find a necessary sheathing in a voice that delivers facts in an objective tone of reportage— as, for instance, when she recalls the murder of her husband with journalistic detachment (*Jasmine* 78). Characterizing this "war correspondent" technique of first-generation immigrant writers, Susan Jacoby in "World of Our Mothers: Immigrant Women, Immigrant Daughters," reflects on the need to sufficiently remove oneself from the maelstrom, in order to achieve "a quality Lillian Hellman has aptly termed 'a way of seeing and then seeing again'" (118). As the Jasmine-Jane protagonist learns to cast herself in different roles, she finds her initial identity in America immured in the volitional silence and invisibility of a law breaker in two senses. She is an illegal alien who has defied the immigration laws and a murderer who defies the ruthless violence of a male-powered capitalist society. An adept at defiance as a mode of survival from her childhood days, Jasmine-Jane characterizes her voice with the tone of defiance. This defiance, born of inner monologues and reflections, and of the sanity and the capacity of the human will to survive, is distinct. It is at times a brash, willful defiance, at others a quietly enduring one. It is, however, not the one that violates through "unconscionable behavior," as some immigrants' defiance does, such as Dr. Manny Patel's in the story, "Nostalgia," from *Darkness* (Jussawalla 588). On the contrary, it is born of an honest sense of an individual's worth; it is a way of birthing a new self; and it is a way of grappling with the pain and pathos underlying this birth: "There are no harmless, compassionate ways to remake oneself" (*Jasmine* 25). Other immigrants in Mukherjee's short stories echo this realization in terms of both despair and defiance. Panna in "A Wife's Story" expresses it thus: "It's the tyranny of the American dream. . . . No instant dignity here" (*The Middleman* 24).

This process of transformation, figuratively centered in the death of one's old self and the birth of a new self, is a motif that vitalizes the narrative language and structure. Sensory images reiterate at various levels the symbolism of cyclical patterns of birth, death, and new birth, in the context of the postcolonial immigrant woman's life and experiences.

A striking mark of her supposed limitation, as defined by others, is a visible star-shaped scar on Jasmine's forehead. A visual image of physical deformity and, more significantly, of the stamp of fate, this scar is transformed by even the most "silent woman," Jyoti: she regards it as her "third eye" (*Jasmine* 2). The third eye of Shiva, the Hindu God of destruction, "depicts that God [as] all-seeing and wise. Placed in the center of the forehead on which the Yogi concentrates while in meditation, this spot is symbolic as the seat of wisdom. Shiva opens his third eye to destroy evil" (Jagannathan 42). This destruction is a necessary antecedent to the birth of a new universe. In a sense, Jyoti's conviction in herself as powerful and God-like is later expressed by Jasmine in terms of the goddess image Kali, one of several names of the female consort of

Shiva. Like Kali, the Jyoti-Jasmine-Jane protagonist must destroy evil, the external and internal distortions of the woman's self, in order to birth a new wholesome cosmos, a woman complete in herself. She herself constitutes, in her various identities, the two halves of the complete self, depicted in Hindu cosmology as the male and female aspects of the Godhead. Thus transforming a physical scar into the spiritual power of the "third eye," the protagonist reenvisions the roles of fate, destiny, and a woman's will. However, she discovers, the process of transformation is an ongoing, continual one. Even in the more liberated landscape of America there are "potholed and rutted" (*Jasmine* 214) driveways where a Third World immigrant woman might find herself sinking into new forms of old expectations, new ways of exercising old oppressions. Jane in her pregnant condition encounters the underlying biases and assumptions with which mainstream America isolates the immigrant "other," the Third World "you." In her traditional, feudalistic village of Hasnapur in India, girls of fifteen were already married off and pregnant, and at twenty-two might be widowed, old, dead. Having escaped that fate and having defined her destiny through the pain, the chaos, and the uplifting sense of unlearning the old and learning the new, Jane still finds herself struggling against culturally ingrained gender-based stereotypes.

Jane internalizes these problems of self and self-definition in a country of "equal opportunity" through the dialectics of opposing images. One of them is old age versus youth: she acknowledges her youth but realizes that she feels "millennia old, a bug-eyed viewer" (*Jasmine* 30). The "third eye" can easily turn into a "bug-eyed viewer" and therein lies the danger and the despair of the promise that the New World holds. She could actively precipitate change; however, she could as quickly be reduced to the role of a silent, wearied witness of change and turmoil.

Another striking pattern of opposing images that emphasizes the nature of self-transformation in *Jasmine* recurs in the form of associations: death and violence associated with the stench of a floating carcass of a drowned dog (*Jasmine* 3), Pitaji's sudden end, attacked by a bull from behind (*Jasmine* 51), or with the monstrous Half-Face, covered in the blood pouring from Jasmine's slit tongue (*Jasmine* 103). Life and preservation are associated with the sweet smelling sandalwood Ganpati, the Hindu God who removes obstacles, and the red-tongued Jasmine as Kali-figure. While the animal images symbolize the violence and disorder that an external world can impose on an individual, the god/goddess images symbolize the icons of the woman's inner strength to be her own guide and savior. Partaking the strengths of both the male and the female aspects of the Godhead, Jasmine realizes the androgynous nature of human will and courage.

In the large context of the changes that an immigrant undergoes, the references to another cultural symbol, food and food habits, become integral ways to comprehend Jyoti-Jasmine-Jane's several shifting arenas of evolution. The feudalistic Punjab of Jyoti's childhood is rife with class and gender divisions. Her father, living in his dream world of his prosperous past, clings to qualities of class refinement, lacking, as he points out, even in the variety of indigenously grown Bombay mangoes. Desire for and partaking of food is not a simple physical activity; it resonates with the implications of gender divisions and traditionally assigned roles for women: it is by withholding certain types of food, such as onions among other items, that widows in India are relegated to a subclass among women (*Jasmine* 41).

In America, Jasmine encounters two sets of families, the Indian immigrant Vadheras and the American Hayeses. In each household, Jasmine observes the way in which the use or abuse of food concretizes the larger ideologies that define their world. In Flushing, New York, the Vadheras live in their own insulated world. This myopic vision is symbolized in Nirmala's excuse for failing to get pregnant: she blames pollutions in the food. These self-satisfying, often deceptive ways of avoiding reality are reflective of the larger self-deceptions that some immigrants hide behind. Devinder, now "Dave," Vadhera never faces the reality of his failure to prosper in America; he hides behind his pretense-title "professorji," while his family too hides from facing its new immigrant identity behind superficial symbols of "Indian" culture. In this stultifying environment Jasmine entertains elderly Indian visitors with tea and an assortment of snacks. Food is viewed by the old folks, Vadhera's parents, as a deserved compensation for what America has deprived them of—a mother-in-law's tyranny, their son and daughter-in-law's total dedication, and the grandparents' right to play with their grandchildren. In this milieu, where Flushing is a recreation of Jullundhar, Jasmine finds herself gaining weight and sinking into depression. Branded as a widow, she is but a "servant" who cooks and accompanies the elders. Here food and cooking are symbols for the larger entrapments of one kind of immigrant life. The Hayeses, however, provide her with a thoroughly "American" one: Taylor, unlike Vadhera, serves *her* snacks. Here, partaking and sharing of food imply Jasmine's sense of her equality with the Hayeses. Class and gender rigidities relaxed, Jasmine appreciates the freedom and self-worth she experiences, even as she encounters other unfamiliar customs she cannot reconcile herself to, such as Duff, a small child, sleeping in her own room. However, in contrast to her "suspect" position as a competitor to Nirmala in Vadhera's house, here she gains her self-confidence: she feels like a guest at the Hayeses' dinner table.

Jane, in Baden, Elsa County, Iowa, encounters cultural differences by recognizing food differences. Cumin, coriander, varieties of peppers, *gobi aloo,* and *matar paneer* define her Indian heritage, while pot roast signifies mainstream America. Although Darrel, their neighbor, of the Lutz farm, makes overtures at reproducing Jane's concoctions, he succeeds in mangling them as much as he distorts the names of the food items. Other more horrifying results of cross-culturalism, expressed in the form of the effects of food, is encapsulated in the story of Darrel's father Gene's death: he chokes to death on a chunk of Mexican food (*Jasmine* 6). The obverse side of these effects is echoed in the generalized response of the American to Third World immigrants as starving people, veiled women, and natural disasters. Food terminology becomes a reflection of the "language" which, as Trinh Minh-ha points out, "partakes in the white-male-is-norm ideology and is used predominantly as a vehicle to circulate established power relations" (6). Into these categories is impinged the naming of foods that Du, their Vietnamese adopted son, had to eat in the refugee camps: worms and crabs. These several food categories also emphasize and extend the implications of America as a "melting pot" in which the ingredients retain their individual flavor and taste.

Jasmine-Jane, in realizing her potential as a "speaking person" and "teller of tales," creates the new voice and vision of the immigrant woman defining her "changing into" and "transforming of" the world around her. She adapts the oral method of transmitting knowledge and wisdom through short, insightful self-created proverbs, enlivened by brutal honesty and biting candor. Commenting on postcolonial women writers, Ketu H. Katrak elucidates on their "ongoing process of decolonizing culture" (169) which is relevant for postcolonial immigrant writers like Bharati Mukherjee as well:

> Women writers' uses of oral traditions and their revisions of Western literary forms are integrally and dialectically related to the kinds of content and themes they treat. . . . Their texts deal with and often challenge . . . patriarchy that preceded and continues after colonialism and that inscribes the concept of womanhood, motherhood. . . . (173)

Mukherjee indicates the complex blending of traditional and modern forces in Jasmine through the narrator's reinvention of the traditional proverb-telling method of folk speech. Mukherjee in an interview points out this aspect of

Narrative Voice and Gender Roles in Jasmine   123

her technique: "As a Hindu, I was brought up on oral tradition and epic literature. . . . I believe in the existence of alternative realities, and this belief makes itself evident in my fiction" (Carb 651). The Jasmine-Jane narrator-protagonist voices her transformations at multiple levels of self-identity as an "illegal," an "immigrant," a "woman" from the Third World. Crossing boundaries of nation, culture- and gender-centered definitions of self, Jasmine's pithy one-liners, stated in terse American idiom, concretize her insights in terms of immediate experience. It is as if constant living on the borders has given Jasmine/Jane's tongue an edge that challenges the possibility of "unvoicing" her experience. From the communal-centered value of telling truths through proverbs, the narrator-protagonist wrests and creates the new voice of her "speaking" and "telling" self. Her defiance is at the root of her inflexible energy to create her space in the borderland.

By combining impulse with premises, insight with inferences, Jasmine-Jane's truths reflect the forging of the immigrant woman's reality. In voicing this reality and its presentness, her "truths" become skillful weapons, "fists" of language that circumvent the external threats of silencing this voice by assuming its absentness, or as the woman protagonist in "The Lady from Lucknow" reflects, its "not-quite" nature (*Darkness* 25). This emergence of the new type of immigrant woman is voiced in a language which "integrates the old cultural vocabulary with the new one" (St. Andrews 56). Comparing Joy Kogawa, a Japanese Canadian writer and Bharati Mukherjee, St. Andrews makes an important observation:

> Language therefore becomes a metaphor both of belonging and not belonging. Kogawa and Mukherjee create characters who wrestle with the idea of how language enfranchises and disenfranchises them.
>
> Focusing on immigrant characters . . . Mukherjee too warns society about this tactic of imposing silence or of using language to misrepresent experience [by which] . . . society clings to an outdated, static version of itself. (56–57)

The Jasmine-Jane protagonist, like Leela in "Hindus," encounters this "othering" experience when Darrel confuses "Hindi," a language, with "Indian," a nationality (*Jasmine* 8), or Thad, the mailman, blithely assumes "Hindu," a religion, is Hindi, "your language" (*Jasmine* 185). However unintended, these glib confusions place Asian immigrants from "hot, moist continents" (*Darkness* 2) in the sphere of "out there" (*Darkness* 18), as Mother Ripplemeyer characterizes, where missionaries go to save the destitute.

Jasmine-Jane, the immigrant woman, is the new pioneer who uses language to confront and challenge this characterizing of self through mainstream America's rhetoric of "other." She uses her language to control and direct her choices. Knowing what she does not want to turn into, Jasmine-Jane retains those values of her Hindu heritage that sustain her life in America—a strong faith in the importance of all individual life. She concretizes the concepts of Hindu *dharma* and *karma* in simple, contemporary, life-affirming terms. Her beliefs strengthen her ability to survive, to discard debilitating aspects of traditional customs, to open herself to change, to the transforming fluidity of American life and American personality. Mukherjee effectively poses this simultaneity of the immigrant woman's identity through the Jyoti-Jasmine-Jane stages of the protagonist who is both "I" as well as "the other"—"a set of fluid identities to be celebrated" (*Darkness* 3).

The rubric of Mukherjee's narrative force in *Jasmine* infuses the energy of reality to academic discussions of multiculturalism in America, as well as exposes the "cerebral" acceptance of difference. Jasmine's life is a whirlwind and so are the lives of most immigrants. While we debate and question and confer, like the professor friends of Taylor, America has already changed in form, appearance, even the timbre and accent of its speech. As the immigrant slowly adopts "an intensity of spirit and quality of desire" which, according to Mukherjee, is being "American in a very fundamental way" (Steinberg 47), the very history, physiognomy, psychology, and language that define America are undergoing revision. The value of the narrative voice that delineates the reality of both ethnicity and gender in such a context is unquestionable. "Greedy with wants and reckless from hope" (*Jasmine* 214), Mukherjee's narrator-protagonist validates all aspects of her immigrant experience: "silent woman," "speaking person," and "teller of tales." In *Women, Native, Other*, Trinh Minh-ha powerfully echoes the value of this "selving" process of the immigrant woman:

> You who understand the dehumanization of forced removal-relocation-reeducation, redefinition, the humiliation of having to falsify your own reality, your voice—you know. And often cannot say it. You try and keep on trying to unsay it, for if you don't, they will not fail to fill in the blanks on your behalf, and you will be said. (80)

WORKS CITED

Carb, Alison B. "An Interview with Bharati Mukherjee." *The Massachusetts Review* 29.4 (1988): 645–654.

Jacoby, Susan. "World of Our Mothers: Immigrant Women, Immigrant Daughters." *Ethnicity and Gender: The Immigrant Woman*. American Immigration and Ethnicity, Vol. 12. Ed. George E. Pozzetta. New York: Garland, 1991.

Jagannathan, Shakuntala. *Hinduism: An Introduction*. Bombay: Vakils, Feffer and Simons, 1984.

Jussawalla, Feroza. "Chiffon Saris: The Plight of South Asian Immigrants in the New World." *The Massachusetts Review* 29.4 (1988): 585–591.

Katrak, Ketu H. "Decolonizing Culture: Toward a Theory for Postcolonial Women's Texts." *Modern Fiction Studies* 35 (1989): 157–179.

Leong, Liew-Geok. "Bharati Mukherjee." *International Literature in English: Essays on the Modern Writers.* Ed. Robert L. Ross. New York: St. James Press, 1991.

Minh-ha, Trinh T. *Woman, Native, Other.* Bloomington: Indiana University Press, 1989.

Mukherjee, Bharati. *Darkness.* New York: Penguin, 1985.

———. *Jasmine.* New York: Fawcett Crest, 1989.

———. *The Middleman and Other Stories.* New York: Fawcett Crest, 1988.

O'Flaherty, Wendy Doniger. *Hindu Myths: A Sourcebook Translated from the Sanskrit.* New York: Penguin, 1975.

Ramanujan, A.K. "Telling Tales." *Daedalus* 118.4 (1989): 239–261.

Rustomji-Kerns, Roshni. "Expatriates, Immigrants and Literature: Three South Asian Women Writers." *The Massachusetts Review* 29.4 (1988): 655–665.

St. Andrews, B.A. "Co-Wanderers Kogawa and Mukherjee: New Immigrant Writers." *World Literature Today* 66.1 (1992): 56–58.

Steinberg, Sybil. "Immigrant Author Looks at U.S. Society." *Publishers Weekly* (25 August 1989): 46–47.

THE AESTHETICS OF AN (UN)WILLING IMMIGRANT: BHARATI MUKHERJEE'S *DAYS AND NIGHTS IN CALCUTTA* AND *JASMINE*

Anindyo Roy

To assign a specific tradition to the literature written by and about the new Indian diaspora is also to acknowledge that this tradition is marked by the presence of a "postcolonial" discourse. The terms "diaspora" and "postcolonial" belong to a specific historical condition that is released by India's emergence as a "free" nation and by her entry into a new transnational geopolitical sphere. If "colonial" discourse, maintained throughout India's two hundred years of colonial rule, operated across an "ensemble of linguistically-based practices unified by their common deployment in the management of colonial relationships" (Hulme 2), "postcoloniality" reflects the extension, multiplication, and negotiation of these managerial operations within the newly constituted decolonialized and cosmopolitan space of Third World nationhood. Functioning within the spheres of culture and politics, these operations reproduce those elements of colonial ideology which support a postcolonial politics of "truth."

Within the domain of such politics, the immigrant subject and experience are given a certain "truth" status. In the literary production of the immigrant experience, for instance, this status is achieved through the projection of specific aesthetic norms that are narrativized to give a cosmopolitan shape to the experience of "diasporic" exile in the New World. In other words, such construction serves as a means to mediate and appropriate the "truth" about the postcolonial consciousness as "immigrant" subjectivity, defined across a new transnationality. Both the writer's as well as the fictional agent's positions are marked by this territory of truth. My aim in this essay is to examine the construction and production of such aesthetics in Bharati Mukherjee's *Days and Nights in Calcutta* (1977) and to inquire into the specific deployments of these aesthetics in the novel *Jasmine* (1989). I will seek to demonstrate how the author's representation and production of the aesthetics of exile as a transnational and cosmpolitan "epic theme" (*Conquering*) elide the deep contradictions built within the space of postcoloniality. The discursive basis of postcolonial diasporic writing appears to be inextricably tied to those aesthetic projections that are utilized to fabricate and authorize an "epic" truth about the immigrant experience. This experience is made possible as fictive construct by circumventing and suppressing the historical exigencies of Third World immigration.

In the concluding sections of *Days and Nights in Calcutta*, Mukherjee delineates her personal aesthetics as an immigrant writer. Such aesthetics help determine the territory of "difference" within which the author can locate and narrate the experience of Third World exile and displacement to the First World. She claims that her aesthetic "must accommodate a decidedly Hindu imagination with an American craft of fiction." She further asserts that since narrative structures influenced by the Hindu imagination are "non-causal, non-western," her "concepts of what constitute a 'story'" are radically different from those of the Western writer: "A Hindu writer who believes that God can be a jolly, potbellied creature with an elephant trunk, and who accepts the Hindu elastic time scheme and reincarnation, must necessarily conceive of heroes, of plot and pacing and even paragraphing in ways distinct from those of the average American" (*Days and Nights* 286). In these assertions, Mukherjee attempts to clear a space for her aesthetics in order to posit a system of easily recognizable forms of "identity" and "difference." These forms are clearly indicative of the stabilization and commodification of a colonized culture by a postcolonial writer whose own authorial gaze corresponds to that of the Orientalizing West.

In seeking to work out the specifics of this system of identity and difference, Mukherjee places the idea of a "Hindu imagination" as the mark of her "identity" as a non-Western writer. But this notion of identity is little more than a standardized and "Orientalized" figure of a colonial, cultural self-definition. She marks her own "difference" by introducing the idea of an "American craft of fiction," projecting it as a source of literary "influence," rather than an effect of literary colonization, a process that was initiated in the author's own English-medium missionary upbringing in Third World but upper-class Calcutta. Her subsequent entry into the First World literary culture transforms her into a cosmopolitan artist, enabling her to mark her own cultural difference in purely Orientalist terms. Her world is the realm of "the potbellied God," "elastic time," "reincarnation." Indeed, her authority to "speak" from this new space depends on her eliding the very colonial difference, which allows her to enter this Orientalist discourse and to participate in it as a cultural alibi. The critical implications of her authorial position are, to a great measure, reflected in *Jasmine*, whose "magical" narrative reflects some of the elements of this Orientalist discourse, particularly the "non-causal, non-western" narrative form that is employed to fictionalize Jasmine's entry and her wanderings as an illegal immigrant in the New World.

As this narrative is packaged in its foolproof, urban, transnational, and cosmopolitan shape, the aesthetics that undergirds such packaging not only reproduces what Spivak calls "the legitimizing narrative of cultural and ethnic specificity" (Spivak, "Who Claims" 13), but also helps reduce the noise and heterogeneity of the postcolonial inscription of this experience. With the authority to sustain this form of cosmopolitan aesthetics, Bharati Mukherjee not only suppresses the complex realities of economic, political, and historical exigencies of immigration, but also "forgets" the implications of the post-colonial subject's authorizing of such aesthetics. This is clearly highlighted in the author's Introduction to *Darkness* (1985). While she declares that she has "joined imaginative forces with an anonymous, driven, underclass of semi-assimilated Indians," she situates her own authorial self "in the tradition of other American writers whose parents or grandparents had passed through Ellis Island" (*Darkness* xv). By subsuming her postcoloniality in this Euro-centered aesthetic rite of passage, Mukherjee seeks to legitimize her own romantic "epic" imagination, seemlessly weaving it into the archetypical European immigrant experience in the New World. No other differences and contradictions are significantly allowed to interrupt, at any conscious level, the continuity of the narrative. Although she acknowledges her own post-coloniality, she can only use "Indianness" as a "metaphor" (*Darkness* xv). In her interview with Bill Moyers, she expresses her faith in this metaphorical/epic theme: "If Conrad had the 'Heart of Darkness,' I'm exploring the heart of light, through Jasmine." She celebrates her own Whitman-like spirit as the singer of "fluid identities" (*Darkness* xv) and she sees herself as the newly initiated writer of the diasporic epic romance.

As she enumerates her own aesthetics in *Days and Nights* across what appears to be a rather self-conscious projection of the personal dilemma of a Third World immigrant writer situated in the First World, the assumptions of Mukherjee's postcolonial position become increasingly evident. Under the imperative to speak the "truth" about her own status as an artist in exile, she expresses her wish to be able to represent, like V.S. Naipaul, the "pain and absurdity of art and exile . . . among the former colonizers." But all she sees in herself is a "pale and immature reflection" of the writer (*Days and Nights* 287). In the belated postcolonial world of creative initiation, Mukherjee wrests her supplemental authority to write about the pain of exile from an established, urban, postcolonial writer. She further consolidates that authority by rejecting other homegrown Indian writers writing in English, claiming that they had abandoned the "complexities the voice cannot encompass." Indeed, she cannot accept the "limpid naivete" of a writer like R.K. Narayan. Her insistence on the "complexity" of voice reflects a modernist aesthetic concern that is close to Joyce's celebration of the exiled artist's God-like, polyphonic creativity. But beyond this modernist concern lies another aspect of the postcolonial aesthetic position: a "complex" voice can faithfully represent the experience of exile only through the unremitting projection of a heterodox, urban, cosmopolitan aesthetics. In *Days*, Mukherjee can do no better than present herself as the belated protector of this ethos of "voice." In Mukherjee's aesthetic schema, the voice's complexity parallels the endless refashioning of the self, which she claims lies at the heart of the new immigrant experience. Not only does Mukherjee fail to question how this freedom to reinvent one's self stems from her own urban, English educated, upper-class, postcolonial background, but she also conflates the imaginary representation of the American pilgrim-as-quester with the new myth of the eager immigrant ready to slip into such an archetypal role.

Even the idea of the "mongrelization" in immigrant culture (*Conquering*) which she expresses fourteen years after the publication of *Days and Nights*, in the interview with Moyers, reflects the ethos of such cosmopolitan aesthetics. Claiming that her interest lies in delineating the "dense lives" of the new immigrants seeking to find their place in the New World, she hopes to capture the dangers and uncertainties of their existence. What makes Mukherjee's assertions ironic is that the epic theme she adopts to dramatize these dangers does not allow her to consciously represent them in any other form than the one mandated by her own managerial, postcolonial imagination.

This kind of aesthetics also fosters, in *Jasmine*, a peculiar relationship of identification and misidentification—between the immigrant writer as the holder of an urban cosmopolitan ethos and the immigrant protagonist as a Third World subject pursuing the dream of cosmopolitan romanticism. Although Mukherjee's protagonist, Jasmine, is made to embody the urban spirit and feistiness of the new immigrant, the author refuses to acknowledge the fact that her heroine does not share the same social and economic sphere as herself. Indeed, as fictional "subject," Jasmine's identity is subjected to an objectifying authorial gaze that unproblematically reproduces the only kind of alterity that Mukherjee can access in her postcolonial imagination—that of the upper-middle-class subaltern, caught up in the dream of freedom and liberty. Kwame A. Appiah, quoting Sara Suleri, the author of *Meatless Days*, refers to this gaze as "otherness machine" (356), a system that simply reproduces what the postcolonial imagination posits as the "other," without acknowledging how this "otherness" is itself a construction of the postcolonial imagination. Mukherjee's education and socialization in India's post-Partition, insular, upper-middle-class environment (she was partly educated in Swiss and British schools) and her achievement of artistic reputation in the West (she counts as her personal friends John Bart Gerald and Bernard Malamud) place her own creativity on a privileged ground that Jasmine does not share. From this site, Mukherjee can reject the insularity of her own upbringing with a cavalier sense of dismissal ("I felt when I came to Iowa City from Calcutta that suddenly I could be a new person. I didn't have to be the daughter of a very upper-class patriarch, a daughter who was guarded every moment of her life by bodyguards and so on" [*Conquering*]) and euphorically celebrate her religion of cosmopolitan freedom made possible by her own immigrant experience. What she ignores is the fact that this privileged site for self-declaration is also an enabling site from which she can access and project a specifically urban, cosmopolitan aesthetics and subsequently package Third World exile for the First World through her epic theme.

The idea of the epic suits the Western imagination because it easily plays into the latter's "grand" narratives. Moreover, the epic narrative, resting on a new heteroglossia of the melting-pot idea, operates by eliding the postcolonial difference, reproducing a colonial ethos in its new shape as cosmopolitan creativity. Such an artistic credo also suits the critical imagination of the West, which sees in the new immigrant's epic position the possibility of sustaining the dream of freedom in the chaos of the new immigrant's life. The reading public in the West and the literary press are quick to seize the opportunity of promoting a Third World artist who is also a believer in the American Dream. Moreover, an immigrant writer's work like Mukherjee's narrative contains enough exotic elements to preserve the curious differences posited by an Orientalist discourse, which can be easily appreciated by the Western reading public. In view of these possibilities, one can assert that the novel *Jasmine* is not the work of a single author, but is the product of what Foucault refers to as the "author function" (*Language* 124–126). This function is made possible by the collusion of the institutionized forces of postcoloniality and the West, and the immigrant author, who with her portable imagination can easily suppress her own authorizing position and fabricate the new immigrant's epic of freedom. The idea of the portable imagination also guards the ethos of the diasporic writer in the West from facing and dealing with the overdetermined reality of its own authorial position. With the commodification of the denseness and complexity of the immigrant life as cosmopolitan quest-motif, the urban, diasporic writer can unproblematically produce her epic for consumption by the First World.

The novel *Jasmine* offers a fine example of the utilization of a "portable imagination," within the economy of an Orientalist discourse, to fashion such an epic. Deployed by the author to reduce the complexities of immigration to the simple dream of escape from a confining world, the novel projects Punjabi society and contemporary Indian history as perfect sites for potential Third World emigration. But such projections are nothing more than simulations, made possible by the poetic license of "open and assemble" techniques. History is represented, with the right balance of verisimilitude and fantasy, from a journalistic acquaintance with the political events in civil strife-torn Punjab. The general descriptions of the Punjabi society wasted by the realities of post-Partition and by the vulgar versions of Western "development" it aspires to, are not "un-historical." What is intriguing (and perhaps predictable) is Mukherjee's selective portrayal of such a society: it is a world peopled by warring, superstitious women, by fortune-tellers, by victims of social injustice and religious factionalism, by a nostalgia-ridden father who still dreams of returning to a colonial Lahore, by aspiring young men who waste their lives learning to be trained technicians, by a young groom who instills in his young bride the dream of emigrating to America. The repertoire is quite endless. The politics of Mukherjee's aesthetics of immigration are evident in these selected representations; they are clearly deployed to highlight Jasmine's difference so that she can be constructed as the perfect agent of immigration. The lonely girl who seeks liberty *and* loves English fails to realize her desires in her own society—she has no other option but to emigrate. In the midst of the chaos that Punjab represents, the author seeks to project the lonely, singular voice of Jasmine's quest for freedom. But Jasmine can only enter the writer's epic imagination by participating in the latter's cosmopolitan dream. She has no other way of asserting her difference in the immigrant writer's fictive world.

Once Jasmine is objectified as the immigrant subject, Mukherjee can safely validate her own authority to represent the experience of exile. This authority stems from the writer's own quest, expressed in *Days*: to "find a voice that will represent the life that I know in a manner that is true to my own aesthetic" (*Days and Nights* 287). One of the primary ways in which the "truth" of such aesthetics is established is by regulating and deploying a "voice." In *Jasmine*, Mukherjee deploys this voice in two ways: as a voice emanating from Jasmine's centered consciousness and as an authorial voice that attempts to represent the former. However, the overlapping of the two voices, and their interactive and appropriative dynamics in the novel dramatize the kind of identification/misidentification that typifies the contradictions within Mukherjee's postcolonial commodification of the immigrant experience. As Jasmine goes to live with Taylor and Wylie in New York, she declares that she has begun to view herself as an American. In her interview with Moyers, Mukherjee claims, "I feel very American. . . . I knew the moment I landed as a student in 1961 . . . that this is where I belonged." Despite the close parallel in the two positions, it is impossible to regard Jasmine's and Mukherjee's feelings about "belonging" to America as identical because they belong to two very different social spheres. However, if the author intends us to regard Jasmine's naive declaration ironically, how can her own pronouncements in the interview escape the same irony? Questioned in this way, the novel appears to be no longer seamless. It becomes clear that Mukherjee cannot always sustain her authorial privilege of maintaining the irony in the novel. Though her cosmopolitan aesthetics demands that she be able to retain this privilege, Mukherjee's own position is always in the danger of being intersected by the larger irony induced by the postcolonial discourse. The author's own mediated and ironic position as a postcolonial writer of the "free" First World is marked by the same codes of middle-class freedom that she seeks to represent in her fiction. But these codes cannot be "re-presented" without their further differentiating the very authority from which the writer operates.

The aesthetic system that dictates the stability of identification and authority in *Jasmine* offers some interesting insights into the making of the exiled imagination. Two images of the exiled subject emerge in the novel: one, the immigrant writer as the cosmopolitan author of exile who commands and writes in the language of the First World and, two, the poor, young bride from the wasting stillness of Punjab, whose romantic aspirations to master the English language and conquer the world represent a postcolonial consciousness shared by the author's upper-class sensibility. Mukherjee appears to have ignored the possibility that such romantic aspirations to the mastery of a colonial language are always preconstructed in the form of a "lack," which all postcolonials carry as part of their own legacy, and that is often inscribed on the register of bourgeoisie freedom and self-mastery. This "lack" makes Jasmine into an ideal, urban, postcolonial subaltern. As Spivak notes, the ideology behind this lack is "what a group takes to be neutral and self-evident," denying "any historical sedimentation" in its constitution (*In Other* 118). All other forms of difference have to be eliminated so that through this "lack," the immigrant can recognize her difference from the rest of her immediate social environment. Furthermore, this recognition, forced on her by the author, makes her into a "good subject" whose self-identification consists in freely consenting to the power of Mukherjee's upper-class, postcolonial ethos.

Mukherjee uses this condition of lack to narrativize Jasmine's story of salvation through exile. With Jasmine's identity secured across this space, she can be safely used as the "subject" of the author's cosmopolitan, immigrant *Bildungsroman*. By being situated in the same ideological domain in which the author is interpellated as a free and modern subject of the West, Jasmine becomes the medium for the aesthetic reproduction of such mentality. The reality of such reproduction is often concealed under the mystique of the writer's statement that "the immigrant's soul is always at risk" (*Conquering*). Indeed, what we see in the novel is the metonymic figuration of Jasmine's identity within the ideology of the author's urban, cosmopolitan credo. Furthermore, by presenting Jasmine as an intelligent and sensitive human being, whose only aspirations after her husband's death are to realize the dream of free enterprise—"Vijh and Wife"—Mukherjee inserts her completely within the enclosure of a postcolonial capitalism. Her journey to America begins with this dream but it gradually evolves into a series of fantasies, induced by the cosmopolitan dream of endless self-improvisations.

The fictional production of such transformations is neither new nor surprising. In *Days and Nights*, we find Mukherjee wondering about the "fate of those millions of young women . . . who were sensitive enough to feel cheated [in their middle-class worlds] but neither pretty nor smart enough to arrange for their own salvation" (271). One cannot help but think of the narrative impulse behind *Jasmine* as a significant staging of a rescue mission: the First World artist reconstructs the Third World subject as the First World inheritor of the American Dream, thereby saving it from "the continent of cynicism and irony and despair" (*Conquering*). Once Jasmine enters this free world, she is made to undergo a series of transformations so that she can identify with this dream— the dream of an urban, cosmopolitan freedom. As the novel evolves into a story of the immigrant wanderlust, we witness Jasmine's evolution into the full-blooded subject of the West, perpetually stirred by the urge to move from the peripheries to the centered frontier.

If Jasmine's immigrant, epic identity is made to proliferate in all its fantastical forms, her "otherness" is strictly controlled and regularized by the author. Jasmine's supplemental and fluid selves remain, within the logic of the genetic change that she claims separates her from the Vietnamese Du's hyphenated selves, nothing more than a series of coded forms of otherness that the author can unproblematically construct in her postcolonial, aesthetic world. Retaining the forms of identity and difference, which were earlier identified in *Days and Nights*, the narrative depicts Jasmine as she moves through the New World, being constantly refashioned by the logic of the postcolonial author's aesthetics. In India, she is "Jyoti," her name reflecting the ironic reversal of the dark world she inhabits, a world without hope or salvation. It is a confining world of the petty bourgeoisie and the peasantry, caught between feudalism and post-Independence modernity. Yet, she carries her third eye, the symbol of her arrogant refusal to be sealed by her fate (the astrologer symbolizes the larger social fate that Jasmine fights against). The only forms of freedom she enjoys in this world are when she steps out into the fields for her early morning ablutions and when she amuses herself by reading the books given to her by her English-language teachers. As "light," Jasmine transgresses the world of fate, darkness, and death. As she is renamed "Jasmine," by her liberal husband, she transcends the stench of the dead pools of Hasnapur (the name itself evokes the sweetness and exotic qualities of the Orient). This marks her entry into the world of Prakash, the man who dreams of escaping to America to study at an American university and be a private entrepreneur. Though Prakash is killed in a terrorist attack, Jasmine, infected by her husband's dreams, resolves to carry on his legacy.

After her strangely "magical" passage into the New World—she leaves in an anonymous airliner and then travels from Europe in a cargo boat that carries other immigrants of the postcolonial world—Jasmine is made to confront the "evil" of America. Attacked by a sailor belonging to the crew of the ship that carried her to Florida, she assumes the wrath of Kali, the Hindu goddess of destructive energy, and kills him in a divine frenzy. This feminine, mythical power is evoked again as Jasmine is

Aesthetics of An (Un)willing Immigrant 139

wooed by Bud Ripplemeyer, the Iowa farmer: she feels like a goddess. In both instances, the power of the Orientalist discourse of "otherness" is deployed by Mukherjee to mark Jasmine's difference as an exotic subject of the West.

In New York, Jasmine becomes "Jase," her name abbreviated by two young, urban professionals, Taylor and his wife, Wylie, who appoint her as the nanny to their child, Duff. By offering her a "home" away from the Vadhera household in Flushing and by approving her command of the English language, including her accent, the couple allows Jasmine to experience the first taste of cosmopolitan freedom. This is the initiating moment of her passage into the New World. Subsequently inducted into the city-bred Taylor's universe of humor, she is reminded that her knowledge of English is not only adequate to make her qualified to be part of his world, but also to participate in New York's world of unlimited opportunity. Jasmine gradually overcomes her fear of "losing" English which had haunted her ever since she moved into the Vadhera household. In her abbreviated form as "Jase" she is, thus, empowered as a subject of the West. Overcoming her difference and yet ironically reconstructing it within the cosmopolitan scene (she works as a translator of Indian languages), Jasmine is able to assert her economic freedom and the liberty to experience the true spirit of American urban life.

As the narrative unfolds, Jasmine is made to undergo another transformation. In Iowa, Jasmine is rebaptized as "Jane" by the farmer/banker, Bud Ripplemeyer, in whose alternatively stable and unstable life of middle America Jasmine discovers the possibility of recreating exotic Indian dishes with unpronounceable names. She also assumes the role of a chronicler, witnessing the slow decline of the American farm. But, as her own life gets caught up in what appears to be little more than the fantasy of daytime television miniseries, we are presented with the seemingly poignant dramas of love-triangles, pregnancy, and suicide. The concluding moments of the novel capture Jasmine in flight to

California with her former lover, Taylor. In all these dramatizations of Jasmine's improvised "lives," Mukherjee seeks to sustain her own aesthetics of identity and difference by forcing Jasmine into the same blind spot that she, as the postcolonial subject, occupies. This blind spot is also an enabling condition for Jasmine to be the new diasporic subject, one who constantly seeks out and celebrates only those differences that are mandated by Mukherjee's cosmopolitan aesthetics. As a willing immigrant, Jasmine stands poised on the American Dream, confident that she can freely refashion her life by obeying its dictates. In Jasmine's final decision to be the new agent of the frontier experience, one discerns the postcolonial implications of Mukherjee's aesthetic delineation of her life: the gaze of the West that has successfully encoded her as "Jane" can only leave her at the edge of the New World—it is her "home" as well as her unfulfilled, but glorious, destiny.

WORKS CITED

Appiah, Kwame A. "Is the Post- in Postmodernism the Post- in Postcolonial?" *Critical Inquiry* 17.2 (1991): 336–357.

Conquering America with Bharati Mukherjee. Videocassette. Prod. Bill Moyers. Public Affairs Television, 1990. 58 min.

Foucault, Michel. *Language, Counter-Memory, Practice.* Ed. Donald F. Bouchard. Ithaca, N.Y.: Cornell University Press, 1977.

Hulme, Peter. *Colonial Encounters.* New York: Methuen, 1986.

Mukherjee, Bharati. *Darkness.* New Yor: Fawcett Books, 1985.

———, and Clark Blaise. *Days and Nights in Calcutta.* Garden City, N.Y.: Doubleday, 1977.

Spivak, Gayatri C. *In Other Worlds: Essays in Cultural Politics.* New York: Methuen, 1987.

———. "Who Claims Alterity?" Unpublished essay, 1989.

TOWARD AN INVESTIGATION OF THE SUBALTERN IN BHARATI MUKHERJEE'S *THE MIDDLEMAN AND OTHER STORIES* AND *JASMINE*

Alpana Sharma Knippling

It would be no exaggeration to say that Bharati Mukherjee is primarily recognized in United States academic circles for her challenge to mainstream American literary-cultural productions. A well-articulated instance of this challenge occurs in her 1988 *New York Times Book Review* essay called "Immigrant Writing: Give Us Your Maximalists!" in which Mukherjee claims that "both inside and outside America, 'American fiction' has become synonymous with the mainstream, big advance, well-promoted novel or story collection . . . and . . . American fiction—clever, mannered, brittle—has lost the power to transform the world's imagination."[1] According to Mukherjee, the literary decline of the United States is largely due to its refusal to see that "an epic was washing up on its shores" (28), in the form of the hundreds of untold stories of "nontraditional" (i.e., Asian) immigrants. It is their stories that Mukherjee sets out to write in a self-professed radical and new project. But the question remains: precisely how radical is her project? At the outset, I will suggest that this question is more insistently relevant to those of Mukherjee's readership who include themselves in the very Asian immigrant body in the United States that constitutes Mukherjee's own subject. As an example of such a reader—or, to be more specific, as an example of an Indian diasporic "academic"—I offer my interpretation of Bharati Mukherjee's fiction (specifically *The Middleman and Other Stories* and *Jasmine*) in order to make the point that its assertedly radical critique of mainstream American literary-cultural productions is not as radical as it might be. I do so by demonstrating, first, that Mukherjee ignores the role that representation (of the Other) plays in the textual production of her writing and, second, that she homogenizes her ethnic minority immigrant subjects, instead of calling attention to the actual heterogeneity of ethnic minority immigrant subjects in the United States. Two (autobiographical) assertions by Mukherjee help frame the two parts of my demonstration.

I

> I would rather we all cashed in the other legacy of the colonial writer, and that is his or her duality. From childhood we learned how to be two things simultaneously: to be the dispossessed as well as the dispossessor. . . . History forced us to see ourselves as both the "we" and the "other," and the language reflected our simultaneity. . . . Perhaps it is this history-mandated training in seeing myself as the "the other" that now heaps on me a fluid set of identities denied to most of my mainstream American counterparts. ("Immigrant Writing" 29)

In this passage, Mukherjee is discussing a kind of contradictory colonial legacy, according to which the colonized subject sees herself as both "we" (the British colonial subject) and "other" (the colonized Indian native). In a postcolonial analysis such as this one, it seems to me important to underscore that the "other" to whom Mukherjee refers is still not the wholly other (the tribal or

The Subaltern in The Middleman and Jasmine

the rural illiterate Indian, for instance) but the Other of Western creation and appropriation in the imperialist (also Orientalist) mission. When Thomas Babington Macaulay, in his colonial, administrative capacity, recommended English as the language for adminstration and education in India, it was precisely the creation of the West's Other that he had in mind: "We must at present do our best to form a class who may be interpreters between us and the millions we govern; a class of persons, Indian in blood and colour, but English in taste, in opinions, in morals, and in intellect."[2] This West's Other is, in Mukherjee's frame of reference, the "other." There can, in other words, be no claim for a pure space that is truly Indian in the colonial landscape. The textbooks Mukherjee read as a child violently enact the fact that Indian history itself was largely the product of British arrangement; Partha Chatterjee has shown how even the nationalist quest for difference from the British was itself imbricated in Western rational discourse.[3]

In the context of these kinds of colonialist determinations, it is telling that Mukherjee's professed literary influences are E.M. Forster and V.S. Naipaul: Forster because he validated the fictional world of India, Naipaul because he taught her that "a postcolonial consciousness" involved a state of "unhousing and remaining unhoused and at the same time free."[4] V.S. Naipaul's influence on Mukherjee is especially interesting in light of the fact that, in her interview of him in 1979, Naipaul took recourse to his typical foreclosing of any reasonable view of the Indian subcontinent: "It takes a long time in India to come to the simple conclusion that, by God, these people are just extraordinarily stupid!" (Mukherjee and Boyers 13). That Mukherjee could ignore the weighted political dismissal of such a pronouncement and refer to Naipaul in 1982 as her "literary model" is an index of her own colonial legacy.[5]

Further, Mukherjee herself has typified her social determinations as bourgeois. In "Immigrant Writing," she alludes to her "Brahminical elegance" as constituted by "top family, top school, top caste, top city" (28). In an interview, Mukherjee describes her educational background: first, a school run by Protestant missionaries; then "a fancy Sloane Square school" in England; next, "a very special girls' school called Loretto House run by Irish nuns in independent Calcutta."[6] She also describes herself as the daughter of "a very rich factory owner" and claims a rather suspect access to Calcutta's labor class because she was chauffeur-driven to school during labor riots with military policemen and bodyguard in tow, looking, along with her sisters, like "pretty maidens in gondoliers (sic)" (Connell 8).

My purpose in locating Mukherjee among the urban upper-class bourgeoisie is not to make her own privileged background in India the sole determinant for a "politically correct" reading which eventually denounces her. Indeed, this background is a typical one among many of the educated elite in colonial and postcolonial India; it constitutes even a norm among professional Indian immigrants in the United States. The question of privilege, I want to suggest, becomes important when Mukherjee claims to represent the Other as the *wholly other* in her writing. No wholly other is susceptible to representation; when it is represented, it immediately ceases its transgressive function and becomes the domesticated other (which I am referring to, in this case, as the West's Other). In his project to deconstruct the bases of Western metaphysics, Derrida might refer to this wholly other as the "*tout-autre*" (the "quite-other"); the West's Other is what he might, and Spivak indeed does, call the "self-consolidating other":

> Derrida does not invoke "letting the other(s) speak for himself" but rather invokes an "appeal" to or "call" to the "quite-other" (tout-autre as opposed to a self-consolidating other), of "rendering delirious that interior voice that is the voice of the other in us."[7]

The passage seems to suggest that one way out of the inherently fraudulent attempt to give the other a voice may

The Subaltern in The Middleman *and* Jasmine   147

lie in gesturing at—not speaking for—what remains consistently out of reach, namely, the "quite-other," or what, in a postcolonial reading, constitutes the subaltern. In an earlier essay, "Three Women's Texts and a Critique of Imperialism," Spivak formulated a similar idea:

> No perspective critical of imperialism can turn the Other into a self, because the project of imperialism has always already historically refracted what might have been the absolutely Other into a domesticated Other that consolidates the imperialist self. (253)

Given her bourgeois background, coupled with her desire to tell the stories of marginalized Asian immigrants in the United States, Mukherjee tends to uncritically reproduce the imperialist project of "selving the Other" (turning the Other into a self, giving the Other a voice, speaking for the Other). What is more, in the process of doing so, she claims to speak for nothing less than the "quite-other," the subaltern, a point which I discuss later in this section.

The question of privilege also becomes important when Mukherjee renders herself, her own self-representation (a crucial part of any representation, particularly the ethnic minority writer's) transparent in the act of representing the Other. A curious example of what I mean occurs in her previously quoted essay, "Immigrant Writing": "All around me I see the face of America changing. . . . But where, in fiction, do you read of it? Who, in other words, speaks for us, the new Americans from nontraditional immigrant countries?" (1). Here, we see a shift from the highly personalized "I" of the first sentence to the generalized "us" of the next one. In the first sentence, the eye/I figures first as an agent that separates itself from others in order to observe them: "All around me I see the face of America changing." But in the next one, it locates itself among the very people it observes: "Who . . . speaks for us?" What seems to occur in this passage is a telling example of the author first giving herself the authority to speak for others, then concealing it. "To render thought," says Spivak, again elaborating on Derrida, "or the thinking subject transparent or invisible seems . . . to hide the relentless recognition of the Other by assimilation."[8] By disguising the thinking function of the writer, Mukherjee also suppresses the (urban upper-class bourgeois) agency that is busily domesticating the Other.

To sum up: Mukherjee is a product of British imperialism (herself the West's Other). It is in this already Western context that we can discern her problematic reproduction of a fundamentally Western project: of making the Other accessible to representation by turning the Other into a Self. In the process of doing so, she disguises (makes transparent) her own particular position of privilege instead of accounting for it and systematically exploiting it as, for instance, Spivak herself does.

It may be worthwhile to keep in mind that it is not only the object of representation that is in question; representation is itself a problematic concept. For quite some time now, certain poststructuralist critical practice has sought to undo the Western metaphysical language of presence. Its most radical formulation has been that presence is itself unknowable except as *re*-presentation. A particular ideological charge has also been brought to bear upon representation: representation does not survive as only an epistemological challenge when it bears upon ideological questions of how to represent the Other, because one is necessarily involved in representing that which cannot represent itself.[9] Mukherjee is engaged in both acts, of re-presenting and representing that which cannot represent itself. For my purposes, the first is perhaps obvious; it is played out whenever language is invoked. The second—insofar as it concerns representation of the West's Other, not the wholly other—concerns us here. How does Mukherjee represent that which cannot represent itself?

Clearly, Mukherjee's project in both *The Middleman and Other Stories* and *Jasmine* is to represent that which cannot represent itself. In the essay, "Immigrant Writing," she asks, who will tell the stories of new Asian immigrants

The Subaltern in The Middleman *and* Jasmine   149

in the United States? It seems to follow that she will. Indeed, by the time of this volume, she already has.[10] Her short stories (1987; 1988) cover a gamut of ethnic, minority, immigrant characters in America (the United States in particular) across the cultural registers of race, ethnicity, gender, and class: Iraqi Jews, Afghanis, Indians from India, Uganda, and Trinidad, etc. Similarly, her novel, *Jasmine* (1989), is about a Punjabi peasant woman's "rebirth" in the Midwest of the United States. At first glance, these various racially, sexually, socially underprivileged characters appear to be subaltern subjects. I use the word "subaltern" with two meanings in mind: the first derives from Gramsci, who calls the "masses" the subaltern classes and who opposes those to the dominant, hegemonic class in society; the second usage comes from the Subaltern Studies scholars who, in their project to rewrite colonial Indian history from the point of view of the subaltern, mean by the word not only the "masses" or "the people" but also an enormous, heterogeneous range of rural groups, including even "the lowest strata of the rural gentry, impoverished landlords, rich peasants and upper-middle peasants."[11]

Most of Mukherjee's characters seem to be subaltern in that they are both heterogeneous and socially marginalized in one way or another. But when these seemingly subaltern characters speak—eight of the eleven stories in the short story collection are from the first-person point of view, the other three from the limited third person—we need to see that they lose their subalternity and assimilate themselves into (are assimilated by) recognizable patterns of conformity/nonconformity; and they induce in us correspondingly recognizable responses of pity and compassion. The transgressive function of the "real" subaltern, the wholly other, however, consistently lies beyond the realms of organizability, and, *from there*, points to the "lack" of the enterprise at hand.

In "Fathering," for instance, a double mode of representation is mobilized. Mukherjee represents a white Vietnam veteran, who in turn represents his newly emigrated Vietnamese daughter. The former representation is not very problematic in that it takes its assumptions from the Western side of the world's geoeconomic division into "West" and "East"; the arena here is neo-imperialist, late capitalist United States, in which both Mukherjee and her white Vietnam vet, Jason, may be situated. But the latter representation is problematic. Eng, the Vietnamese daughter, is attributed a great strangeness: she comes from the outside; she engages in strange acts, such as inflicting injury on herself or eating when she isn't hungry. But her strangeness does not become the fundamentally indeterminate site of the story. It is, instead, assimilated into a recognizable formulation: *naturally*, a Vietnamese survivor will suffer trauma of this sort. What is also "naturalized" is the fact that father and daughter will be united in their common Vietnamese experience, which is, in fact, Jason's American experience of Vietnam. The process by which Jason assimilates his daughter into his American discourse is dramatized strikingly in this passage: "'Get the hell out, you bastard!' Eng yells. 'Vamos! Bang bang!' She's pointing her arm like a semiautomatic. . . . My Rambo. . . . My Saigon kid and me: we're a team" (*Middleman* 122). How Eng is translated from the Vietnamese site to "Rambo" and "my Saigon kid" is precisely the process of translation of the wholly other, the subaltern, to the self-consolidating other, the West's Other. In *Jasmine*, the representation of Jasmine follows a similar domesticating translation. As a Punjabi member of the Indian peasantry, Jasmine is positioned as subaltern; but her subalternity is lost when she becomes the self-willing subject of the West.[12]

What is also at stake in Mukherjee's writing is the fact that she does not explicate the agency which renders the Other accessible to her. There is a particular self-representation at work here that is elided. This is another way of saying that we do not get, with her, the point of view of the point of view. The "I" of her fiction, after all, implicates the "I" of the writer. When this latter "I" removes itself from the scene of representation, it is still

The Subaltern in The Middleman and Jasmine   151

doing the work of representation. It is representing those who cannot represent themselves, with the added illusion that those who cannot represent themselves are, here, at any rate, representing themselves. There is a specific density of activity here that needs pointing out: Mukherjee's ethnic minorities seem to represent themselves directly, when, in fact, they can only be understood in terms of her representation of them; her representation of them begs the question of her own self-representation (she is the minority equipped to represent them). Now, it does not necessarily follow that if I am a member of an ethnic minority group, then I am the best person to represent minorities. We have seen how Mukherjee speaks from a position of bourgeois privilege. It is the exercise of this privilege that needs accounting. The responsibility of the 'Third World" privileged intellectual in the United States is both precarious and immense. It is not given justice in a project which easily assumes that the Other can be turned into a Self. I have tried to show that this project is at work in Mukherjee's writing, calling particular attention to the fact that representation of the Other is an ideological act which, further, renders self-representation problematic in the process.

II

> [T]he rickshaw puller near Nizam's was suddenly not just a Muslim resident of a Calcutta slum, but he was also me, a timid, brown, naturalized citizen in a white man's country that was growing increasingly hostile to "colored" immigrants. (*Days and Nights in Calcutta* 250)

In this scene from the autobiographical *Days and Nights in Calcutta*, a well-to-do acquaintance of Mukherjee in Calcutta sets upon a poor wage laborer, degrading him by making him "perform" for the benefit of Mukherjee and her American husband. Mukherjee watches and is curiously ashamed for the sake of the laborer. At this moment, she discovers that what unites her with the rickshaw puller is their common marginalization in a dominant culture. What is suppressed in the interest of commonality is Mukherjee's own privileged social and intellectual status. We have, in this passage, an impossible unification of the subaltern and the upper-class bourgeois writer; but this unification is one, according to Mukherjee, which not only occurred but also made possible her unquestioned access to all ethnic minorities in the United States, regardless of race/class/gender stratifications: "Chameleon-skinned, I discover my material over and across the country, and up and down the social ladder" ("Immigrant Writing" 29).

Given that economically determined and ideologically enforced differentiations cannot be homogenized without a certain will-to-power, we find that Mukherjee exerts exactly such a will-to-power in her treatment of all ethnic minorities as identical. Consequently, not only do we need to see that representation in Mukherjee's writing is ideologically situated, we also need to see that what facilitates representation is Mukherjee's notion of the *sameness* of the minority condition. This knowledge, which is somehow communicated to her by the encounter with the Calcutta rickshaw puller, is communicated by her to her characters in a privatized vein. We are, Mukherjee seems to whisper, along with her characters, all of us minorities together; our stories, our struggles, are the same. This highly privatized, intuitive language is everywhere present in her stories and it repeatedly tells the same story of survival against the odds, a sort of tooth-and-nail, gut-wrenching acquisition of individuality in a dominant culture that is now bemused at cultural otherness, now ready to stereotype it. Even Mukherjee's white characters, who attain minority status by dint of being Vietnam veterans, articulate the pathetic cost of individuality in a similar manner. But perhaps nowhere is the privatized communication of sameness across minority registers both clearer and more problematic than in Mukherjee's most recent novel, *Jasmine*.

The Subaltern in The Middleman and Jasmine 153

Jasmine narrates, again from the first person, the story of a Punjabi Indian peasant woman, Jasmine, who marries an American Midwestern banker and adopts a Vietnamese boy, Du. Du and Jasmine communicate silently in a no-questions-asked relationship of strong identification: they come from the same "Third World" and share a common legacy of suffering and survival. Silently united by this identification, they are able to identify with other minorities also. They watch, with unspoken disgust, a racially biased TV news item of an INS bust of illegal Mexican laborers in Texas (*Jasmine* 22-24). The racism to which Du is subjected in high school by his teacher Mr. Skola has already been "known" by Jasmine (*Jasmine* 24-26).

When notions of sameness are privatized in this communication-by-blood/race manner, they begin to function as essentializations which must be challenged by raising questions of historical and cultural specificity. Ethnic characters such as Jasmine and Du are themselves accessible to representation precisely because their "real" counterparts emerge from very different histories and cultures. Vietnam entered the world stage at a particular Cold War moment when the imperialist cards had been reshuffled, while India underwent imperialism of the old order. Du's and Jasmine's "real" counterparts—dare I say, the "real" subalterns?—would not relate, consequently, to the United States in the same manner. We see again the seemingly transparent/disguised stamp of the assimilating writer whose Western program allows her the imaginative leap.

The fact that heterogeneity of this order is elided by Mukherjee is tellingly demonstrated in two versions of the same story about Jasmine. One is a short story, "Jasmine," in *The Middleman and Other Stories* and the other is the novel, *Jasmine*, that developed out of the short story. There is no question that both texts deal with the same "main" character, Jasmine, and the same story: an Indian girl enters the United States illegally; after working at a menial, demeaning job, she ends up as a babysitter for a white professional American couple and sets about "remaking" herself.[13] It matters little that the cultural specificity of Trinidad differs from the cultural specificity of India in ways that are too numerous to list here. When differences in the two versions occur, they only serve to further a typically Western "self-reflexive," "self-marginalized" narrative of the subject. For instance, the short story is narrated from the limited third person, the novel from the first. In the short story, Jasmine comes to the United States from Trinidad; she is the daughter of Indian parents in the Caribbean. In the novel, Jasmine comes to the United States directly from India. The two characters even enter the United States from different geographical points: the Trinidad Jasmine enters from the Canadian border; the Indian Jasmine from the Gulf coast of Florida. There are several consequences of these differences. In the impersonal third-person narrative mode of the short story, Jasmine is more controlled by the social forces around her than controlling them. Her diction is both objectified and simulated as peculiarly Caribbean: "'I don't know what happen, girl. . . . feel all crazy inside. Maybe is time for me to pursue higher studies in this town'" (*Middleman* 127). In the first-person narration of the novel, Jasmine is at once a superior, intensely privatized character, very much in charge of her life, very aware of even the unspoken ways in which she is being appropriated by others. Even the act of cooking *gobi aloo* for the Lutheran Relief Fund craft fair or *matar panir* in the microwave as an accompaniment for pork is laden for her with dark, political, subversive meaning.

To thus homogenize the Other (Jasmine-Du; Trinidad Jasmine-Indian Jasmine) is to discount heterogeneity as a viable condition of ethnic minorities in the United States. Heterogeneity is, moreover, not only viable, it is the condition under which to most successfully resist the imperialist program of assimilation, appropriation, and domestication. If what the Other "is" can be seen as having dispersed itself in a radically indeterminate way across cultural registers and specificities, it might refuse to claim its space in an already named and designated field of inquiry: "[T]o read this multiple plot," say Pathak and Rajan of another text, "is to recognize that the space of the 'other' has no permanent occupant" (577).

III

I have tried to show that readings of Mukherjee will need to take into account her representations and homogenizations of the Other. I have critiqued her not out of whim but out of a particular necessity that involves our current moment both in United States history and in academia. It is a well-known fact that new kinds of immigrant literatures are being produced in the United States today. The question needs to be asked: can these literatures be read and taught in such a way that they can function as resistant? Already, English departments across the country are absorbing these new literatures by creating new subfields, variously titled "Anglophone literature," "Commonwealth literature," "Third World literature," "world literature," "postcolonial literature," "Asian American literature," "non-Western literature," "multicultural literature," and, most strangely, even "non-canonical literature." This new literary production of immigrant literatures is itself, of course, also a cultural production that reminds us of recent demographic changes registered by, among other agencies, the United States Immigration and Naturalization Service: namely, the drastic decrease of a traditional European influx of immigrants to the United States and the simultaneous increase in United States metropolitan centers of such non-European immigrants as Latinos, Filipinos, Indians, Koreans, Japanese, Chinese, and Vietnamese, to name only a few. At the very time that ethnic minority literary-cultural productions are being generated, circulated, and taught, we need to test their resistance. We need to ask what these literary-cultural productions are offering by way of a radical challenge to traditional epistemologies. Perhaps one "measure" of their resistance lies in how effectively they escape easy consumption (as "authentic, from-the-horse's-mouth" accounts) by calling into question our own reading practices. As for the actual ethnic minority immigrant subjects, the subalterns who are subjected to the writer's and the critic/teacher's functions, we need to point to how and why they remain outside these fields of inquiry.

NOTES

1. Bharati Mukherjee, "Immigrant Writing: Give Us Your Maximalists!" *New York Times Book Review*, 28. Henceforth, I will refer to this essay as "Immigrant Writing."

2. Thomas Babington Macaulay, "Minute on Indian Education," *Macaulay: Prose and Poetry*, 729. Another way of describing the West's other, "Indian in blood and colour, but English in taste," is to describe this subject as the "Orientalized Oriental." The definitive text that comes to mind is, of course, Edward Said's *Orientalism*, in which he shows how the Orient was created by the West as an object of investigation and control. I try here to extend Said's argument by making the point that Orientalism also produced the Orientalized Oriental who received Oriental definitions of himself or herself as self-evident, non-problematic "truths."

3. See Partha Chatterjee, *Nationalist Thought and the Colonial World: A Derivative Discourse?*

4. See "Writer's Panel," *E.M. Forster: Centenary Revaluations*, ed. Judith Scherer Herz and Robert K. Martin (Toronto: University of Toronto Press, 1982), 291, and "A Conversation with V.S. Naipaul," *Salmagundi* 54 (Fall 1981), 5.

5. "Writer's Panel," 292.

6. See Connell, et al. "An Interview with Bharati Mukherjee," *The Iowa Review*, 20, 3 (Fall 1990), 9. Mukherjee further elaborates on this school: "And during the school-days we were taught to devalue—I was going to say sneer at, but that's putting it a little too strongly—Bengali plays, Bengali literature, Bengali music, Bengali anything" (9).

7. See Gayatri Chakravorty Spivak's "Can the Subaltern Speak?" 271–313. The essay constitutes by far the most exhaustive treatment given to the wholly other vs. the West's other. Jacques Derrida's statements are quoted by Spivak in the same essay. For his astute reading of Spivak's essay, I am indebted to Joseph Flanagan of the English department at the University of Delaware.

8. Ibid.

9. The poststructuralist critique of presence derived from several heterogeneous sites: Derrida, Lacan, Foucault, to name a few. The ideological charge to representation comes primarily from Marx. See *The Eighteenth Brumaire of Louis Bonaparte*, in which the peasant proprietors "cannot represent themselves; they must be represented." See Karl Marx, *Capital: A Critique of Political Economy*, 302. Spivak discusses the play of "represent"/*vertreten* and "re-present"/*darstellen* in the Marx passage in "Can the Subaltern Speak?" 276–279.

10. See Mukherjee, *The Tiger's Daughter*, *Wife* (Boston: Houghton Mifflin, 1975), and *Darkness*.

11. See, for instance, Antonio Gramsci, "History of the Subaltern Classes," *Selections from the Prison Notebooks*, 52–55. The exercise of hegemony is not limited to the dominant class; it extends, according to Gramsci, to parties representing socially subaltern classes also (see 189); hence, I do not mean to suggest a strict opposition between subaltern classes and the dominant group in terms of hegemony. The Subaltern Studies definition of "subaltern" comes from Ranajit Guha's key essay, "On Some Aspects of the Historiography of Colonial India," *Selected Subaltern Studies*, 37–44. *Selected Subaltern Studies* comprises an excellent selection of essays drawn from the Subaltern Studies group's journal, *Subaltern Studies: Writings on South Asian History and Society*, which started in 1982.

12. In this context, it is interesting to note that Mukherjee deliberately set out to write the story of a Punjabi peasant girl, to, in other words, mark Jasmine as subaltern: "Whereas with Jasmine, a village girl who's used to quite literally fighting the enemy . . . there's a kind of gutsy village quality" (Connell et al., "An Interview with Bharati Mukherjee," 24). Of course, Jasmine's subalternity in India is itself privileged. She is the daughter of an impoverished but "refined" landlord and, against all odds, learns to speak English at an early age.

13. Says Mukherjee, "I didn't know when I finished the story that it would become a novel. It was just that this was a character that I fell in love with. . . . She became a deeper, more complicated character in my head, over the months, so I had to give her a society that was so repressive, traditional, so caste-bound, genderist, that she could discard it in ways that a fluid American society could not" (Connell et al., "An Interview with Bharati Mukherjee," 18–19). At no point does Mukherjee clarify the implications of the conflation of Jasmine-from-Trinidad with Jasmine-from-India.

WORKS CITED

Chatterjee, Partha. *Nationalist Thought and the Colonial World: A Derivative Discourse?* London: Zed Books Ltd., 1986.

Connell, Michael, Jessie Grearson, and Tom Grimes, "An Interview with Bharati Mukherjee." *Iowa Review* 20.3 (Fall 1990): 7–32.

Gramsci, Antonio. *Selections from the Prison Notebooks*. Ed. and trans. Quintin Hoare and Geoffrey Nowell Smith. New York: International Publishers, 1971.

Guha, Ranajit, and Gayatri Chakravorty Spivak, eds. *Selected Subaltern Studies*. New York and Oxford: Oxford University Press, 1988.

Macaulay, Thomas Babington. "Minute on Indian Education." *Macaulay: Prose and Poetry.* Ed. G.M. Young. Cambridge: Harvard University Press, 1952.

Marx, Karl. *Capital: A Critique of Political Economy.* Trans. Ben Fowkes. Vol. I. New York: Vantage Books, 1977.

Mukherjee, Bharati. *Darkness.* New York: Penguin Books, 1985.

——. "Immigrant Writing: Give Us Your Maximalists!" *New York Times Book Review* (28 August 1988): 1, 28–29.

——. *Jasmine.* New York: Fawcett Press, 1989.

——. *The Middleman and Other Stories.* New York: Grove Press, 1988.

——. *The Tiger's Daughter.* Boston: Houghton Mifflin, 1971.

——, and Clark Blaise. *Days and Nights in Calcutta.* Garden City, N.Y.: Doubleday, 1977.

——, and Robert Boyers. "A Conversation with V.S. Naipaul." *Salmagundi* 54 (Fall 1981): 4–22.

——, et al. "Writer's Panel." *E.M. Forster: Centenary Revaluations.* Ed. Judith Scherer Herz and Robert K. Martin. Toronto: University of Toronto Press, 1982.

Pathak, Zakia, and Rajeswari Sunder Rajan. "Shahbano." *Signs: A Journal of Women in Culture and Society* 14 (Spring 1989): 558–582.

Spivak, Gayatri Chakravorty. "Can the Subaltern Speak?" *Marxism and the Interpretation of Culture.* Ed. Cary Nelson and Lawrence Grossberg. Urbana: University of Illinois Press, 1988.

——. "Three Women's Texts and a Critique of Imperialism." *Critical Inquiry* 12 (Autumn 1985): 242–261.

"IN THE PRESENCE OF HISTORY": THE REPRESENTATION OF PAST AND PRESENT INDIAS IN BHARATI MUKHERJEE'S FICTION

Debjani Banerjee

Bharati Mukherjee's is a familiar voice in the Indian literary diaspora. As the spokesperson of a minority immigrant community in North America, her novels and short stories have been steadily winning acclaim in literary circles. With this critical and popular recognition providing new definitions of literary contexts for postcolonial[1] writing, certain issues involving Mukherjee's use of anecdotal versions of Indian history, her affiliation with North America, and her relationship with her target audience demand close exploration. This essay will touch on these issues related to Mukherjee's commitment as a postcolonial intellectual while focusing on her construction of Indian history in her fiction. The question of representing history is doubly significant in the context of India's colonial past and in the context of contemporary global politics in the era of multinationalism. Mukherjee's exploitation of Third World historical material for a First World audience has important political implications. In the words of Fredric Jameson, the hierarchical relationship between "First and Third World countries, and in particular the way in which this relationship—which is now very precisely what the word 'imperialism' means for us—is one of necessary subordination or dependency" (Eagleton, Jameson, and Said 48). Does Mukherjee's fiction take sufficient account of or address the problems of this inequitous relationship while narrativizing history? Fragments of histories are encountered in the gaps and the hyphens of her writings, woven into a sequence of events extrapolated from their context, masquerading as history. Mukherjee's failure to contextualize the historical and political events of India arises from her inability to perceive the complex workings of postcolonial and neocolonial forces.

The texts privileged in this essay may not be overtly concerned with political movements; yet works such as *The Tiger's Daughter* provide the matrix in which historical and political events can be reenacted fictionally. The main thread of the narrative, pertaining to Tara's first vacation in Calcutta after seven consecutive years in America, coexists uneasily with the depiction of the contemporaneous political movement in the city. The "actualities" of the political events that Mukherjee refers to may not be her intended subject, but the political juncture is perceived by the author and her protagonist as an epistemic moment, the fragments of which are interspersed throughout the narrative. Listening to the radio broadcasts about bomb blasts, Tara feels herself "in the presence of history" (*The Tiger's Daughter* 46). And yet, the Naxalite movement, the political context invoked in the text, is consistently undermined; destruction and loss of lives are emphasized while the revolutionary tenor which rocked Calcutta in the late sixties and early seventies is overlooked. This representation of an ideologically charged juncture in Indian history is not as untrue as it is monolithic. As an Indian sociologist has pointed out: ". . . the word Naxalite was . . . a word loaded with nameless fears and aspirations, stirring hopes or despair, and always strong passions" (Ray 3). Like other radical political movements in postcolonial countries, this one inspired a certain ambiguity which is eschewed in Mukherjee's rendition by way of the focus she chooses.

In *The Tiger's Daughter*, the protagonist belongs to and associates with the privileged bourgeois class. It is the perspective of this class that the author uses as a segue into the exploration of political forces. In an interview with Ameena Meer, Bharati Mukherjee expresses her intention thus: "In *The Tiger's Daughter*, I was writing about my class at a certain period in Calcutta's history, about a class and a way of life that's become extinct" (Meer 26).

Mukherjee's interpretation of the historical context is unifocal, drawing on the hegemonic point of view. As is evident from the extract above, there is some conflation of perspectives between the author and her protagonist based on almost identical class affiliations, which prompts the uniformly negative portrayal of the political movement within the narrative. Perhaps Mukherjee's text pleads ignorance of the "Other," the undifferentiated, subaltern classes of Calcutta, as a reason for the gap created in the text by their nebulous presence. And yet, by locating her text at a sensitive nodal point at the crossroads of historical change, Mukherjee is compelled to represent, even if perfunctorily, the participants of the Naxalite movement. They are of course constantly marginalized from the consciousness of Tara and her friends, trivialized as puerile rather than militant. Mukherjee's portrayal of several such vignettes of political riots as framing moments in her narrative makes her vulnerable to the charge of appropriation. While the fracturing effects of the movement resonate throughout the novel, Mukherjee makes no attempt to foreground the Naxalite movement from the perspective of those participating in it and/or those who have internalized its ideals. This, like Tara's consistent othering of Macdowell, the African American student visiting from California, is an assertion of the inflexibility of difference which makes communication impossible across categories of gender, class, and race. Sara Suleri feels that "the very insistence on the centrality of difference as an unreadable entity can serve to obfuscate and indeed to sensationalize that which still remains to be read" (Suleri 11). Mukherjee's reading of postcolonial history polarizes the two classes: in her narrative, one is threatened by the impending revolution; the other is perceived as the perpetrator of the revolution. Through her persistent effort to erase the rebellious insurgents of Calcutta from her text, while focusing on the privileged sectors, Mukherjee perpetuates silence and lack of communication between two groups of people. Trinh Minh-ha writes, "The understanding of difference is a shared responsibility, which requires a minimum of willingness to reach out to the unknown" (85).

By abjuring a multivalent perspective in her novel, *The Tiger's Daughter*, Mukherjee indicates her indifference to the task that Trinh Minh-ha outlines; in her narrative, lines of communication remain unbridged between the two classes.

The author deserves commendation for her sympathetic but perceptive recreation of the elitist establishment of Calcutta which could have been more effective politically had the juxtaposing vision of the revolutionary energies of the Naxalites not been so relentlessly negative. As it stands, a real attempt has been made to empathize with the problems of Tara and her friends. The threat faced by this class of people as landowners and businessmen is the focal point; the nostalgic imperative of the narrative underscores the tragic implications of their imminent dispossession, the destruction of their Calcutta, and the concomitant prerogatives of their position. Tara's friends, insulated from their surroundings, make desultory conversation on the terrace of a plush hotel while a procession of demonstrators passes by; filtered through their vision, the riot on the main thoroughfare of the city is reduced to a spectacle. This group of people is part of the national bourgeoisie whose ideological bankruptcy has come under scathing criticism by postcolonial theorists like Frantz Fanon. Their "intellectual laziness, spiritual penury and profoundly cosmopolitan mould" (Fanon 122) are what

Fanon identifies as impediments in the war waged by newly decolonized nations against the pervasive effects of colonialism.

In *The Tiger's Daughter*, the indigenous elite who usurp power after decolonization can be seen as surrogates for the colonizer. As the African writer Ayi Kwei Armah puts it, the bottle of colonialism has remained intact while the black top has replaced a white one (26). In a sense, Mukherjee does not interrogate the status quo of the power structure at all. She foregrounds their nostalgia, their collective yearning for "the peaceful times" (*The Tiger's Daughter* 39) with ironic distance and a mild disparagement. She does not perceive them as a threat to the country or as a class of power-mongers who make desperate bids to maintain their power through ideologies of cultural and economic inequality. As clones of their British predecessors, characters like Mr. Tuntunwala work with the police force to consolidate the nexus of power and perpetuate the evils of colonial oppression. In his book, *Writers in Politics*, Ngugi wa Thiong'o writes about a common occurrence in newly independent countries

> where a client indigenous government is ruling and oppressing people on behalf of American, European and Japanese capital. Such a regime acts as a policeman of international capital and often mortgages a whole country for arms and crumbs from the master's table. It never changes the colonial economy of development and uneven development. (Ngugi 119)

What Ngugi is gesturing toward here is the phenomenon of neocolonialism that is a potent threat in Third World countries today. In reconstructing Indian history in her fiction, Mukherjee does not seem to acknowledge such a threat. In *The Tiger's Daughter*, she valorizes, not uncritically, the quasi-colonial milieu of Calcutta and sees the Naxalites, the ostensible agents of the imminent extinction of this class, as a more immediate menace. This representation marks a reenactment of colonial anxiety which Sara Suleri discusses as a recurrent theme in

Anglo-Indian fiction in her book, *The Rhetoric of English India*. The anxiety, Suleri argues, results in

> the ostensible unreadability of the colonized subcontinent.... This unreadability is of course simply one instance of a discursive transfer of power, which fetishizes a colonial fear of its own cultural ignorance into the potential threats posed by an Indian alterity. (Suleri 6)

Roughly translated into the Indian context, this is the threat posed by the Naxalite movement for the elite classes of Calcutta. Their challenge to dominant sociopolitical structures produces a fear within the bastions of power; Mukherjee who enshrines her privileged background as constituted by "top family, top school, top caste, top city" ("Immigrant Writing" 28) is not untainted by this fear and reacts to it by accomplishing the erasure of the rebellious insurgents from her fictional microcosm. Another relevant fact worth mentioning here is that by the time this book was published in 1971, the Naxalite movement had largely failed; although a Communist government was voted into power, the composition of the indigenous elite changed only slightly as establishments of power remained undisrupted. So Mukherjee's paranoia seems largely exaggerated and misplaced.

Mukherjee's consciousness of a Western audience manifests itself in interesting ways in her representation of India. She sensationalizes Tara's visit to the slums; the Indian bourgeois and Western reader alike are taken on a guided tour of the urban slums in Calcutta. Western mediation also enters the novel in less immediate ways. Tara's epistolary exchanges with her American husband provoke her into self-justificatory explanations of her inertia with respect to the turbulent political situation in India. On the one hand, the disturbing suggestion is that the relationship between a privileged Indian and her political circumstances must be mediated by a white, American male. On the other hand, Tara's opinion, expressed in her letters, is that the problems of Calcutta are too numerous and too complex to be categorized and dealt with. Like the "prehistoric" lizards in her father's house, Calcutta in Tara's vision is always already entrapped within a stasis; its political exigencies are naturalized, in a sense, and denuded of history. Once concretized as a static body of knowledge, history can degenerate into a mere compilation of data, from which certain events can be selectively used. This essentialized view of Indian history is paraded for a preeminently Western and Westernized audience, for whose consumption the book is written. As a postcolonial writer affiliated to the West, Bharati Mukherjee cannot evade the responsibility of representing India in her fiction although she does not declare any degree of commitment. In this context, it would not be irrelevant to invoke Chandra Mohanty's comments on feminist writing in the United States:

> Western feminist writing on women in the third world must be considered in the context of the global hegemony of Western scholarship—i.e., the production, publication, distribution and consumption of information and ideas. Marginal or not, this writing has political effects and implications beyond the immediate feminist or disciplinary audience. (Mohanty 55)

Given Mukherjee's unhesitating proclamation of her kinship with American fiction, my concern about her construction of Indian history as a stratified body of knowledge rather than as a crossroad of dynamic historical movements is rendered more urgent.

Within the context of the society of Calcutta, Mukherjee perceives the class privileges and its accoutrements as contested territories, but she portrays them as part of an unchanging monolith where problems proliferate but no solutions can be sought; like her protagonist Tara, Mukherjee probably feels that fighting for justice can be fatal. Tara attends a debate in the British Council, Calcutta, which questions the validity of English as an official language in India; but the evening ends with the guests singing, "For He's a Jolly Good Fellow." The ironic vision provides a refuge which trivializes the vexed issues surrounding English, the most important constituent of colonial debris. In the Indian context, English and the cultural attributes it articulates have proved to be intransigent opponents in the war against residual components of colonialism, mainly because of the sustenance they have received from the Anglicized section of society, who have internalized these attributes. The inculcation of a language and the way of life it signifies begins—as in Tara's case—at an early age, under the aegis of well-endowed missionary schools and other institutions modeled on them. The introjection of the language and the Anglocentric values causes the first stirrings of the "foreignness of spirit" which Mukherjee refers to in *The Tiger's Daughter*.

It can be safely concluded that this alienation is a pervasive postcolonial phenomenon in India where the introduction of English, putatively for educational purposes, was accompanied by a desire to create a chasm within Indian society. In his famous Minute of February 1835, Macaulay, then the President of the Committee of Public Instruction, advocates the study of English in India, in preference to the indigenous languages. He formulates his recommendation thus:

> . . . [I]t is impossible for us with our limited means, to attempt to educate the body of the people. We must at present do our best to form a class who may be interpreters between us and the millions whom we govern; a class of persons, Indian in blood and colour, but English in taste, in opinions, in morals, and in intellect. (Macaulay 729)

Mukherjee's perpetuation of differences between the two classes in *The Tiger's Daughter*, which I have discussed earlier, can be regarded as an act in connivance with these imperial interests.

The "foreignness of spirit" induced by language is explored thoroughly in *Jasmine* where the language of the erstwhile masters continues to connote a circumscribed circle comprised of the quasi-colonialists. The protagonist's desire to learn English is an elitist impetus which has a transformative effect on her life. When she meets the man she wants to marry, her prime criterion is his fluency in English. She regards this peculiarly postcolonial inheritance as a signifier of desire. The language appears to be the source of dreams while really channelizing dreams and desires in particular directions and providing them with a Western orientation. In her discussion of the historical origins of English in India, Gauri Viswanathan writes:

> British colonial administrators, provoked by missionaries on the one hand and fears of native insubordination on the other, discovered an ally in English literature to support them in maintaining control of the natives under the guise of a liberal education. (Viswanathan 17)

The ideological formations molded by the study of English in India remain as compelling four decades after political decolonization as they had been in colonial times. Through her sojourns in the fictional worlds of Jane Eyre and David Copperfield, Jasmine learns to project herself imaginatively into landscapes beyond her parochial parameters, which, esconced in her memory, control her desires. But Jasmine's special affinity for an American novel, *Shane*, presages her preference of America over Britain. The fictional landscape is innately bound up with desire which can be fulfilled by actual immigration to the country.

Desire for immigration to the First World can also be induced in the inhabitant of the Third World through advertisements which display plenitude, the weapon of a consumerist society. In *Jasmine*, the protagonist is enticed by colorful brochures of American universities. While America disseminates the message of consumerism through advertisements which function as a neocolonial weapon, the Third World country gets more and more entangled in its multifarious problems. In *Jasmine*, Mukherjee's reconstruction of the political scenario in India is such that immigration can posit itself as an alluring option. Floundering in a traumatic world of postcolonial reconstruction, caught literally in terrorist cross fires, immigration for Jasmine becomes an ideal to aspire to as differentiated from an expedient escape. The novel insistently portrays a monochromatic picture of violence; Sikh activists, for example, are reduced to mere terrorists and murderers. Mukherjee clearly does not regard political unrest in India as a necessary step in the fortification of a newly independent nation. It is more likely, however, that Mukherjee does not want to acquaint her audience with the fractured histories of Third World countries, which, if analyzed closely, often reveal uncomfortable moments of complicity for any Westerner. Evidently, her refusal to contextualize the political events of India while emphasizing the violence can be construed as a trivializing of the complexities of the postcolonial condition. What is problematic is her implication in *Jasmine* that one must escape from the disillusionment and treachery of postcolonial history. This suggestion takes on ominous proportions if one were to agree with Fredric Jameson's proposition:

> Third-world texts, even those which are seemingly private and invested with a proper libidinal dynamic— necessarily project a political dimension in the form of national allegory: the story of the private individual destiny is always an allegory of the embattled situation of the public third-world culture and society. (Jameson 69)

While I share with Aijaz Ahmad a certain anxiety about Jameson's totalizing impulse with regard to the Third World, Jameson's point seems relevant here as it helps us to see how Jasmine's individual life may be symbolic of that of a whole nation. Jasmine's complete erasure of her Indian past once she is embroiled in the melting-pot dynamic of North America is interesting. As she assimilates into the dominant culture, she casts aside her identity as an Indian. Employing Jameson's allegory, it is easy to see how Indian history is to be obliterated from the text. Mukherjee here is complicit in what Dipesh Chakrabarty describes as "the tendency to read Indian history in terms of a lack, an absence or an incompleteness that translates into inadequacy . . ." (Chakrabarty 5). This ostensibly deficient Indian past is easily subsumed in *Jasmine* by First World forces, thus enacting cultural colonization.

It is, I contend, to resist this imperialism that a sense of nationhood must be promoted among postcolonial subjects. In *Jasmine*, the protagonist feels she can rip herself free of the past as she assimilates in American society. She acquiesces to her own exoticization as an Indian princess; she is resigned to her lover's uneasy silence about her histories; she does not protest even minimally against the normative core of the patriarchal and ethnocentric society that has been dangled in front of her as the site of wish-fulfillment. Along these lines, Jasmine's unquestioning acceptance of the Americanized versions of her name, Jase and Jane and Jazzy, gives rise to discomfort. But this is probably not surprising given the fact that even in India, Jasmine shuttled between her identities as Jyoti, a simple peasant girl, and Jasmine, the Anglicized urbanite who spoke English and internalized litanies of "independence, self-reliance" (*Jasmine* 76). The colonial heritage fosters a catatonic split and eventually an erosion of the sense of self in the individual, which marks him/her as an easy target for neocolonizing forces.

It is precisely in this context that this issue of national consciousness[2] assumes importance. In the Indian context, the concept of nationalism has outgrown its utility since the nationalist struggle and can be perceived as moving into obsolescence. But a newly independent country which is reeling from the attenuating effects of colonization and simultaneously fighting to stabilize its position against the imperializing forces of the First World powers needs a site of resistance which can claim participation from a large and diverse body of people. At critical junctures in postcolonial history, national consciousness can imbue a certain resilience which would help combat the tyranny of imperial forces. Terry Eagleton's position on this issue can be summed up thus: "To wish . . . nation away, to seek to live sheer irreducible difference now in the manner of some contemporary post-structuralist theory, is to play straight into the hands of the oppressor" (Eagleton et al. 23). National consciousness can provide a platform to generate discursive practices against postcolonialist and neo-colonialist exploitation and prevent the oppression that Eagleton hints at.

The concepts of nation and nationhood have been criticized and dismissed by several critics, one of the most persuasive arguments being articulated by Benedict Anderson in his book *Imagined Communities*. According to him, the nation is an international norm that is being imposed upon Third World countries:

> Twentieth century nationalisms have . . . a profoundly modular character. They can, and do, draw on more than a century and a half of human experience and three earlier models of nationalism. Nationalist leaders are thus in a position consciously to deploy civil and military educational systems modelled on official nationalisms; elections, party organizations, and cultural celebrations modelled on the popular nationalisms of nineteenth century Europe; and the citizen-republican idea brought into the world by the Americas. (Anderson 135)

It is true that the problematics raised by the concepts associated with that of the nation can assume hazardous proportions: the nation can be used as a tool to yoke together heterogeneity at various levels; Third World nations can reenact imperialism by claiming to emulate nationalism. In spite of these ambiguities, I would like to insist on national consciousness as a rubric under which possible interventionist strategies can be devised and subsequently employed by literary practitioners from the Third World in order to resist imperialist endeavors of the First World. To underscore its difference from nationalism, it is imperative that national consciousness be regarded as a construct. It is a position that the postcolonial subject can identify with while being aware of its deconstructibility. Refusing the gamut of narrow nationalisms ranging from apparently spontaneous patriotic loyalties to the more stern vision of nationality as a normative allegiance, national consciousness offers a space for self-reflexivity and self-critique which thwarts its crystallization into aggressive authoritarianism. What is important for our purposes is that the postcolonial subject finds a way to define him/herself in relation to colonial histories and neocolonial ventures that is mediated by national consciousness. Within the realm of literature, the postcolonial subject can historicize his/her existence without dismissing the impact of colonialism or underestimating the menace of neocolonialist projects.

It is important at this point to trace the relationship between national consciousness and international relations in the context of Bharati Mukherjee's position as a writer catering to a First World audience while still mining the Third World for fictional material. While discussing this issue, Fanon writes, "National consciousness, which is not nationalism, is the only thing that will give us an international dimension" (198).

This international dimension which prevents national consciousness from degenerating into sterile separatism is qualitatively different from Mukherjee's cosmopolitanism. By reading a temporal sequence into the extract above, I can deduce that it is Fanon's argument that the postcolonial subject must have a certain degree of national consciousness before s/he can deal with the world of global networks. To reverse this pattern is to be in Jasmine's position, totally devoid of a historical past and vulnerable to colonizing forces; in other words, it is the contemporary phenomenon of cosmopolitanism with its shallow internationalist glitter and its casual repudiation of histories of oppression. In his essay "Cosmopolitans and Celebrities," Tim Brennan evaluates the situation astutely when he posits:

> It is altogether innocent, then, that metropolitan critics are eager to embrace the "pluralism" of the new cosmopolitan just when defensive nationalism is on the Third World agenda? . . . What we are seeing is a process by which Western reviewers are selecting as the interpreters and authentic public voices of the Third World, writers who, in a sense, have allowed a flirtation with change that ensures continuity, a familiar strangeness, a trauma by inches. (Brennan 6)

Whether the primary responsibility of commitment devolves upon the critic or the author is a polemical issue which need not be delved into here. Suffice it to say that Brennan's comment takes us into the heart of the matter at hand by politicizing the process of literary production and gesturing toward the necessarily asymmetric power relations between the First World and the Third World. Under the guise of universalist catch phrases like "artistic freedom" with respect to choosing their material, Bharati Mukherjee and other cosmopolitan intellectuals from the Third World may be complicit in the process of neocolonization. By her dismissive attitude toward Indian history, by her failure to provide historical contexts for significant political events while referring to them peripherally in her fiction, she appropriates and represents Indian pasts for an audience which can claim to read Indian history through her work. In fact, Mukherjee's modest popularity and her acceptance within academic circles as the spokesperson for a new group of immigrants enhances the anxiety about the interpretations generated by her text.

Until the last two decades, post-Independence emigration from India, especially among bourgeois writers and intellectuals, had been largely channeled toward England. Mukherjee belongs to the first generation of immigrants to align themselves with America. Unlike her protagonist Jasmine who is, in a sense, compelled to leave India, Mukherjee claims that she had a semblance of choice in leaving India; the ramifications of this choice are worth exploration. Discussing the heritage of the postcolonial writer, Edward Said describes the past "as scars of humiliating wounds, as instigation for different practices" (Said 55). Mukherjee's hierarchization of America and the Old World (symbolized by Canada whose associations with Britain are overdetermined) is part of her political practice; she exercises the simulacrum of a rational choice thus rupturing the instinctual bonds that are presumed to exist between the postcolonial subjects and the world of colonizers and colonies. It is evident that Mukherjee, in defining herself in contradistinction to the Old World, is trying to write her way out of postcolonial nostalgia in which the bourgeois characters in her novel *The Tiger's Daughter* are trapped. In an interview for *Iowa Review*, she says, "America represented a kind of glitziness—as in *Jasmine*—a chance for romantic reincarnation, whereas moving to Canada was like going to England, a step backward to an old world, a hierarchical society" (Connell 11).

In Mukherjee's fiction, America is no Eden; but what is important in her estimation is that the romance overshadows the "glitziness." Mukherjee's categorical rejection of Britain and the Old World can be perceived as a well-defined political position, although she presents it as a "culmination of a long process of searching for a home" ("Immigrant Writing" 28). Unlike writers like V.S. Naipaul who identify their positions as permanent exiles, Mukherjee positions herself emphatically within America and as a part of what she asserts is the "ethnic and gender-fractured world of contemporary American fiction" ("Immigrant Writing" 28).

For Mukherjee, her past identity as an Indian is something she has left behind, although she has internalized it. De-linked from the ongoing processes of Indian history, she situates herself firmly within American culture. In a recent interview, Mukherjee asserts, "I totally consider myself an American writer . . . now my roots are here and my emotions are here in North America" (Meer 27).

Her unambiguous relationship with her identity as an American writer denies her the strategic distance that is needed to comment on and critique the dominant ideologies that pervade American society. Her affiliation with America blinds her to the implications of America's centric and supremacist position among world powers. She is critical of racism in America, but with a certain naivete: her fiction overlooks the fact that the America she clamors to belong to is the prime mover of colonialism today with its proclaimed goal of setting up a new world order, undoubtedly with America at the helm. In this context, her valorization of America as a locus for positive change in novels like *Jasmine* problematizes her position as a postcolonial intellectual. In attempting to escape from what she considers the deterministic landscape dominated by disruptive, postcolonial forces, Mukherjee has sentimentalized her attachment to her new homeland; her fiction does not bear any traces of her interrogation of the political implications of her alignment with this new set of power structures which has displaced the colonialist powers but retained similar configurations of domination and subordination. Evidently, she does not perceive the colonizing potential of America as an immediate threat and therefore her dependence on the power structure is unquestioning to a large extent. Given the sensitive nature of her political praxis, however, this misty vision can make her work susceptible to neocolonizing forces.

In her over-eagerness to consecrate the melting-pot theory of assimilation that America subscribes to, Mukherjee declares the demise of material from the Third World in an article:

And (Third World) material is dead.
Let it die, I want to shout. We're all here and now, and whatever we were raised with is in us already. . . . That's enough. Turn your attention to this scene, which has never been in greater need of new perspectives. ("Immigrant Writing" 29)

Her cosmopolitan politics is clearly stated; her use of Third World material in her work as a tangential referrent evidently obligates her in no way to energize it as a vexed crossroad of history. Since the Third World constitutes a former phase of her life, attempts to activate its history can only become "self-imitative and predictable" ("Immigrant Writing" 29). Therefore, Mukherjee argues, the immigrant writer must transfer allegiances to the contemporary scene exclusively, while "the native society marches onward and perhaps downward" ("Immigrant Writing" 29).

This dismal vision of postcolonial history enshrined in Mukherjee's fictional work finds as its target audience other international cosmopolitans and natives of the First World. When writing for the First World, historical specificities can be viewed as encumbrances which are easily dissipated in a cauldron of romance; in *Jasmine* romance is the "universal" trope which cuts across the First World–Third World binary. Mukherjee's protagonists, Tara and Jasmine, disentangle themselves casually from the homogenized versions of the history of their nation to become American, while within the parameters of the text, Indian history is erased altogether. Mukherjee's accusation of regression leveled against the native nation stems from her inability or unwillingness to comprehend the complex mesh of political problems facing the nation; textual and paratextual readings of Mukherjee's writing make clear that the cumulative effect of colonialism coupled with neocolonial forces offers a very narrow conduit for the Third World nation to operate in.

In her novels, *The Tiger's Daughter* and *Jasmine*, Mukherjee grapples with the evil effects of colonialism in her own elitist way; what she does not seem to perceive at all is the threat of neocolonialism. Consequently she does not see that her cosmopolitan agenda which dilutes history and sanitizes difference is complicit in the process of neocolonialism. Clearly, she wishes to evade the responsibility of representation. Nowhere in her writings does she actively engage with the issue of her commitment as a postcolonial intellectual. In this context it would not be irrelevant to invoke Salman Rushdie; by drawing on the Orwellian metaphor of the whale, Rushdie makes a cogent argument about the possible ways in which postcolonial intellectuals can mediate the relationship between the First and the Third Worlds:

> Outside the whale is the unceasing storm, the continual quarrel, the dialectic of history. Outside the whale there is a genuine need for political fiction, for books that draw new and better maps of reality, and make new languages with which we can understand the world. Outside the whale we see that we are all irradiated by history, we are radioactive with history and politics. (Rushdie 100)

Fiction resonating with history can be one way of representing postcolonial histories; it would be to belabor the point to say that these histories need to be represented in order to be analyzed and critiqued and thus develop their resilience within contemporary global contexts. The onus is, therefore, clearly on the postcolonial intellectual whose writings provide the terrain on which this resistance to imperialist efforts can be enacted. It is not my intention to set up a prescriptive agenda for Mukherjee; however, I cannot vindicate her lack of insight into the sensitive nature of her political praxis, the consequences of which can result in her reenacting colonialism through her fiction.

NOTES

1. I use the term "postcolonial" to talk about processes and moments following political decolonization.

2. I borrow the term from Fanon but not entirely in the sense in which he takes it to be almost synonymous with

national culture. Later in this essay, I give a rough definition of what I mean by national consciousness.

WORKS CITED

Ahmad, Aijaz. "Jameson's Rhetoric of Otherness and the 'National Allegory.'" *Social Text* 6.2 (1987): 3–25.

Anderson, Benedict. *Imagined Communities: Reflections on the Origin and Spread of Nationalism.* New York: Verso, 1991.

Armah, Ayi Kwei. "African Socialism: Utopian or Scientific?" *Présence Africaine* 64 (1967): 6–30.

Brennan, Tim. "Cosmopolitans and Celebrities." *Race and Class* 31.1 (1989): 1–19.

Chakrabarty, Dipesh. "Post-coloniality and the Artifice of History: Who Speaks for 'Indian' Pasts?" *Representations* 37 (1992): 1–26.

Connell, Michael, Jessie Grearson, and Tom Grimes. "An Interview with Bharati Mukherjee." *Iowa Review* 20.3 (1990): 7–32.

Eagleton, Terry, Fredric Jameson, and Edward W. Said. *Nationalism, Colonialism and Literature.* Minneapolis: University of Minnesota Press, 1990.

Fanon, Frantz. *The Wretched of the Earth.* Trans. Constance Farrington. New York: Grove Press, 1963.

Jameson, Fredric. "Third World Literature in the Era of Multinational Capitalism." *Social Text* 5.3 (1986): 65–88.

Macaulay, Thomas. "Indian Education, Minute of the 2nd of February, 1835." *Macaulay: Prose and Poetry*. Selected by J.M. Young. London: Reynard Library, 1952.

Massa, Daniel. "The Post-colonial Dream." *World Literature Written in English* 20.1 (1981): 135–149.

Meer, Ameena. "Bharati Mukherjee." *BOMB* 29 (1989): 26–27.

Minh-ha, Trinh. *Woman, Native, Other: Writing, Postcoloniality and Feminism*. Bloomington: Indiana University Press, 1989.

Mohanty, Chandra. "Under Western Eyes: Feminist Scholarship and Colonial Discourses." *Third World Women and the Politics of Feminism*. Ed. Chandra Mohanty, Ann Russo, and Lourdes Torres. Bloomington: Indiana University Press, 1991. 51–80.

Mukherjee, Bharati. "Immigrant Writing: Give Us Your Maximalists!" *New York Times Book Review* (28 August 1988): 1, 28–29.

———. *Jasmine*. New Delhi: Viking, 1990.

———. *The Tiger's Daughter*. New Delhi: Penguin, 1987.

Ngugi wa Thiong'o. *Writers in Politics*. London: Heinemann, 1981.

Ray, Rabindra. *The Naxalites and Their Ideology*. New Delhi: Oxford, 1988.

Rushdie, Salman. "Outside the Whale." *Imaginary Homelands*. London: Granta, 1991. 87–101.

Said, Edward W. "The Post-colonial Intellectual." *Salmagundi* 70–71 (1986): 44–64.

Suleri, Sara. *The Rhetoric of English India*. Chicago: University of Chicago Press, 1992.

Viswanathan, Gauri. "The Beginnings of English Literary Studies in British India." *Oxford Literary Review* 9.1–2 (1987): 2–26.

BORN AGAIN AMERICAN: THE IMMIGRANT CONSCIOUSNESS IN *JASMINE*

Gurleen Grewal

> The dialectic between change and continuity is a painful but deeply instructive one, in personal life as in the life of a people. To "see the light" too often has meant rejecting the treasure found in darkness.
>
> —Adrienne Rich

Bharati Mukherjee has insisted on being read not as an Indian, or expatriate, writer, but as an immigrant writer, whose literary agenda is to claim the America that is being improvised by newcomers from the Third World. Evident in Mukherjee's self-definition is a refusal to be marginalized as a writer of alien material, an insistence that her themes are central—not marginal—to contemporary American society. *Middleman and Other Stories* (1988) and her latest novel *Jasmine* (1989) support her claim, demonstrating Mukherjee's evolving belief that "expatriation [is] the great temptation, even the enemy, of the ex-colonial, once-third-world author" ("Immigrant Writing" 28). However, it is important to note that the experience of expatriation gave Mukherjee the material for more than half her work to date: *The Tiger's Daughter*

(1971), *Wife* (1975), *Days and Nights in Calcutta* (1977), and *Darkness* (1985). According to Uma Parameswaran, a central tension in expatriate Indian writing stems from the writers' inability to either "wholly repatriate" or "wholly impatriate themselves into their adopted country" (46). We could better appreciate the entirety of Mukherjee's writing if we view it as chronicling the transitions from an expatriate sensibility to an immigrant one. A novel of migrancy and belonging, *Jasmine* is the culmination of a literary trajectory initiated by *The Tiger's Daughter*, a semi-autobiographical novel reflecting a postcolonial expatriate consciousness. The latter consciousness also characterizes Mukherjee's memoir *Days and Nights in Calcutta*, which records, with ironic distance, the painful experience of negotiating identities across various borders of alienation. By the time Mukherjee writes *Jasmine*, she is ready to celebrate: "I'm one of you now" ("Immigrant Writing" 1). *Jasmine* is an ebullient novel offering a spiced-up version of the classic recipe of assimilation into the dominant culture. However, the central problem of the novel is that it is silent about the conditions that make such assimilation possible.

Despite the epigraph from James Gleick's *Chaos*, *Jasmine* is very orderly; what is being ordered is a new identity. The novel is inscribed in what Adrienne Rich has called the "old American pattern, the pattern of the frontier, the escape from the old identity, the old debts, the old wife, to the new name, to the 'new life'" (143). The reader is led from one consciousness to another as the illegal immigrant woman from the farmland of Punjab, India, blazes a trail of identities (Jyoti-Jasmine-Jazzy-Jase-Jane) on her way to the frontier of California, "greedy with wants and reckless from hope" (*Jasmine* 214). The novel is an immigrant *Bildungsroman* and, like most narratives of *Bildung*, it posits a norm of self-development. For the immigrant there are only two possibilities in *Jasmine*: either the ghetto where ethnic identity is tightly secured by a minimal interaction with the outer alien world—an option that has its obvious shortcomings—or assimilation into the dominant white culture, requiring nothing less than the radical rupture with the past. If expatriation is the great temptation and enemy of the "once-third-world" author, the preferred state of impatriation as it is described in *Jasmine* requires nothing less than the extinction of the "once-third-world" self.

Caught in the dialectic between the Third World and the First, between the past and the present, *Jasmine* does not attempt a resolution by a complex synthesis; it simply dissolves the claims of the past. The novel bedazzles the reader with its protagonist's chameleon identities matching her changing locales: Hasnapur, Jullundhar, Florida, Queens, Manhattan, Iowa. However, this quick succession of ever-progressive identities in *Jasmine* flattens what is, in effect, a long and complicated process of negotiating cultural dispositions, experiences, allegiances, and memories (a process that has absorbed Mukherjee's own writing for nearly two decades). Proceeding through a series of jump-cuts, the narrative conceals the violent disjuncture at the heart of the novel: the (il)logic by which the identity of Jyoti, a peasant woman who has only just made the transition to an Indian city, yields—without the benefit of the requisite elite education—to the identity of the narrator, Jane Ripplemeyer, a middle-class American woman consorting with a white banker. To the extent that the novel does not consider this an anomaly, it is complicitous with the myth of the American Dream: it suppresses the issue of class.

By jettisoning continuity, the narrative also muffles a critical question at the heart of the novel. The question is whether the dispositions wrought by one's class, culture, and education (or, as in Jasmine's case, the lack of a certain kind of education) can be discarded like so much baggage; and whether a new set of dispositions, pertaining to another class and culture and education, can be externally assumed, put on in the manner of a new dress. The motto of the novel is clear: "There are no harmless, compassionate ways to make oneself. We murder who we were so we can rebirth ourselves in the images of dreams"

(*Jasmine* 25). This is the story of Jasmine who cuts her tongue, burns her past, sheds her cultural baggage, changes her clothes, alters her walk and her name, and instead of becoming in this violent process of nullification a nonentity, a husk void of self, she acquires the desired and desirable identity of Jase or Jane, the identity of a white banker's or professor's wife. Mukherjee endorses what Adrienne Rich called the "two powerful pressures in present-day American culture": "one is the imperative to assimilate; the other, the idea that one can be socially 'twice-born'" (141).

If, as Rich says, "to assimilate means to give up not only your history but your body" (142), Mukherjee's heroine is ready to give up both. Mukherjee makes much of the fact that Third World immigrants are able to live and compress in one lifetime the development of centuries: hurtling through time, they move from a feudal village to the global metropolis. But she makes very little of the fact that her protagonist's provincial origins and lack of credentials might intractably condition her life in America. The unlikelihood of Jyoti-Jasmine's trajectory being congruent with Jane's jars the realistic composure of the narrative. Finally, it is the success of Mukherjee's own investments, literary and otherwise, in America, that Jasmine registers through the narrative consciousness of Jane.

The account of the protagonist's speedy and spectacular progression from Jyoti to Jane, from the farmland of Punjab to the other farmland of Iowa is the core of the novel. The first nodal point of change is Jullundhar, Punjab, where Prakash, Jyoti's husband, turns her away from the feudalism of her village, Hasnapur, and sets her on the emancipating path to self-assertion and self-reliance, America's self-proclaimed virtues. However, before he can take off for the engineering school in Florida, which was to have given them both new lives, he is killed in a Sikh terrorist bomb attack. Jyoti-Jasmine spends all her husband's savings on a fake visa to America. Oddly enough, her goal is to commit sati on the campus of her husband's would-be school; in her suitcase is her husband's brand new suit and a white sari of the traditional widow, both of which she intends to burn along with herself. However, after a tortuous, illegal immigrant's journey to Florida, she falls into the hands of a white man who rapes her in a motel in Florida. Sullied, she surrenders her vision of sati and settles for a symbolic burning instead: she sets the suit and sari on fire in a trash can behind the motel and takes to the road.

Henceforth, all her encounters with strangers in the United States are miraculously benign; naturalism gives way to romance. A kind Quaker lady, Lillian Gordon, shelters her, calls her Jazzy, teaches her how to walk American-style and sends her on her way to Queens, New York, where Jasmine contacts an Indian professor who is well disposed to her husband. His home in Flushing, Queens, is part of a Punjabi immigrant ghetto; after spending five depressing months there and acquiring a fake green card, she leaves. Lillian Gordon's sympathetic daughter guides her to her new home in Manhattan; a young, liberal couple, Taylor and Wylie Hayes, employ her as an *au pair* and nanny to their adopted daughter Duff. Taylor, a physics professor at Columbia University, names her Jase, and during her two years with them she becomes an American. Then, Wylie leaves Taylor for another man and Taylor himself falls in love with Jase. However, the presence in New York of a Sikh terrorist from her village frightens Jasmine into running away to Iowa, the next station of change.

In Baden, Iowa, she is fortunate to run into Mother Ripplemeyer, a Lutheran of German stock, who promptly takes her to her son's bank. The aging banker Bud Ripplemeyer is swept off his feet by the Indian princess; six months after working as a teller in his bank, she is Jane Ripplemeyer, living with the banker who has divorced his wife for her. He names her Jane and her Americanization is complete. As part of his midlife crisis, Bud adopts Du Thien, a fourteen-year-old Vietnamese boy from a refugee camp. However, this multiethnic American family is short-lived. Violence also characterizes this flatland, where dispossessed farmers kill themselves; one of them shoots Bud and cripples him. Meanwhile, the frontier beckons the immigrants. Rugged individualism dissolves personal debts: Du leaves for Los Angeles and Jane, pregnant, leaves for Berkeley with Taylor.

The starkness of the rapid linear development from village to metropolis, of Jyoti reborn as Jane, is disguised by the nonlinear narrative techniques of montage and jump-cuts, shuffling us back and forth in time. However, from the opening page, the narrative constructs the native woman, Jyoti, as a becoming figure marked for exile and deliverance from the dark and static Being of India. Structuring the novel are the polarities of fate and will, with Jyoti-Jasmine/India locked into the inertia of stasis, the land of Yama/Death, and Jase-Jane/America equated with freedom from fate, poverty, and a repressive gender identity. Adrienne Rich parallels the "twice-born" notion with the Christian fundamentalist model of "a soul once drenched in sin—in negativity—which through some charismatic encounter comes to see the truth, rejects its former 'path'" for a new "'path' of innocence," leaving "sin and shame behind" (143). To many readers of *Jasmine*, the erasure of the immigrant's Indian past would not seem a loss because this quintessential "Third World" occupies the negative term in the binary of First and Third Worlds. The novel opens with two images that emblematically sum up the novel's representation of India. The first image is of an astrologer sitting under a banyan tree in a village; by predicting the doom of fate upon seven-year-old Jyoti, he symbolically and actually inflicts a star-shaped wound on her forehead. The second image is of this girl paddling furiously against fate in a dirty river carrying the stinking carcass of a dead dog. Recalling the stench, the young first-person narrator, Jane Ripplemeyer of Elsa County, Iowa, defines herself by negation: she says that she knew what she did not want to become (*Jasmine* 3).

The narrating consciousness proceeds to dissociate itself not only from India but from Jyoti as well. Jane

Ripplemeyer, the narrator, declares that she was named Jyoti, which means light, but she has transformed herself into Jane—a fighter and survivor (*Jasmine* 35). Thus, the survivor's spirit in Jyoti belongs more to Jane than to Jyoti herself. However, Jyoti, insofar as she is a part of Jane, is a singular character, superior to the other peasant women, who cannot fend for themselves. In a village scene Jane recollects, the village women are caught with their pants down as their morning toilet ritual in the fields is disrupted by the arrival of a mad dog; interestingly, while adult women—presumably hardy peasants—"crouch" or "crab-crawl" (*Jasmine* 48–49) before the reader, the girl Jyoti (in her capacity as Jane) dramatically fights the mad dog and rescues them from danger. Being a survivor, Jyoti is less like the Indian women, who "fell into wells," and "got run over by trains" (*Jasmine* 36); she is more like Jane. When she is herself (not Jane), Jyoti/light is powerless against the feudal darkness of India; likewise, Jasmine/fragrance is weak before the land's stench.

Thus, in the portrayal of her immigrant heroine, Mukherjee reinforces images of the Third World Woman who is constrained by her gender and by the "backward" culture and economy of the Third World: she is ignorant, traditional, domestic, in short a victim awaiting rescue. As Chandra Mohanty has pointed out, such an image of the Third World Woman posits "western women as secular, liberated, and having control over their own lives" (81). Mukherjee is of course careful to suggest that America is no Eden: it is a brave new world that includes the violence of rape, murder, and suicide. However, America saves Jasmine from Yama. By laughing at Jasmine's mission of death (sati) and rendering it impure, the American rapist in Florida liberates Jasmine from tradition. Instead of burning herself, she throws her suitcase into a trash can and sets it on fire. Thus, it follows that when a self-immolating Third World Woman is an immigrant to America, she has nothing to preserve of her identity, which is symbolic of and synonymous with oppression. The novel's cover jacket praise by *The Baltimore Sun* for the

Ballantine edition of *Jasmine* is not surprising: "POIGNANT . . . The story of the transformation of an Indian village girl, whose grandmother wants to marry her off at 11, into an American woman who finally thinks for herself"!

In fact, the novel seems to suggest there are women who might travel half-way round the globe to the United States to commit sati. Jasmine has no other motive. We share with Half-Face, the rapist, his incredulity and contempt when he finds out her motive for coming to America. Willing to suggest some obscure piety for Jasmine's bizarre motivation, Mukherjee fosters a gross misperception. Reading *Jasmine*, one might think sati was being practiced as a matter of routine and choice by contemporary Hindu widows. To an Indian reader it is clear that Jasmine's desire for sati—let alone her desire for sati in America—is incomprehensible. The will to live that she exhibits at all other times is conveniently repressed; her husband's considerable savings that could have supported her are squandered on a passport to death. Mukherjee's protagonist is neither coerced by relatives avaricious for her husband's money, nor so bereft of options that death is her only alternative. Extricated from relations of power and property, the practice of sati, as an arena both of oppression and of women's resistance to oppression, is rendered meaningless in *Jasmine*.

However, apart from this affront to social and psychological realism, the symbolic performance of sati allows Mukherjee to mark the violent transition from the old to the new. The intractable issue of continuity, from the past to the present, is literally trashed. The fire marks the extinction of an oppressive gender identity, for the notion of both purity (the virtuous woman) and impurity (the raped woman) is destroyed: henceforth Jasmine can define her own desires, unhampered by conventional duty or morality. Further, if a progressive immigrant identity is a matter of shedding Old World baggage and clothing, Jasmine begins her first morning in America by "traveling light" (*Jasmine* 108). She is now a *tabula rasa* upon whom the names of Jase and Jane can be inscribed. Jyoti-Jasmine leaves Florida for Flushing, New York, but what gives her the sensibility or the disposition to stay aloof from the ethnic ghetto is never specified. She seems to have an antipathy to her culture's practices although, we are told, she came to America in allegiance to sati, the most orthodox of practices.

The two most critical points of change in Jyoti-Jasmine's life are awkwardly maneuvered. The first big shift is from India (Punjab) to America; the second move is from the Punjabi ghetto to Manhattan. Both are comparable in magnitude in that they require a transition to a Western world view, one for which Jyoti-Jasmine has not been prepared. However, it is not anomalous, within the novel's terms, that an Indian woman who can bring to America her vision of sati can discard that sensibility overnight and assume the consciousness of individualism. Changing world views appears to be a matter of changing clothes; Jasmine becomes Jase, an Americanized woman who wears silk pants and glittering shoes.

In her haste to Americanize Jasmine and dress her up in the images of dreams, Mukherjee neglects a significant immigrant story, that of the Vadhera family in Flushing that provides her a home, no questions asked, on the strength of old connections in the homeland. Little sympathy is wasted on Mr. Vadhera, an unemployed Indian professor who makes a living literally splitting hairs in the basement of a cheap hotel—hair that could well come from Jasmine's own village. His plight elicits from the ironic and composed Jasmine no outrage. Mukherjee allows her little empathy for the Vadheras, certainly little solidarity on the basis of their shared predicament as immigrants. Newly arrived in America, Jasmine, having lived the better part of her life in a village, faults the Vadheras for living in a Punjabi ghetto, where she finds herself "deteriorating" (*Jasmine* 131). From her perspective, the Vadheras are cast in a one-dimensional world of nostalgia and inertia. Later, in marked contrast, the narrator tells us that she declined the opportunity to maintain a continuity with her past: "I changed because I wanted to. To bunker oneself inside nostalgia, to sheathe the heart in a bulletproof vest, was to be a coward" (*Jasmine* 165). Adrienne Rich has traversed this terrain before and has articulated what needs to be said here:

> By constructing an ideal of Americanization and equating this with virtue, progressiveness, decency, and worth, the assimilation imperative has also assured that those least able to assimilate—most often because of skin color or gender but also because of ethnicity or religion—could be cast as absolute Other, sentenced to live by different laws, treated as victims of inferior biology. (141–142)

Representing the retention of ethnic identity as cowardice or failure on the part of these first-generation immigrants, the novel seems obtuse to their conditions of existence. As Sucheta Mazumdar notes, "Asian ethnic ghettoes" are "a genuine response to the needs of the new immigrants who live, work, or find support services there. Even highly trained professionals may find . . . their foreign credentials unacceptable here and be forced to turn to low-income housing and semi-skilled jobs in ethnic markets, restaurants . . . in order to survive" (14).

However, Jasmine makes her separate appeal to the reader: "Can wanting be fatal?" (*Jasmine* 126). Individual desire propels her away from the confining roles of gender in the immigrant ghetto. As Mazumdar notes, "For immigrant women arrival in America can be liberating. Societal norms of the majority community frequently provide greater personal freedom than permitted in Asian societies" (15). The inscription of an Indian woman into the frontier pattern is exotic as well as heroic and makes for some dramatic moments. Some readers may commend Mukherjee for creating a vital female figure who combines the force of the Hindu trinity with her own uninhibited powers of feminine creating, wrath, and sexual desire. "I feel so potent, a goddess" (*Jasmine* 12), says Jane Ripplemeyer. As the female Brahma, she is her own creator, pregnant with new life; as caregiver, she matches Vishnu, the preserver; as Siva's counterpart, Kali, she has killed the demon Half-Face, her rapist.

However, Jasmine's active, willful, individualistic persona notwithstanding, the reader must examine to what extent Mukherjee's character is a self-defining immigrant woman. As exotic caregiver, homemaker, and temptress, Jane is the model immigrant woman who says and does nothing to challenge the authority or ethnocentrism of the white American male. She makes no mention of her past because it is unacceptable to Bud and Mother Ripplemeyer. She tells us that Bud has never shown any interest about her life in India which frightens him; in fact, he construes Jane's memories as a mark of disloyalty to him. However, he endows her with a predictable foreignness: Jasmine points out that it is her mysterious and inscrutable exoticism that entices Bud so much. Although a case could be made for the ambivalence and irony of this statement (as of many others), Jasmine readily complies as the exotic Other. In fact, this compliance is her ticket to the American Dream. As Rich notes, of non-Anglo-Saxon immigrants in "quest of a middle-class standard of life," the "pressure to assimilate" could say various things: "change your name, your accent," "don't make trouble," "defer to white men," and "be ashamed of who you are" (142). Mukherjee's heroine complies.

Adrienne Rich astutely observes that in "the desire to be twice-born" is "a longing to escape the burdens, complications, and contradictions of continuity." Jane Ripplemeyer, pregnant with new life, asserts that she hardly sends out or receives any mail because she wants to disconnect herself from her past (185). Maintaining a life of continuity implies carrying the burdens of history; Jane only carries her own new life. It is significant that Du, the adopted son, is not considered twice-born. In making a distinction between the Vietnamese-American Du and herself, Jane makes the perplexing statement: "My transformation has been genetic; Du's was hyphenated"

(*Jasmine* 198). While the "hybrid" Du departs for the frontier to work on behalf of his Vietnamese family and community in America, the singularly Americanized Jane, pursuing "[a]dventure, risk, transformation," has no responsibility to anyone.

As the novel erases the history and ethnic identity of the immigrant woman, it also ignores the realities of race and class distinctions in American society. The unskilled immigrant woman, if she is also an illegal alien like Jasmine, is "frequently powerless and marginalized" (Mazumdar 21). Because Jasmine's employers, the liberal New York couple, call her a "caregiver," not a maidservant, we are led to assume there are no class boundaries or distinctions. The Anglo-Saxon banker in Iowa runs toward her the minute he sees her and excitedly invites the "maharani" (*Jasmine* 31) to lunch. She magically leaves behind her roles as *au pair*, nanny, and bank teller simply by being the Oriental Woman to the American male.

Finally, it seems clear that Mukherjee blurs the distinction between someone like herself, a member of an Indian elite, well groomed in British colonial education, and a peasant woman like Jyoti-Jasmine. The reader is led to believe that Jane's success story is Jyoti's, that the peasant Jyoti and the Westernized Jane share the same "I" of the first-person narrator. However, two divergent trajectories are made to intersect in the titular figure of Jasmine. Mukherjee attributes to an underprivileged immigrant woman (Jyoti-Jasmine) the dispositions and options available to an Indian woman privileged by class and education (Jazzy-Jane). For women of the class and education of Mukherjee, assimilation into the American mainstream is possible. However, to assume that unskilled, illegal women immigrants like Jasmine—who are not fluent in the English language—have the same opportunities as upper-class, educated immigrant women is to make a mockery of their lives. It is to brush aside the realities of class, whose lines of hierarchy in both America and India can be as unyielding as the Indian astrologer's lines of fate. It is, in short, to write a romance novel.

Born Again American 193

The struggles of immigrant women corresponding to the figure of Jasmine are ultimately misrepresented, for both the consciousness and the trajectory of Mukherjee's heroine have their origins not in peasant Punjab but in an elite postcolonial India. The trajectory of a system may be chaotic but it is not arbitrary; it is always sensitive to the starting point of the system. It is difficult for the reader to believe that Jasmine and Jane can share the same trajectory. Jyoti-Jasmine's formative years are spent in the village—a place untouched by Western influence. Jasmine, we recall, has not passed the sixth grade. How, then, does she acquire the consciousness of Jane, someone who is an alien in the Punjabi ghetto, who is at home in the place of middle-class white women? Mukherjee attempts to conceal the incongruity by having her protagonist be both educated and uneducated, learned in English and unlearned. A novel about a peasant woman's life, *Jasmine* is unable to shake off a Western-oriented postcolonial consciousness, which most clearly manifests itself in literary allusions to English texts: *Jane Eyre*, *Great Expectations*, and *Pygmalion*. We are told, in fact, that Jyoti could not understand the Victorian novels her village tutor gave her to read. Yet, Jane Ripplemeyer (whose last name rhymes with Jane Eyre) can make an intimate reference to Charlotte Brontë's novel. In other words, if Jyoti is not familiar with these texts, who is the one aware of the fact that her life has corresponded to their plots?[1]

How does she gain that awareness? The mask has slid and authorial consciousness makes its presence felt; Mukherjee is unable to suppress the trace of the education that allows her narrator to assimilate into the Anglo-Saxon world of the United States. The two distinct starting points of Jyoti and Jane are revealed. We have seen that the narrator Jane Ripplemeyer both is and is not Jyoti/Jasmine. This double coding of identification and denial occurs throughout; its source is in Mukherjee's own postcolonial identity as an elite Indian woman. Mukherjee's Jane grafts her own story of becoming American onto the Punjabi peasant woman's. For Jane, "the images of dreams" are within reach; in fact, she has no need to murder herself, for they are "Taylor-made" for her.

As a writer, Mukherjee has claimed a special legacy for herself. She calls it the colonial writer's "legacy" of "duality": the "learned" ability "to be two things simultaneously; to be the dispossessed as well as the dispossessor" ("Immigrant Writing" 29). A "history-mandated training," one conducted through colonial "textbooks," has thus bequeathed on her "a fluid set of identities" to "enter" at will ("Immigrant Writing" 29). There is, however, a certain ingenuousness in the claim which discounts the imbalance of power between the two simultaneous selves; for one cannot be both without some violence done to the dispossessed. *Jasmine* illustrates this well. The narrator Jane Ripplemeyer is both Jane and Jyoti. Yet, as we have seen, Jyoti is consistently subordinated to the consciousness of Jane. As a member of the educated Indian elite, Mukherjee is closer to Jase's and Jane's subjectivity than to Jyoti's. In a very telling moment, the narrator explains her own inability to identify with the Vadheras: had she "been a different person with a different set of experiences," her stay with them "would be life-affirming, invaluable, inexpressibly touching" (*Jasmine* 143). That is precisely my point. What may be life-affirming for Jyoti is life-denying for Jane. And since it is Jane's experience that *Jasmine* affirms, Jyoti-Jasmine's perspective is being denied. Consequently, there is a certain untruth in Jane's statement, "We murder who we were so we can rebirth ourselves in the images of dreams." For the self murdered is not Jane but Jyoti. The narrator casually remarks that Jyoti died when she started the fire in the trash can in Florida. From the perspective of the dispossessor (Jane), a peasant woman (Jyoti-Jasmine) has/is nothing to lose; merely oppressive, her past is expendable. The pattern of Jyoti yielding to Jane is a colonial legacy; Mukherjee, however, does not acknowledge this psychic violence in the legacy she claims.

In a significant way, *Jasmine* continues the story of the Bengal tiger's daughter. *The Tiger's Daughter* is a candid, barely concealed account of the author's own displacement through education: tutored by nuns in Calcutta, having studied in America and married an American, Tara Banerjee Cartwright returns home to recognize the impossibility of repatriation: specifically, the difficulty of resuming the role of a wealthy patriarch's daughter—over-protected and escorted, hemmed in by the very privileges accorded women of her class. The novel ends with Tara in a car surrounded by a mob, immobile in her class privilege. The dislocation and the entrapment of gender and class in *The Tiger's Daughter* gives way to the relocation and emancipation of the Indian woman in *Jasmine* whom we see, in the novel's last scene, heading for the car that will transport her to the California frontier. Freed from the constraints of gender but endowed, like Tara, with the comforts of class, Jane is mobile.

One applauds the heroine's tenacity and her determination to belong, but one wishes Jane's story had not been told in Jyoti-Jasmine's name.

NOTE

1. A self-reflexive novel, *Jasmine* incorporates elements of all three texts, *Jane Eyre*, *Great Expectations*, and *Pygmalion* and molds them into an immigrant romance: Prakash, her Indian husband, is the Professor Higgins in G.B. Shaw's *Pygmalion* who corrects and modernizes her image and sets her on the path to modernity (America); Charlotte Brontë's story of the orphaned governess finding a rich benefactor and a home, of Jane Eyre finding Mr. Rochester, is paralleled: Jasmine becomes the caregiving Jane to the banker, Bud Ripplemeyer, who like Rochester is older and crippled. Mukherjee, however, not Victorian, extricates her Jane, an immigrant who has great expectations (we recall that she is literally expectant), from the

dutiful role and lets her elope with Professor Taylor. This instance of intertextuality is also an instance of the power of the colonial education to shape native subjects.

WORKS CITED

Mazumdar, Sucheta. "General Introduction: A Woman Centred Perspective on Asian American History." *Making Waves*. Ed. Asian Women United of California. Boston: Beacon, 1989. 1–22.

Mohanty, Chandra. "Under Western Eyes: Feminist Scholarship and Colonial Discourses." *Feminist Review* (Autumn 1988): 61–88.

Mukherjee, Bharati. "Immigrant Writing: Give Us Your Maximalists!" *New York Times Book Review* (28 August 1988): 1, 28–29.

———. *Jasmine*. New York: Ballantine, 1989.

———. *The Tiger's Daughter*. Boston: Houghton Mifflin, 1971.

Parameswaran, Uma. "What Price Expatriation?" *The Commonwealth Writer Overseas: Themes of Exile and Expatriation*. Ed. Alastair Niven. Brussels: M. Didier, 1976. 41–52.

Rich, Adrienne. "Resisting Amnesia: History and Personal Life." *Blood, Bread and Poetry*. New York: W.W. Norton, 1986. 136–155.

LOVE AND THE INDIAN IMMIGRANT IN BHARATI MUKHERJEE'S SHORT FICTION

Mitali R. Pati

> Th'expense of spirit in a waste of shame
> Is lust in action; and till action, lust
> Is perjured, murd'rous, bloody, full of blame,
> Savage, extreme, rude, cruel, not to trust;
> Enjoyed no sooner but despised straight.
> —William Shakespeare, Sonnet 129

Love, desire, and romance as experienced by immigrant men and women from the Indian subcontinent in the New World appears as a recurring theme in Bharati Mukherjee's short fiction collections of the eighties, namely, *Darkness* (1985) and *The Middleman and Other Stories* (1988). Desire, both for material advancement and for sexual fulfillment, becomes the central motif in the South Asian immigrants' self-fashioning in the New World.[1] Such self-fashioning is necessarily self-dividing, especially in the context of Old World romantic texts versus New World social practices.

Mukherjee's art of characterization depends heavily upon contrasting the public and private selves of her principal characters in "Angela," "The Lady from Lucknow," "A Father," "Nostalgia," "Visitors" in *Darkness* and "A Wife's Story," "The Tenant," "Danny's Girls," and "The Management of Grief" in *The Middleman and Other Stories* to depict the unusual dilemmas that confront Mukherjee's men and women when they face their hitherto secret desires in the new country. Mukherjee's South Asian immigrants both fashion and seek new selves and a fresh "truth" as their Indian paradigms of love, desire, and romance are deconstructed by their American experiences. Images of romance and sexuality in Indian texts and contexts are frequently juxtaposed in the rhetoric and actions of Mukherjee's characters with American views of romance and passion. This "migration of texts" in Mukherjee's fiction is essentially ironic, almost parodic. The conflict in the social and cultural codes of the East and the West, the old and the new shows the hopelessly binary nature of all human desire. For the diasporic Indian, love symbolizes the anarchy of the self.

Mukherjee's narrative method is best described as social satire, if one applies Northrop Frye's definition that "satire is irony which is structurally close to the comic: the comic struggle of two societies, one normal and the other absurd, is reflected in its double focus of morality and fantasy" (224). Mukherjee's diasporic Indians struggle with the cultural codes of their old and new countries indulging in behaviors that border on the absurd. In Mukherjee's short fiction, the satiric narrative contrasts interior monologues with public actions as the principal device by which characters confront their own concealed desires. By this process, Mukherjee's protagonists discover the new, at times fragile, identities that they have fashioned in the new country.

Bharati Mukherjee identifies closely with the Indian immigrants when she states that she sees aspects of her own self as an expatriate Indian in the narratives of her diasporic South Asians in the United States (*Darkness* 2–3). However, Mukherjee is sociologically inaccurate when she states that immigrant Indians constitute an "underclass" (*Darkness* 3). Recent research on the South Asian community in the United States reveals that Indian immigrants in the United States are often professionals, and most are middle class (Bhardwaj and Rao 199–200). Nevertheless, Mukherjee's satire is based upon social realism. An instance of this realism is evident in her interest in the import of brides from the old country. Sociologists find that during the early seventies, female Indian immigrants outnumbered males because immigrant males began to bring in Indian brides (Bhardwaj and Rao 199). This import of brides shows the male immigrants' desire to continue the "convenient" practices of South Asian patriarchy amid the freedoms of the New World. Ghetto entrepreneurs such as Mukherjee's Danny Sahib make profit from this practice by importing mail-order brides from the old country for lonely white American males.

Some ethnic and gender stereotyping remains in Mukherjee's characterization. Mukherjee's sympathetic Indians are largely female. Her Indian men are unromantic, overwhelmingly acquisitive, and slightly ridiculous. Their rejection by their romantic, sensual, and sensitive women in Mukherjee's short fiction emphasizes the crumbling masculine power structure in the South Asian immigrant community in the United States. However, Mukherjee's social critique remains politically oblique in that her satire bypasses the feminist emphasis on women's anger.[2]

The immigrants who seek to refashion themselves materialistically and romantically are predominantly educated professionals. Among the male characters, the physicians Vinny Menezies ("Angela"), Manny Patel ("Nostalgia"), Ashoke Mehta ("The Tenant"), the physicist Rabindra Chatterjee ("The Tenant"), and the engineer Bhowmick ("A Father") typify Mukherjee's immigrant Indian men in that the orderliness, success, and prosperity of their public lives contrast sharply with the self-division, deprivation, and turmoil of their emotional lives. On the fringes of the public "stability" of these middle-class men stand the uncontrolled passions of the graduate students Poltoo ("The Tenant") and Rajiv Khanna

("Visitors"), the ghetto character Danny Sahib, and the teenage narrator of "Danny Sahib," a diasporic Indian from Uganda. The stereotypical "blind" patriarch appears in Iqbal of IBM ("The Lady from Lucknow") who is cuckolded, and the accountant Sailen Kumar ("Visitors") who may be a potential cuckold.

Mukherjee's Indian men are brought to life either through the satiric narratives of immigrant women or through the omniscient eyes of a first-person immigrant narrator. In this way, narrator and characters subscribe to the same values, and Mukherjee's telling becomes a showing, a social and psychological revelation from the inside, the satirist's moral selection of absurdity (Frye 224). The Indian traditional practice of arranging marriages is juxtaposed with the Western idea of romance culminating in matrimony. Marriage displays the romantic and erotic conflicts of Mukherjee's male characters to the fullest degree.

Within and without their marriages, Mukherjee's men are often as sober, greedy, and scholarly as Manny Patel (*Middleman*, "Nostalgia" 103), and their material acquisitiveness usually supersedes their desire for romantic and sexual fulfillment. Typically, in midlife these repressed desires get out of control and lead up to the culminating episodes of Mukherjee's satiric plots. Desire brings shame upon Mukherjee's characters.

Vinny Menezies is the most sympathetic of Mukherjee's Indian physicians; he is both innocuous and ridiculous. Menezies is depicted through the point of view of Angela, the teenaged orphan high school student from Bangladesh who has been adopted into a white Midwestern family. This immigrant physician from Bombay is old-fashioned but cultured. He routinely appreciates Angela's Sunday afternoon piano playing with exclamations of "bravo" (*Middleman*, "Angela" 17). In the manner of the old country, Menezies seeks a bride in a marriage of convenience. He seeks to combine this search with altruism. Therefore, the object of his affections becomes the Old World orphan Angela. As there are no go-betweens or marriage brokers in the American Midwest, Menezies proposes to Angela in a bumbling, self-conscious manner. In her narrative, Angela feels no passion for Menezies, but being an orphan from the East, she realizes that her middle-aged suitor offers financial security and the secret desire of his raw and wild heart. As she contemplates accepting Menezies, she is aware of her own body mutilated in childhood by soldiers. The South Asian immigrant woman in Angela betrays no passion or desire for Menezies, nor any desire for a more erotic relationship for herself. The cutting off of her nipples at the age of six has left her unable to feel positively about her own sexuality. Between the war atrocity which she has left behind her and the powerful call of the traditional male in Menezies, Angela remains enmeshed in the net of Old World patriarchy. Her belief in her own assimilation into the American melting pot is therefore ironic.

Vinny Menezies is a caricature, but a kindly healing figure. Another Indian physician appears in "The Tenant" in the person of the ear-nose-throat specialist from Connecticut, Ashoke Mehta, to whose dubious matrimonial advertisement the promiscuous college professor Maya Sanyal responds. Maya harbors a secret desire to sleep with an Indian man, and she has had no such opportunity. The date from the immigrant weekly *India Abroad* is a wealthy playboy of unaccountable behavior. Mehta is the physical image of a Hindu god with ungodly lusts. The gods of Hindu mythology are polygamous and impulsive; so is Mehta. In a parody of South Asian matrimonial advertisements and social practices, Mehta's ad is for a freewheeling relationship without marriage.

Similar to Ashoke Mehta is the New York psychiatrist Manny Patel ("Nostalgia") who cheats on his white American wife Camille in numerous secret encounters with call girls on business trips. Though middle-aged, Patel is incurably romantic, and like Maya he harbors the secret desire for a relationship with an Indian of the opposite sex. Amid the chaos of New York's "Little India" on a busy afternoon, Patel is smitten by a youthful sales clerk in an Indian grocery store. Nostalgia for the subcontinental romantic fantasies of his youth grips Patel. His romantic desires have been long suppressed in his stable marriage to the nurse Camille (who had done most of the pursuing during their courtship). Seeking an escape from his expensive and highly organized life in the suburbs, Patel experiences a sharp desire to sleep with the Indian beauty Padma.

Manny Patel's adultery is the literal rendering of a series of South Asian cultural clichés. Padma is named for the tropical flower lotus. The lotus-like beloved of medieval Indian courtly poetry is analogous to the rose of English poetry. The sales clerk has the curvacious body of a Bombay film star. The old country's visual ideal of female beauty is different from more slender women of the American popular media. The omniscient third-person narrator stresses that Patel is a loving husband and father dominated by acquisitiveness. In his affair with Padma, Patel combines his acquisitiveness with nostalgia for the style of life in the old country where he continues to own a home. He is divided in his desire to be within both cultures, Eastern and Western, simultaneously.

The lotus-like heroines of Indian medieval courtly poetry were often praised by their middle-aged lovers in an earlier polygamous society. In his nostalgia, Patel returns to a fantasy past where he sees himself as a maharaja on a new romantic conquest, seeking to bestow silk, gold, pearls, rubies, and emeralds on the sex goddess of his erotic daydreams. After a stereotypical spicy dinner in an expensive Indian restaurant, Patel's inevitable sexual encounter with Padma takes place. In a mockery of the traditional Hindu woman's passivity, Padma (as she has warned Patel) does not "come." However, there comes the criminal waiter from the restaurant masquerading as Padma's uncle who corners the lustful Patel with successful blackmail. Manny Patel's erotic daydream disintegrates, in the typical style of Bombay films, with the entry of the cardboard villain. Padma is clearly a prostitute, and the waiter is her pimp. After writing a check for $700 and promising a medical note for immigration officers, Patel defecates in the sink of the motel bathroom and writes WHORE on the mirror and floor with his own feces. This concluding act of release sharply parodies the romantic beginning of this clever satiric narrative.

The self-division experienced by Mukherjee's Indian men as they encounter the sexual liberation of the new country leads to acts of shame, madness, even violence as shown by the conflicts of Chatterjee in "The Tenant" and Bhowmick in "A Father." After an evening in his house with the sexy divorcee, Maya Sanyal, for whom his stout, childless wife has prepared an elaborate meal, Rab Chatterjee is so aroused that he begins to masturbate in his car as he takes Maya home. He overtly laments his loneliness and lack of sexual freedom in his marriage.

A "patriarch" is brought to shame, violence, even madness in America when Mr. Bhowmick contends with his bright, unmarried, engineer daughter's artificially inseminated pregnancy in "A Father." Bhowmick, formerly a provincial from Ranchi, is a henpecked husband who begins by living in awe of his clever professional daughter Babli. Dominated by his wife, whose dowry was Bhowmick's education at Carnegie Tech, he emigrated to the United States because of his wife's nagging.

Despite his lack of power, Bhowmick worships Kali, the goddess of wrath and vengeance. Silently, he watches Babli's pregnancy progress, ready to assimilate a white son-in-law if necessary. But Mr. Bhowmick's aggressive secret desires translate into violent action when he intervenes in a physical conflict between his wife and Babli. Babli's sarcastic comparison of her artificially inseminated pregnancy to the practice of marriages of convenience in India brings her father's violence upon her amid her mother's hysteria. Finally, Mrs. Bhowmick calls the police.

Kali brings about destruction as her devotee Bhowmick becomes metamorphosed into an agent of cultural and moral vengeance when he brings down the rolling pin—a phallic object—upon his daughter's belly. Mr. Bhowmick's violence symbolizes patriarchy gone mad in its own powerlessness. We can contrast this assault upon Babli's stomach with the recollection of the lady from Lucknow, who recalls the tale of a girl who died of a broken heart when beaten by her stern Muslim father ("The Lady from Lucknow").

If Mr. Bhowmick is broken from maladjustment, Rab Chatterjee's nephew Poltoo and Rajiv Khanna are bright Indian graduate students whose emotions get out of control when they discard the traditional gender segregation of young people in their original culture. Poltoo falls in love with a black Muslim at the international student adviser's party, a ritual in North American universities. Such a ritual also introduces the lady from Lucknow to her white lover James Beamish. On the pretext of publicizing an Indian classical dance recital, Khanna invades the home of the newly imported bride Vinita, confesses his passion for her, and grabs at her breast. Khanna's uncouth act awakens Vinita to her own need for passion.

Although she rejects Khanna, Vinita can no longer be the same. Vinita's sober, successful accountant husband sleeps unaware and ugly, while his much younger bride tosses restlessly with the desire to experience America first hand, to run off into the "alien American night" (*Darkness* 176). The smugness of Sailen Kumar is comparable to the unawareness of Iqbal, the husband of the Lucknow lady, in that both husbands seem ignorant of their wives' sensual cravings.

As a contrast to the educated, upper-middle-class Indian immigrants, Mukherjee creates the wily Danny Sahib who procures Indian mail-order brides in a New York ghetto. The narrator of "Danny Sahib" is a teenager whose struggling mother aspires to send him to engineering school at Columbia University. The narrator is infatuated with Rosie, an imported Nepalese mail-order bride-to-be. Danny's American entrepreneurship totally parodies South Asian marriage practices because Danny is both a marriage broker and a quasi-pimp who sells the South Asian "brides" to very unattractive men. Women's historical enslavement in marriage thus continues as Old World methods are "bought" by New World men.

If the destitute, rickety beauty Rosie has been sold by her parents to Danny Sahib, the Bangladeshi orphan Angela is given up for adoption by Christian missionaries. Both young women assimilate easily into their new lives, Angela into farmhouse respectability, and Rosie presumably into ghetto prostitution. The adaptability of South Asian women is emphasized by Mukherjee, when Panna in "A Wife's Story" soliloquizes that she has been trained to adapt.

The adaptability of Mukherjee's women is traceable to their conditioning within the strongly patriarchal society of their origins. The women's adaptability contrasts sharply with the men's lack of assimilation and self-division as their masculine codes are undermined in the challenges Hindu and Islamic patriarchy encounter in the North America of the seventies and eighties. The boy narrator in "Danny Sahib," for example, implies that Rosie intends to break her contract with Danny Sahib. Mukherjee's fiction reveals how these historically underprivileged South Asian women discard their traditional sexual passivity in the new country and fashion new selves that are romantic, sensitive, and sensual.

Angela and Rosie have an upper-class counterpart in Vinita. Mukherjee presents Vinita in "Visitors" as an imported bride from Calcutta who is beginning to confront her own secret desire for passion. Shame comes in the form of the disturbing graduate student Khanna who declares his attraction to her. Much like the poor mail-order brides, Vinita has been imported by Sailen Kumar to do the housework and bear his children. All her life Vinita has been trained to reject passion and to adapt, these being the requisites of successful marriages in the old country.

Like Rosie's ghetto "house" to which she is restricted by her "importer" Danny Sahib, Vinita too is confined to traditional "female" space in Sailen Kumar's condominium. The image of a caged tropical bird is evoked when Vinita (whose name means "meek") serves her dinner guests in the atrium. The mail-order bride and the professional's wife operate within the same traditional paradigms. Rosie's captivity is lightened by the attentions of the teenaged narrator, but Vinita's boredom and restlessness invite the unwelcome attentions of Khanna who sees Vinita as a lusty temptress after the fashion of Bombay films. Khanna confronts Vinita with her own deviance from the traditional Indian codes of social decorum in which a wife would not allow a gentleman into the house in her husband's absence (*Middleman,* "Visitors" 172). The house, therefore, becomes a sexual metaphor of female space in Mukherjee's narrative.

If the boy narrator's romantic feelings help Rosie to consider breaking her "contract" with Danny Sahib, Khanna's clumsy caress causes Vinita to lie awake at night and ponder her own lack of romantic fulfillment. These undefined sensual longings of the imported brides are more fully explored by the protagonist in "The Lady from Lucknow." A homemaker in Atlanta with two children, Nafeesa was married at the age of seventeen in Pakistan, and as a dutiful Muslim wife has followed her husband in his diasporic wanderings. This female protagonist's first-person narrative indirectly contrasts the puritanical upbringing of Islamic women with her own craving for romantic and sexual fulfillment. Her husband alerts her to the dangers of what he considers the sex-obsessed society of America. However, she eagerly assimilates into the sexual freedom of the new country when she buys daring intimate apparel and commits adultery with James Beamish. Nafeesa is a literary descendant of Madame Bovary with a difference.

Mukherjee's South Asian Madame Bovary's romance crumbles as she is discovered in bed unexpectedly by Beamish's wife who is too used to her husband's infidelities to care. As lovely and voluptuous as a Goya nude, Nafeesa changes nothing by her passion and has no desire to die either. One recalls that women's adultery can be severely punished by the old Islamic law of the Lucknow lady's origins. In Atlanta, there is no anger, no violence, no vengeance as there might be in Lucknow where the beaten romantic teenage girl died of a broken heart in Nafeesa's opening flashback.

Suddenly the protagonist Nafeesa sees herself caught in a different patriarchal paradigm, that of the white man's colored mistress in a new version of the colonial era. Her self-realization of her own exploitation as a sexual object is ironic because she has only exchanged the polygamous code of Islamic tradition for white male patriarchy in America. After the wife and the mistress confront each other, Mukherjee's satire significantly allows the affair to continue. Desire triumphs over romance in the new country.

Desire and not romantic love motivates the conquests of Maya Sanyal in "The Tenant." Maya, whose name means illusion, pursues illusory sexual fulfillment through various indiscriminate encounters with white men. After a while, Maya craves an erotic relationship with an Indian man. Through a dubious personal ad in the immigrant Indian weekly, Maya locates her male counterpart in Ashoke Mehta, a sexually liberated professional also divided between romantic love and sexual promiscuity. Mukherjee's social satire significantly points out that in graduate school Maya had been a problematic member of a women's group. Divided between cultures, Maya, the eternal enchantress, corrupts the ethos of both East and West. As with Poltoo and Khanna, desire was an act of liberation/rebellion for Maya when she slept with John Hadwen at Duke University. From then onward, and after her divorce from Hadwen, she fashions a new promiscuous but independent identity, eventually becoming the tenant of an armless lover Fred. Mukherjee's satire indicates that Maya is comfortable only with this freak lover whose armlessness signifies his castration and powerlessness.

Unlike Maya whose singleness brings on promiscuity, the protagonist of "A Wife's Story" also arrives in the United States as a woman graduate student. But the attractive Panna (whose name means emerald) is married. She is "a wife" in that she is wedded to the traditional value system of the old country as well as to her husband. This first-person narrator lives in New York on her doctoral stipend. Panna is attractive to a variety of men—from her fellow graduate student Imre to the Lebanese man behind the ticket counter. Panna is a virtuous Hindu wife in a traditional arranged Hindu marriage whose life has been untouched by romance or passion.[3] In the main episode of her story, Panna's husband comes to New York to vacation. In the privacy of a New World apartment devoid of extended family and domestics, they discover passion and romance. Panna contrasts her married love to the meaningless sexual encounters of her roommate Charity Chin. Their romantic New World vacation—again much like Bombay films—ends abruptly when Panna's husband is recalled by his employer. Divided loyalties surface at the conclusion when Panna refuses to quit school and return with her husband (40). While Panna's refusal may signify an expatriate future for her, in "A Wife's Story" her refusal illustrates her stability and intelligence. Panna clearly discerns the differences in the old and new countries and judiciously chooses the Indian romance-as-married love and the American work ethic to circumvent the self-division faced by many of Mukherjee's men and women.

If Panna avoids the anarchy of the self through her economy of passion and her acceptance of the role of the traditional Hindu wife, the actions of Mrs. Bhowmick in "A Father" parody both the pious Hindu wife and the material ambitions of the average Indian immigrant in pursuit of the American Dream. Caught between the East and West in her ethos, Mrs. Bhowmick is a nagging plain woman, ill at ease in both Ranchi and Detroit. In Ranchi, her Americanized housekeeping angers her mother-in-law and the women of their neighborhood. Unlike Panna, she has never been attractive to her husband. While her husband prays to Kali, she performs her morning ritual of making him breakfast in the form of an unappetizing French toast with a filling of marshmallows, apricot jam, and maple syrup. But when she discovers her daughter Babli's pregnancy, she becomes hysterical and violent in a manner reminiscent of the old country. While satirizing the Bhowmicks, Mukherjee also reveals the deficiencies of the new country's freedom of choice and worship of technology in Babli's choosing a bottle and syringe instead of a man's love to conceive her child. A contrast to all of Mukherjee's satirical portraits appears in the deeply moving tragic monologue of Shaila Bhave, the thirty-six-year-old narrator of "The Management of Grief." This woman character loses her husband and two sons in an airplane crash caused by terrorist bombing. The narrative is based on a disastrous Air India crash in 1985, in which many Indo-Canadian immigrants lost some or all of their families. This character's emotional control surprises those around her, and she becomes a resource for the inexperienced social worker whose project is "the management of grief" among the Indian immigrants. Shaila Bhave presents a counterpoint to the anarchy and confusion of Mukherjee's other Indian immigrants and the Canadian authorities. This contrast is heightened by Mukherjee's satiric method which ridicules through innuendo white Canadians' inability to comprehend Indian grief. Mukherjee's ridicule of Canadian society in "The Management of Grief" is clarified in her open critique of Canada in several of her nonfiction prose works.

Outwardly calm, Shaila ceaselessly mourns her sons and her husband to whom she had never spoken of love. She travels to Ireland and cannot find her family in the bodies dredged from the sea. She journeys to her parents' home in India to recover and discovers her own displacement in the old country where newly bereaved husbands rapidly take new wives. She returns to Canada to continue her life which she now views as an endless journey begun with her husband. Her journey includes a quest for truth and for self-realization according to the tenets of Hindu scripture. Shaila Bhave's journey becomes symbolic of the wanderings and indecisions of all of Mukherjee's diasporic Indians who do not know which direction they will take in the future in the New World.

By virtue of her own identification with the Indian diaspora, Mukherjee probes deeply into the inner conflicts of well-educated, sensitive adults whose traditional codes of economy of passion and material desire collapse amid their inadequate comprehension of the American paradigms of life, liberty, and the pursuit of happiness. Mukherjee shows the diasporic Indian as living in between two cultures, constantly journeying into new meanings and fashioning new identities.

NOTES

1. The notion of self-fashioning as a bourgeois Western cultural construct is taken from Stephen Greenblatt, *Renaissance Self-fashioning: From More to Shakespeare.*

2. The characterization of anger as being predominant in feminist writing comes from Jane Marcus, *Art & Anger: Reading Like a Woman* (Columbus: Ohio University Press, 1988).

3. The religiously and culturally prescribed duties and behaviors of Hindu married women are elaborately discussed in Julia Leslie, ed., *Roles and Rituals for Hindu Women.*

WORKS CITED

Bhardwaj, Surinder M., and N. Madhusudana Rao. "Asian Indians in the United States: A Geographic Appraisal." *South Asians Overseas: Migration & Ethnicity.* Ed. Colin Clarke, Ceri Peach, and Steven Vertovec. Cambridge and New York: Cambridge University Press, 1990.

Frye, Northrop. *Anatomy of Criticism: Four Essays.* Princeton, N.J.: Princeton University Press, 1957.

Greenblatt, Stephen. *Renaissance Self-fashioning: From More to Shakespeare.* Chicago: Chicago University Press, 1980.

Leslie, Julia, ed. *Roles and Rituals for Hindu Women.* Rutherford, Madison, Teaneck, N.J.: Fairleigh Dickinson University Press, 1991.

Mukherjee, Bharati. *Darkness.* Markham, Ontario: Penguin, 1985.

———. *The Middleman and Other Stories.* New York: Grove Press, 1988.

THE SHORT FICTIONS OF BERNARD MALAMUD AND BHARATI MUKHERJEE

Carole Stone

> I see a strong likeness between my writing and Bernard Malamud's, in spite of the fact that he describes the lives of East European Jewish immigrants and I talk about newcomers from the Third World. Like Malamud, I write about a minority community which escapes the ghetto and adapts itself to the patterns of the dominant American culture. Like Malamud's, my work seems to find quite naturally a moral center.
> —Bharati Mukherjee (Carb 650)

Bernard Malamud was born in Brooklyn in 1914. Twenty-six years later, in 1940, Bharati Mukherjee was born in Calcutta. Both write about immigrant experience in America, about the struggle to overcome being viewed as "the Other." While definitions of otherness abound, for my essay, I define "the Other" as those who embody difference, primarily religious or racial, that separates them from mainstream American culture.[1] True, Malamud and Mukherjee write about different immigrants— Malamud's Jews are humble shoemakers, tailors, and bakers, and Mukherjee's Indians are doctors, university professors, businessmen, and women married to upwardly mobile professionals—and their stories are set in different times—the 1930s and 1940s in Malamud's, the 1970s and 1980s in Mukherjee's—but the similarities are striking and it is those that I examine here.

I have chosen to compare Malamud's and Mukherjee's work because each speaks about the diasporic experience of cultural alienation and addresses the remaking of oneself as an American. Moreover, a comparison between the two writers' fictions foregrounds the post–World War II immigration from the East to the United States and also allows us to read the narrative of Americanization from both the male and the female perspectives. While Malamud keeps his male immigrant character within the Yiddish tradition of the *shlemiel*, a loser who earns our empathy through his humanity, Mukherjee breaks her readers' identification by portraying the female immigrant as a conquering heroine. For while Malamud's fiction is essentially tragic and his male protagonists' lives relatively fixed—only his humor saves them from total despair—Mukherjee brings to her fiction, despite its often tragic tenor, a joy that Julia Kristeva has characterized as "jouissance."[2] This joy has much to do with Mukherjee's open-ended plots that suggest female fluidity, making rebirth possible.

Through a comparison of Malamud's and Mukherjee's fiction, I show the movement of the margin in America from European immigrants to Asian immigrants. As Norma Claire Moruzzi shows in her discussion of the Jewish experience of marginalization in Europe in the twentieth century, "The margin moves outside of Europe, both historically and in the text," as "[t]he identity of the shadowy other to the self-representation of European identity is effectively transferred from the Jews to the indigenous colonized people" (113). As a discussion of Mukherjee's and Malamud's work demonstrates, a similar loss of old patterns of dominance and marginalization takes place as these formerly colonized people emigrate to America.

That Mukherjee's and Malamud's writing bear comparison should be no surprise. Mukherjee knew Malamud; her husband, Clark Blaise, studied with Malamud at a Harvard Summer School Writing Workshop (Blaise 36). She acknowledges his influence: "Immersing myself in his work gave me the self-confidence to write about my own community" (Carb 650). In fact—and this is the point I want to make in this essay—by adopting Malamud as a Western literary model, Mukherjee distances herself from her former diasporic literary models, V.S. Naipaul in particular, to accelerate her assimilation into the American cultural center. Her literary journey is from the East of her first two novels, *Wife* and *The Tiger's Daughter*, to the West of her two collections of short stories, *Darkness* and *The Middleman*. By entering Malamud's literary space, Mukherjee moves her fiction from the constantly shifting margin to the unstable and shifting center which has no fixed place. Her texts can be seen as emissaries, occupying what Jonathan Crewe describes as the "middle ground" which can also be characterized as a "borderland," "buffer zone," "shield," "filter," "staging post," and "negotiating table" between the old diasporic literature and the new (128).

For as the Jewish immigrants assimilate and move into mainstream America, other marginal groups replace that community on the margins. In a postcolonial age of jet travel, these new refugees come from more remote parts of the world and include, in contrast to Malamud's pre–World War II immigrants, professionals as well as the poor. They are the immigrants of Mukherjee's fiction, arriving from Asian countries. Like Oskar in Malamud's "The German Refugee," one of the few professionals in his fiction, who is part of an exodus from Hitler's Germany, they confront "displacement, alienation, financial insecurity, being in a strange land without friends or a speakable tongue" (*Idiots First* 205), and like Bessie, the baker's wife, in Malamud's "The Loan," they carry the past with them along with hope for the future. Mukherjee speaks for them; she creates their voice in the first-person narrators who appear to collectively and instantly adapt to American values. The problem of speaking for these new immigrants has been raised by Gayatri Chakravorty Spivak who warns that postcolonial literature is in danger of replacing the old Orientalism (Edward Said's study) of the world as exhibition with a new Orientalism of the world as immigrant. I cite her not to deconstruct my discussion of Mukherjee's speaking for the marginal, but to draw attention to the issue of the privileged site of postcolonial writers from formerly colonized countries who, Spivak points out, have had access to the culture of imperialism, while establishing marginality as a subject (223). Thus, one of the reasons for Mukherjee's adoption of Malamud as a literary mentor can be seen as a strategy to place herself in the working-class Jewish tradition and to lend authenticity to her delineation of her socially, if not always economically, marginal characters.

The voice of Malamud's stories is colloquial, down-to-earth, simple and spare, a voice Sidney Richman sees as belonging "to a tradition so old that its appearance is slightly unnerving . . . sounding like an immigrant out of night school translating the prophets" (72); Mukherjee's voice is also colloquial, but goes beyond Malamud's everyday tone, is indeed trendy, using brand names like Advil and Reebok, as if her characters had bypassed night school. It is a street-smart voice that derives its slangy tone from television, films, and other forms of popular culture and replaces what Mukherjee calls the "rather British feel" of her first novel, *The Tiger's Daughter*, with "American English" (Carb 649).

In her first collection of stories, *Darkness*, which she dedicates to Bernard Malamud, Mukherjee says she writes "as an American writer in the tradition of other American writers whose parents or grandparents had passed through Ellis Island" (Carb 650). She separates herself from the postcolonial expatriate writer, V.S. Naipaul, "in whom I imagined a model" (*Darkness* 2) and other writers of the Indian diaspora, such as Anita Desai and Kamala Markandaya. Like Naipaul, they maintain a voice of ironic detachment in the English literary tradition, Markandaya in *Nowhere Man* and Desai in *Bye Bye Blackbird*, two novels about Indian immigrants in England. Mukherjee, however, like Malamud, admires Walt Whitman and says, "It's possible—with sharp ears and the right equipment—to hear America singing even in the seams of the dominant culture.... The book I dream of updating is no longer *A Passage to India*—it's *Call It Sleep*" (*Darkness* 3). Homi Bhabha describes the "scenario . . . of the sudden, fortuitous discovery of the English book . . . a moment of originality and authority . . . a process of displacement . . . a signifier of colonial desire and discipline" (163). I see Mukherjee's displacement of Forster with Roth as a revisionist scenario which gives the literature of the American immigrant the authority formerly held by postcolonial exile literature, and "creates the conditions for a beginning, a practice of history and narrative" (Bhabha 164).

Having placed herself in the American-Jewish literary tradition by citing Malamud and Henry Roth, Mukherjee moves away from her exilic identity as she frames "stories of broken identities and discarded languages, and the will to bond oneself to a new community, against the ever-present fear of failure and betrayal" (*Darkness* 3). She shows her belief in the New World by using the present tense to suggest the desire of her characters to eradicate past lives and adopt new ones. Like Mukherjee herself, they are in a hurry to become Americanized, although the weight of their histories remain in their consciousness.

For at the heart of Mukherjee's and Malamud's short stories, the form I have chosen to confine myself to since it is the primary genre for their representations of immigrants, is a memory of the old country, its poverty, its social strictures, its violence, which their characters must erase to become Americans. Often memories of repression burden their characters' new lives, yet the possibility of Americanization exists in their imaginative sources which contain a belief in transformation. While Malamud's transformations are rooted in the Yiddish folk tale about *shtetl* life and Mukherjee's in the reincarnations of Hindu cosmology, both write of the difficult, often tragic, conditions of diaspora which metamorphosis may conquer.

Critics have pointed out the Jewishness of Malamud's humor, part of which, as Jackson J. Benson points out, has to do with "Yiddish acceptance that if something can go wrong it will go wrong" (41). Mukherjee's sense of humor, derived from Hindu fatalism, contains a similar spirit. Their humor provides a means of transcending one's fate in the face of chaos, displacement, and alienation. With their memory of persecution, their stories bear witness to the death camps of Europe which haunt Malamud's survivors and to the rape and violence in Third World countries that Mukherjee's men and women cannot forget. Malamud's Jews and Mukherjee's Asians dream Westward, especially to California, the furthest geographical distance from their Eastern roots, where possibly they can reshape their lives.

Both believe in the American Dream of a new life. (Malamud, in fact, uses these words as the title for his novel, *A New Life*.) In his stories his characters struggle toward new identities, though they don't always find them. Mukherjee carries her belief, even more intensely than Malamud, that one can become an American. She believes, ". . . there are people born to be Americans. By American I mean an intensity of spirit and a quality of desire. I feel American in a very fundamental way, whether Americans see me that way or not" (Steinberg 46).

For Mukherjee, transformation from "the Other" into a mainstream American is an act of the imagination. Her comments on her religious upbringing explain how her belief in the power to change arises out of her cultural tradition. "As a Hindu, I was brought up on oral tradition and epic literature in which animals can talk, birds can debate ethical questions, and monsters can change shapes. I believe in the existence of external realities and this belief makes itself evident in my fiction" (Carb 651).

Like Mukherjee's, Malamud's imaginative sources contain a belief in transformation derived from the mystical Hasidic tradition of Eastern European Jews that prophesied the coming of the Messiah. Their fantastic tales influenced Yiddish authors like Lieb Peretz, Mendele Sforim, and Sholem Aleichem, who in turn influenced Malamud who created characters like angels who intervene in the lives of his powerless immigrants. Moreover, the Hasidic tale, like the Hindu, was shaped in an oral tradition, and this is why dialogue is of paramount importance in both Mukherjee's and Malamud's work.

A good example of a Malamud story which contains dialogue that conveys the elements of immigrant life seen also in Mukherjee's stories is "Idiots First," the title story of his collection, *Idiots First.* Malamud's Yiddish intonation keeps the immigrant father within old margins of the Russian Pale while containing hope for his son's Americanization. Mendel, who is old and poor, has cared for his retarded son, Isaac, now thirty-eight, all his life and has no one to look after him after he dies. The story of his search for money to send Isaac to his Uncle Leo in California unfolds primarily through spare dialogue with a Yiddish flavor that immediately conveys the atmosphere of Jewish immigrant life:

> "Ginzburg, that he came to see me yesterday," he whispered in Isaac's ear. Isaac sucked air.
> "You know who I mean?" Isaac combed his chin with his fingers.
> "That's the one, with the black whiskers. Don't talk to him or go with him if he asks you."
> Isaac moaned. "Young people he don't bother so much," Mendel said in afterthought. (4)

Not until later in the story do we realize that Ginzburg is the Angel of Death whom Mendel is trying to evade until he can settle Isaac with his Uncle Leo in California. Mendel pawns his watch for the train fare, but gets only eight dollars for it from the pawnbroker. He seeks out others; Mr. Fishbein, a rich man, won't give him money, but asks if he "wishes to partake food before leaving the premises" (*Idiots First* 5). Mendel replies, "For what I got chicken won't cure it" (*Idiots First* 5). The humorous dialogue exaggerates rather than softens the indifference and inhumanity of those who refuse him. In terms of our understanding of cultural identity, it is Jewish humor: self-deprecating and absurd, originating in the poverty and suffering of Eastern European ghettos. When Mendel knocks on the door of the synagogue's rabbi, the rabbi refuses him, but promises him his fur-lined caftan. Mendel yanks it away from the rabbi's wife, who is withholding it, and runs off. Finally, at twelve o'clock, he buys the train ticket, but the train station is deserted, the train has just left, and the ticket collector refuses to open the gate. Mendel begs him to open it; a voice says, "Favors you had enough already. For you the train is gone. You shoulda been dead already at midnight. I told you that yesterday. This is the best I can do" (*Idiots First* 13).

While the ticket collector, death's agent, picks his teeth with a matchstick, Mendel chokes Ginzburg asking, "[D]on't you understand what it means to be human?" As Mendel feels his body turning cold, he sees that "Ginzburg, staring at himself in Mendel's eyes, saw mirrored in them the extent of his own awful wrath. He beheld a shimmering, starry, blinding light that produced darkness." Ginzburg, astounded, says "Who me?" and lets go of Mendel, and tells him to take Isaac to the train. He commands a guard, "Let pass" (*Idiots First* 15).

Malamud's portrayal of the dying man's struggle to outwit Death with its suggestion of Job's ordeal, done in Yiddish dialogue, is simultaneously comic and tragic. The story's miraculous turn creates hope, though not much, as the retarded Isaac sets out for California where an eighty-one-year-old man waits for him.

As Ben Siegel points out, "In Malamud the past is never dead" (120), as demonstrated once more in "The German Refugee." A German-Jewish intellectual in America, Oskar Gassner, struggling to learn English so he can deliver a lecture, hires a twenty-three-year-old tutor, Martin Goldberg. But Oskar cannot learn and his plight, as described by Malamud, sums up the situation of the

German-Jewish immigrants of the 1930s: "To many of these people, articulate as they were, the great loss was the loss of language—they could not say what was in them to say. You have some subtle thought and it comes out like a broken bottle" (*Idiots First* 200). Goldberg believes in his pupil and gives him the notes he has taken on Whitman and German literature, the subject of Gassner's lecture. Gassner delivers his talk in perfect English, quoting Whitman's poetry as if he, the quintessential American poet, could transform him into an American. But afterward he receives a letter from his anti-Semitic mother-in-law telling him that his Gentile wife has converted to Judaism and has been killed in a concentration camp. Filled with guilt, he commits suicide. Just as the possibility of Americanization arises in his mastery of the English language, the horrific evil he has fled from in Germany destroys his chance for a new life.

Malamud's "The Loan," is also about the power of past cruelties on Malamud's Jewish immigrants and in this story, as in "Idiots First," transformation occurs through fantasy, a technique Mukherjee emulates. The baker Lieb, old and ill with cataracts, is able to sell his bread after thirty years of failure, after he weeps tears into the dough. Coupled with this fairy-tale transformation which brings hope is Lieb's poverty and his imminent eye operation. When a friend, Kobotsky, whom Lieb hasn't seen for fifteen years, appears and asks for a loan, Lieb's wife Bessie is furious. Kobotsky, after Bessie recites a litany of their woes to her husband, tells them he needs the money to purchase a stone for the grave of his wife who has been dead five years. Lieb, Kobotsky, and Bessie cry after his story, and the baker thinks his wife will let him make the loan. But as they eat together she recites her own litany of woe which evokes terrible evils of her European past:

> her beloved father [going] into the snowy fields without his shoes, the shots scattered the blackbirds in the trees and the snow oozed blood; how, when she was married a year, her husband, a sweet and gentle man, . . . died of

typhus in Warsaw; and how she, abandoned in her grief, years later found sanctuary in the home of an older brother in Germany, who sacrificed his own chances to send her, before the war, to America, and himself ended, with wife and daughter, in one of Hitler's incinerators. (Malamud, *The Magic Barrel* 190)

Afterward, Bessie sniffs the air and "with a cry wrenched open the oven door. A cloud of smoke billowed out at her. The loaves in the trays were blackened bricks—charred corpses" (191). Present misery and past horror collide in this image of the Nazi gas chambers and the destruction of the Jews.

Mukherjee's story, "Angela" illustrates the shift from the Euro-centered Holocaust memories of Malamud's refugees to the memories of more recent Asian atrocities endured by Mukherjee's immigrants. She situates the title character, Angela, in the tradition of Malamud's Holocaust survivors, suggesting the new immigrants' struggle to overcome their colonized identity so that they can be absorbed into mainstream America. Angela is a seventeen-year-old, adopted by an American Christian family in Iowa; as the story opens, Angela is at a hospital visiting her adoptive sister, who is in a coma after an automobile accident. The sister's boyfriend refers to the situation as "like 'Dynasty' only more weird" as he goes for coffee and a diet coke. Mukherjee uses such pop details to show Angela's assimilation, for while Malamud's characters retain their Yiddish accents and become only partly Americanized, many of Mukherjee's immigrants speak and act American. Angela says of herself, "The name I was born with is lost to me, the past is lost to me. I can't remember any of it. The rapes, the dogs chewing on dead bodies, the soldiers" (*Darkness* 13). But though she says she doesn't remember her nipples being cut off by soldiers in Bangladesh, the experience haunts her. She wants to attend college to become a physical therapist, but forces herself to consider the marriage proposal of Dr. Vinny Menezies, a forty-year-old immigrant from Goa. He contrasts with her devoutly Christian American foster mother who crochets and will not read even the Des Moines *Register* on Sundays. Yet it is the safety of this America Angela wants, and she asks "What am I to do? Only a doctor could love this body" (*Darkness* 19). Angela, like Bessie in Malamud's "Loan," remembers the terrible torture she suffered in her past life.

Tortured in the old country, Angela is forced to give up her identity in the new. In danger of falling into the white snowy vastness of the Midwest, which represents America, she occupies a space that is a nowhere-land. In spite of the necessity to become Americanized, Mukherjee sees the loss of the old culture as an impoverishment. In "The Imaginary Assassin," the narrator, a young man born in Yuba City, California, to Sikh parents, worships his grandfather, who was the first to come to the valley to work as a farmer. But his grandfather was homesick, went back to India after a shoplifting episode, and then returned in 1948—a month after the assassination of Gandhi. The narrator, who comes to hate his parents for their "shabby immigrant lives," loves to listen to his grandfather, who tells tales of old India. He doesn't want to take up the ordinary life as an engineer his parents plan for him; instead he dreams of the Sikh warrior tradition and of Sirhan B. Sirhan. His grandfather's tales have magic and miracles; in them "headless ghosts, eager to decapitate, could hide in trees along dark country lanes" (*Darkness* 181).

After his grandfather's story, he has hallucinations and nervous spells that keep him from an aerospace scholarship, as Mukherjee portrays the poverty of imagination in American culture faced by Indians from a tradition rich with magic. Like Malamud, she sees the loss of the old culture's storytelling as an impoverishment and believes in the story's power to entertain, instruct, and witness, as her own fiction does.

In "Orbiting," set in suburban New Jersey, Mukherjee uses Thanksgiving, the quintessential American holiday, to portray culture clash. Renata's Italian-American father is angry when her Afghan boyfriend Ro refuses a drink. Renata explains that Muslims have taboos and her father mutters, "Jews, so do Jews." He knows this "because catty-corner from Vitelli's is a kosher butcher. This isn't the time to parade new words before him, like *halal*, the Muslim kosher" (*The Middleman and Other Stories* 70).

For while Jews have by the eighties become a familiar presence in the American immigrant experience, the new Asian immigrants are viewed with suspicion. Mukherjee's fiction provides these new Americans with a voice which contributes to the discourse of marginality. This discourse, as Holly Laird observes, "speaks most commonly of bringing the margins out of the corners into the center of attention, making the invisible visible" (7). Like the characters of her stories, Mukherjee, too, is a new arrival, pushing from the margins of American literature into the center. Her immigrant stories fill up the space left by Malamud's, as he turns from writing about recently arrived European Jews to writing about first- and second-generation assimilated Jews. Malamud's Old Testament Jobean tales make the suffering of European Jewry their moral center and bring Jewish-American writing into the American mainstream. Mukherjee's fiction energizes moral concerns with its attention to Asian customs, religions, social structures, and political upheavals. The positive moral values of both writers are reflected in their belief that in spite of man's capacity for evil, through hope and persistence, there is the possibility of rebirth. The voices of Mukherjee's narrators add divergent values to America, proposing to share the center in a new way. She believes, "My task as an author is to make my intricate and unknown world comprehensible to mainstream American readers" (Carb 653). While doing so she follows Malamud's advice to "focus on character, make every act, every detail dramatic" (Carb 653). For both writers, "[f]iction dramatizes the multifarious adventure of the human heart" (Blaise 39).

NOTES

1. See Edward Said's *Orientalism* for the earliest and most useful discussion of "the Other" in colonial discourse.

2. In an introductory note in *New French Feminisms* the editors, Marks and de Courtivron, explain that "women's *jouissance* carries with it the notion of fluidity, diffusion, duration . . . a giving, expending, dispensing of pleasure without concerns about ends or closure" which I see in Mukherjee's heroines' possibilities for new identities.

WORKS CITED

Benson, Jackson J. "Bernard Malamud and the Haunting of America." *The Fiction of Bernard Malamud*. Ed. Richard Astro and Jackson J. Benson. Corvallis: Oregon State University Press, 1977. 40–45.

Bhabha, Homi K. "Signs Taken for Wonders: Questions of Ambivalence and Authority under a Tree Outside Delhi, May 1817." *"Race," Writing, and Difference*. Ed. Henry Louis Gates, Jr. Chicago: University of Chicago Press, 1986. 163–166.

Blaise, Clark. "Mentors." *Canadian Literature* (Summer 1984): 35–41.

Carb, Alison B. "An Interview with Bharati Mukherjee." *The Massachusetts Review* 29.4 (1988): 645–654.

Crewe, Jonathan. "Defining Marginality." *Tulsa Studies in Women's Literature* 10.1 (Spring 1991): 121–130.

Laird, Holly. "Discourse of Marginality." *Tulsa Studies in Women's Literature* 10.1 (Spring 1991): 1–9.

Malamud, Bernard. *Idiots First.* New York: Delta, 1965.

———. *The Magic Barrel.* New York: Farrar, Straus & Cudahy, 1958.

Marks, Elaine, and Isabelle de Courtivron, eds. *New French Feminisms: An Anthology.* Amherst: University of Massachusetts Press, 1980.

Moruzzi, Norma Claire. "Re-Placing the Margin: (Non)Representations of Colonialism in Hannah Arendt's *The Origins of Totalitarianism.*" *Tulsa Studies in Women's Literature* 10.1 (Spring 1991): 109–120.

Mukherjee, Bharati. *Darkness.* New York: Penguin, 1985.

———. *The Middleman and Other Stories.* New York: Fawcett Crest, 1988.

Richman, Sidney. "The Stories." *Bernard Malamud.* Ed. Harold Bloom. New York: Chelsea House Publishers, 1986. 41–58.

Said, Edward. *Orientalism.* New York: Pantheon Books, 1978.

Siegel, Ben, ed. *The American Writer and the University.* Newark: University of Delaware Press, 1989.

Spivak, Gayatri Chakravorty. "Poststructuralism, Marginality, Postcoloniality and Value." *Literary Theory Today.* Ed. Helga Geyer-Ryan and Peter Collier. Ithaca: Cornell University Press, 1990. 219–244.

Steinberg, Sybil. "Immigrant Author Looks at U.S. Society." *Publishers Weekly* (25 August 1989): 46–47.

SELECTED BIBLIOGRAPHY

WORKS BY BHARATI MUKHERJEE

Fiction

The Tiger's Daughter. Boston: Houghton Mifflin, 1971.

Wife. Boston: Houghton Mifflin, 1975.

Darkness. Markham, Ontario: Penguin, 1985.

The Middleman and Other Stories. New York: Viking Penguin, 1988.

Jasmine. New York: Viking Penguin, 1989.

Nonfiction

(with Clark Blaise) *Days and Nights in Calcutta.* Garden City, N.Y.: Doubleday, 1977.

(with Robert Boyers) "A Conversation with V.S. Naipaul." *Salmagundi* 54 (Fall 1981): 4–22.

"An Invisible Woman." *Saturday Night* (March 1981): 36–40.

(with Clark Blaise) *The Sorrow and the Terror: The Haunting Legacy of the Air India Tragedy.* Markham, Ontario: Viking Penguin, 1987.

"Immigrant Writing: Give Us Your Maximalists!" *New York Times Book Review* (28 August 1988): 1, 28–29.

"Prophet and Loss: Salman Rushdie's Migration of Souls." *Village Voice Literary Supplement* 72 (March 1989): 9–12.

(with Clark Blaise) "After the Fatwa." *Mother Jones* 15.3 (April/May 1990): 29–31, 61–65.

Interviews

Carb, Alison B. "An Interview with Bharati Mukherjee." *The Massachusetts Review* 29.4 (1988): 645–654.

Connell, Michael, Jessie Grearson, and Tom Grimes. "An Interview with Bharati Mukherjee." *Iowa Review* 20.3 (1990): 7–32.

Conquering America with Bharati Mukherjee. Videocassette. Prod. Bill Moyers. Public Affairs Television, 1990. 58 minutes.

Hancock, Geoff. "An Interview with Bharati Mukherjee." *Canadian Fiction Magazine* 59 (1987): 30–44.

Meer, Ameena. "Bharati Mukherjee." *BOMB* 29 (1989): 26–27.

Steinberg, Sybil. "Immigrant Author Looks at U.S. Society." *Publishers Weekly* (25 August 1989): 46–47.

CRITICAL STUDIES OF BHARATI MUKHERJEE

Boxill, Anthony. "Women and Migration in Some Short Stories of Bharati Mukherjee and Neil Bissoondath." *Literary Half-Yearly* 32.2 (July 1991): 43–50.

Chua, C.L. "Passages from India: Migrating to America in the Fiction of V.S. Naipaul and Bharati Mukherjee." *Reworlding: The Literature of the Indian Diaspora.* Ed. Emmanuel S. Nelson. Westport, Conn.: Greenwood Press, 1992. 51–61.

Jain, Jasbir. "Foreignness of Spirit: The World of Bharati Mukherjee's Novels." *The Journal of Indian Writing in English* 13.2 (July 1985): 12–19.

Leong, Liew-Geok. "Bharati Mukherjee." *International Literature in English: Essays on the Modern Writers.* Ed. Robert L. Ross. New York: St. James Press, 1991. 487–500.

Malik, Amin. "Insider/Outsider Views on Belonging: The Short Stories of Bharati Mukherjee and Rohintan Mistry." *Short Fiction in the New Literatures in English.* Ed. J. Bardolph. Nice: Faculté des Lettres et Sciences Humaines, 1989. 189–196.

Mandel, Ann. "Bharati Mukherjee." *Dictionary of Literary Biography: Canadian Writers Since 1960.* Vol. 60. Ed. W.H. New. Detroit: Gale Research Company, 1986. 266–269.

Nelson, Emmanuel. "Kamala Markandaya, Bharati Mukherjee, and the Indian Immigrant Experience." *Toronto South Asian Review* 9.2 (Winter 1991): 1–9.

Pandya, Sudha. "Bharati Mukherjee's Darkness: Exploring the Hyphenated Identity." *Quill* 2.2 (December 1990): 68–73.

Rustomji-Kerns, Roshni. "Expatriates, Immigrants and Literature: Three South Asian Women Writers." *The Massachusetts Review* 29.4 (1988): 655–665.

Sivaramakrishna, M. "Bharati Mukherjee." *Indian English Novelists.* Ed. Madhusudan Prasad. New Delhi: Sterling, 1982. 71–86.

St. Andrews, B.A. "Co-Wanderers Kogawa and Mukherjee: New Immigrant Writers." *World Literature Today* 66.1 (1992): 56–58.

Tapping, Craig. "South Asia/North America: New Dwellings and the Past." *Reworlding: The Literature of the Indian Diaspora.* Ed. Emmanuel S. Nelson. Westport, Conn.: Greenwood Press, 1992. 35–49.

NOTES ON CONTRIBUTORS

Debjani BANERJEE, a graduate of the University of Calcutta, is currently a doctoral candidate at the State University of New York at Stony Brook. Principal areas of her teaching and research interests are postcolonial and feminist literatures and theory.

Brinda BOSE has studied literature at Presidency College, Calcutta, and at Oxford University, England. She is now a doctoral candidate at Boston University where she is completing a dissertation on gender, race, and silence in postcolonial fiction.

Samir DAYAL holds a doctorate in English from the University of Wisconsin at Madison. Assistant Professor of English at Franklin College, Indiana, he is currently at work on a book-length study of the literature of the Indian diaspora.

Gurleen GREWAL teaches in the department of Women's Studies at the University of South Florida, Tampa. A recent recipient of a Ph.D. in English from the University of California at Davis, she is completing a book on Toni Morrison's fiction.

Alpana Sharma KNIPPLING is Assistant Professor of English at the University of Delaware campus at Newark, Delaware. She has published in the area of pedagogy and multiculturalism; her research and teaching interests range from Indian literature in English to postcolonial critical theory. At present she is writing a book on postcolonial critical practice and editing a volume on immigrant literatures.

Emmanual S. NELSON, Associate Professor of English at SUNY-Cortland, received his doctorate from the University of Tennessee in 1983. During 1984–1986 he was a Postdoctoral Research Fellow in Commonwealth Literature at the University of Queensland, Australia. Author of over two dozen articles on American and international literatures in English, he is the editor of *Connections: Essays on Black Literatures* (1988), *Reworlding: The Literature of the Indian Diaspora* (1992), *AIDS: The Literary Response* (1992), and *Writers of the Indian Diaspora: A Bio-Bibliographical Critical Sourcebook* (1993).

Pushpa N. PAREKH holds a Ph.D. in English from Louisiana State University. A critic as well as a creative writer, she teaches at Spelman College, Atlanta.

Mitali R. PATI teaches at Augusta College, Georgia. She has published on Renaissance drama, South Asian women writers, and Canadian literature.

Janet M. POWERS teaches at Gettysburg College, Pennsylvania. Among her teaching and research interests are multicultural and postcolonial literatures.

Anindyo ROY received his doctorate in the Humanities from the University of Texas, Arlington. A specialist in critical theory and literary modernism, he currently teaches at Southern Methodist University, Dallas.

Maya Manju SHARMA, Assistant Professor of English at Eugenio Maria de Hostos Community College (CUNY), holds a doctorate from Columbia University.

Carole STONE teaches at Montclair State College, New Jersey.

Pramila VENKATESWARAN, a graduate of Sophia College, Bombay, received her Ph.D. in English from George Washington Unviersity in 1988. She now teaches at Nassau Community College, New York.

INDEX

"Angela," 200–201, 222–223
Austen, Jane, 19

Barthes, Roland, 90–107
Bhabha, Homi, 77, 217
Bhagavad Gita, 98
Blaise, Clark, 5, 7, 23, 27, 28, 41

Call It Sleep, 4
Carb, Alison, 59, 215, 216

"Danny Sahib," 204, 206
Darkness, 3–4, 19, 48, 123, 197–204, 222–224
Days and Nights in Calcutta, 23–42, 128–132
"Debate on a Rainy Afternoon," 6

Fanon, Frantz, 78–80, 173
"Father, A," 82, 203, 208
"Fathering," 149–150

Gone with the Wind, 11

Hancock, Geoff, 5, 6, 16

"Imaginary Assassin, The," 223

"Immigrant Writing: Give Us Your Maximalists!" 143, 144, 145–146, 166, 175, 177, 181, 194
"Invisible Woman," 6–7

Jain, Jasbir, 9
Jasmine, 58–60, 65–83, 99–106, 110–125, 132–140, 150, 152–155, 168–171, 175, 176, 177, 181–195

Kakar, Sudhir, 4, 7, 11, 14
Katrak, Ketu H., 122
Kingston, Maxine Hong, 42
Klass, Rosanne, 15, 18

Mahabaratha, 38
"Management of Grief, The," 209–210
Markandaya, Kamala, 10, 216–217
Middleman and Other Stories, The, 148–150, 197–210
Minh-ha, Trinh, 57, 125, 164
Mohanty, Chandra, 187
Moyers, Bill, 89, 128, 131, 132–133

Mukherjee, Bharati: aesthetics of, 79–107, 109–125, 127–140; and biculturalism, 11; and critique of Western feminism, 18; educational background, 5–6, 10–11; and Hindu imagination, 16–17, 24, 25, 41, 129, 218; and Malamud, 213–225; marriage of, 5, 6; and postcolonial subjectivity, 65–83, 127–140, 143–156, 167–178, 182–185; on racism, 6–7, 27; treatment of exile, 8–12, 40, 127–129, 217; treatment of history, 161–178; treatment of immigration, 13–14, 15–16, 40–41, 47–61, 65–83, 89–107, 109–125, 134–140, 143–156, 181–195, 197–210, 222–224; treatment of violence, 53, 65–83

Naipaul, V.S., 10, 13, 145

"Nostalgia," 201–202

"Orbiting," 223–224

Passage to India, A, 4

Rama Rau, Shantha, 10
Ramamyana, 29
Ramanujan, A.K., 109
Rushdie, Salman, 40, 52, 178
Rustomji-Kerns, 112

Sivaramkrishna, M., 10, 21
Spivak, Gayatri, 50, 53, 54, 56, 130, 146, 147, 216

Tiger's Daughter, The, 4–15, 50–52, 162–165

"Visitors," 205, 206

Whitman, Walt, 19, 20
Wife, 15–17, 18–19, 55–57, 92–99
"Wife's Story, A," 208

For Product Safety Concerns and Information please contact our EU
representative GPSR@taylorandfrancis.com
Taylor & Francis Verlag GmbH, Kaufingerstraße 24, 80331 München, Germany

www.ingramcontent.com/pod-product-compliance
Lightning Source LLC
Chambersburg PA
CBHW071823300426
44116CB00009B/1415